OVER 300 SUCCESSFUL BUSINESS LETTERS FOR ALL OCCASIONS

ALAN BOND

BARRON'S

The publisher and the author wish to point out that the names of persons, businesses, companies, organizations, institutions, hotels, service and product names, trademarks, events, situations, places, locales, addresses, zip and postal codes, telephone area codes, e-mail addresses, telephone and fax numbers, which are used in the sample letters, news releases, reports, phrases, and sentences or other examples in this book are entirely fictitious and are for demonstration purposes only. Any resemblance and similarities are unintentional and entirely coincidental.

All inquiries should be addressed to:
Barron's Educational Series, Inc.
250 Wireless Blvd.
Hauppauge, NY 11788
http://www.barronseduc.com

ISBN 0-7641-0322-9

Library of Congress Catalog Card No. 97-33521

Library of Congress Cataloging-in-Publication Data
Bond, Alan J.
    Over 300 successful business letters for all occasions / by Alan J. Bond.
        p.   cm.
    ISBN 0-7641-0322-9
    1. Commercial correspondence—Handbooks, manuals, etc.   2. Letter writing—Handbooks, manuals, etc.   I. Title.
    HF5726.B67   1998
    651.7′4—dc21   97-33521
                                                          CIP

PRINTED IN THE UNITED STATES OF AMERICA
9 8 7 6 5 4 3 2 1

Contents

## CHAPTER 1

BUSINESS CORRESPONDENCE

Business letters are written on the company's letterhead stationery, which includes the organization's full name, full address and telephone, fax, or telex numbers, and (if available) the e-mail address. The parts of a business letter (see the sample letters in this chapter) are:

- Date
- Attention line
- Inside address
- Subject line
- Salutation
- Body of the letter
- Complimentary closing
- Signature
- Reference initials
- Enclosure notation
- Copy notation

Not all of the above components are always used. The "Attention line," "Subject line," and "Enclosure" notations are used only as they apply to a particular letter.

Detailed information about the use of forms of address to dignitaries and officials, punctuation marks, and the rules to capitalize words in correspondence can be found in the Quick Reference Appendix in this book.

The three business letter formats most commonly used in the international business world are:

1. *Block-style format.* There are no indentations in this letter. All lines are typed against the left-hand margin. The block-style letter is very popular, because it is simple and reflects efficiency.

2. *Modified block-style format.* The difference between the modified block-style letter format and the block-style format is the fact that the dateline and the complimentary closing are typed slightly to the right of the page center. There are no indentations.

3. *Semiblock-style format.* In the semiblock-style or indented letter format, the paragraphs are indented five spaces from the left of the margin. The dateline and the complimentary closing are typed to the right of the page center.

(Block-style business letter)

letterhead

ABC COMPANY
00 Wilson Street
New York, NY 00000
Tel. (000) 000-0000
Fax: (000) 000-0000

date

July 12, 1999

attention line

CONFIDENTIAL

inside address

Mrs. Diane Warner
President
XYZ Company, Inc.
000 West 59th Street
Chicago, IL 00000

subject line

<u>Subject: Block-style Letter</u>

salutation

Dear Mrs. Warner:

body of letter

This is an example of a full block-style letter, one of the most frequently used forms for writing business letters in the international business world. As you can see, there are no indentations. All lines are typed against the left-hand margin.

The block-style letter is very popular, because it is not only simple to use but also reflects efficiency. If you have any additional questions about the layout of a block-style business letter, please do not hesitate to call me at (000) 000-0000.

complimentary
close

Sincerely yours,

signature line

John A. Hickman
Executive Vice President

ref. initials
enclosure(s)
copy to

JAH:gws
Enclosure: 1 brochure
cc: Mary Davis

(Modified block-style business letter)

MIRKOVICH COMPANY
00 Levitt Boulevard
Rutherford, NJ 00000
Tel. (000) 000-0000
Fax: (000) 000-0000

August 17, 1999

Mr. Matthew Ridgewood
Director of Human Resources
ABC Company
00 Berkshire Square, Suite 1288
Arlington, VA 00000

Dear Mr. Ridgewood:

Re: Modified Block-style Letter

This is an example of a modified block-style letter. As you can see, there are no indentations. All lines are typed against the left-hand margin with the exception of the dateline and complimentary closing, which are typed slightly to the right of the page center.

If you have any additional questions about the modified block-style business letter, please do not hesitate to contact me immediately.

Cordially,

Sharon B. Tate
Vice President

SBT:pr
Encls. 2 brochures
cc: Alexander Haigh, Marcia Klein

(Semiblock-style business letter)

XYZ INTERNATIONAL
0000 East Park Street
Riverside, CA 00000
Tel. (000) 000-0000
Fax: (000) 000-0000

October 4, 1999

Mr. Steve Fleming
Sales Manager
ABC Corporation
000 Jefferson Avenue
Miami, FL 00000

Dear Mr. Fleming:

   This is an example of an indented or semiblock-style business letter, which many companies use. The semiblock-style gives business letters a more balanced appearance.

   As you can see, the paragraphs are indented: usually five spaces from the left of the margin. However, the dateline and the complimentary closing are typed slightly to the right of the page center.

   If you have any additional questions about the layout of the semiblock-style business letter, do not hesitate to call me as soon as possible.

Sincerely,

William Klass
Sales Director

WK:bls
Enclosure: quarterly sales report
cc: Maria Moralez

Parts of a Business Letter

DATE

The dateline in a letter is typed three or four lines below the last line of the letterhead. The standard dateline in the United States and various other countries is the full name of the month (no abbreviations), followed by the day and the year. A comma separates the day of the month from the year. No period follows the date (example: August 18, 1999). However, in Europe and many other countries the most widely used format to write a date is: day, followed by the month and the year (example: 5 November 1999).

In order to avoid confusion in international correspondence, do not use numerals to indicate a month, but always type out the full name of the month. Thus, do not write 05-09-1999 if you want to indicate the date of 5 September, because an American businessman would assume that you mean May 9 instead of September 5.

ATTENTION LINE

The attention line is sparingly used in business letters. If used, the notation "Personal" or "Confidential" is placed two or three lines below the dateline.

INSIDE ADDRESS

The inside address, which identifies the name(s) of the person(s), and the name and address of the company or organization to whom the letter is addressed, is typed two lines below the date or the attention line.

Examples:

Mr. Kenneth Maxwell
Corporate Planning Department
XYZ Company, Inc.
00 Highwood Avenue
Midland Park, MA 00000

Mrs. Karen Southerland, Director
Consumer Services Division
ABC Company
000 West 12th Street
Toronto, Ont. 000 000

The American Corporation
Attention: Mr. Dennis Rosen
Linsley Building, Suite 000
000 East 23rd Avenue
Dayton, OH 00000

123 Limited
Attention: Head of Accounting
00 Englewood Square
London 0000 000
England

College or University
Attention: Admissions Office
Bergenfield, AL 00000
USA

Dr. Luigi Pirelli
Via Vittor Pisani 00
00000 Milan
Italy

SUBJECT OR REFERENCE LINE

The subject or reference line (which is often underlined) is placed below the inside address. This line is used if you want to include or refer to a file or reference number (e.g., of an order, the name of a special project or a certain date) in the letter. The word "Reference" is often abbreviated as *Ref.* or *Re:*.

Examples:

Subject: Holiday Schedule for 1999
Ref.: Your order No. 2338A
Re: Insurance Policy No. B444-AvZ-MA33-35

It should be pointed out that certain companies place the subject or reference line below the salutation of the letter.

SALUTATION

The salutation of a business or private letter, which greets the addressee appropriately, should use the person's name if at all possible. Always make sure that a person's name is spelled correctly. The salutation in business letters is usually followed by a colon (:). The comma (,) is seldom used in the salutation of business letters, but is instead saved for personal letters and letters of condolence and sympathy. The following are correct salutations used in letters.

Examples:

(For a man)

Dear Sir:	Dear Mr. Johnson:	Dear Dr. Faulkner:
Dear Professor Brown:	Dear Rabbi Goldstein:	Dear Senator Lyons:

(For more than one man)   Dear Sirs: Gentlemen:

(If you know the person well)   Dear Robert,

(For a woman)

Dear Madam:	Dear Mrs. Robertson:	Dear Miss Bloomfield:
Dear Ms. Gruber:	Dear Mayor Kilpatrick:	Dear Professor Madison:

(For more than one woman)   Ladies:

(If you know the person well)   Dear Anne,

Ms. is used as a courtesy title before the surname or full name of a woman or girl. *Ms.* is a blend of *Miss* and *Mrs.* The courtesy title *Mrs.* is often used for a married woman, although many married women nowadays also use *Ms.*

If you are writing a letter to a person with a first name that does not indicate whether the person is a man or a woman (e.g. first names such as Leslie or Terry), use the following salutation: *Dear Leslie Taylor:*.

Detailed information about correct forms of address (in salutation and letter address) of dignitaries and officials can be found in the <u>Quick Reference Appendix</u> in this book.

BODY OF THE LETTER

The body of the letter is the main part of the business letter. It is usually single-spaced and has double spacing between paragraphs and before the complimentary closing.

COMPLIMENTARY CLOSING

The complimentary closing ends the letter. It is typed two lines below the last line of the body of the letter. Only the first letter of the first word of the closing is capitalized. A comma follows the closing. Complimentary closings vary in formality as indicated below.

(formal closing)   Yours truly,   Respectfully yours,

(less formal closing)   Sincerely,   Sincerely yours,   Cordially,

(personal closing)   Regards,   Personal regards,   Kindest regards,

SIGNATURE LINE

The name of the person who signs the letter is typed three or four lines below the complimentary closing. The handwritten signature is placed between the complimentary closing and the signature line. One line below the signature line the position or title of the person who signs the letter is typed.

Examples:

Sincerely,   Yours truly,

Joseph L. Cotton   Marion Nicholson
Director, Marketing Services   Secretary to Mr. Leaman

REFERENCE INITIALS, ENCLOSURE NOTATION, AND COPY NOTATION

Additional information in a business letter may be included below the last line of the signature block. For example, reference initials, enclosure notation, and copy notation.

The reference initials following the signature line usually are preceded by the writer's initials in capital letters and separated by a colon (for example: JAH); followed by the intials of the person who has typed the letter in lowercase letters (for example: gws).

Example:

JAH:gws

The enclosure notation is typed directly below the reference initials. This indicates that something has been enclosed with the letter (for example, a résumé, a brochure, a report, or a photograph). The word "enclosure" or "enclosures" is often abbreviated as *Enc.* or *Encls.*

Examples:

Enc.: 1 résumé   Enc.: credit application   Encls.: 3 brochures

The copy notation is typed directly below the enclosure notation or the reference initials. It indicates that a copy (abbreviated as *cc:*) of the letter has been sent to the person who has been named.

Examples:

cc: Maria Vlady   cc: Susan Griffin, William King

## CHAPTER 2

LETTERS OF INQUIRY

A letter of inquiry is usually written to ask for specific information or sales literature about products and services, price lists, catalogs, terms of business, quotations, discount schedules, dealer prices, the name of a dealer or local supplier, or free samples or materials. Letters of inquiry are also referred to as request letters. Most letters of inquiry are short. They can be sent by mail, telex, fax, or e-mail. If necessary, you can include information about what type of company you are and how you heard about the company that you are writing to. The following types of letters are provided in this chapter:

- Letters of Inquiry and Requests for Information
- Replies to Letters of Inquiry and Requests for Information
- Follow-up Letters

LETTERS OF INQUIRY AND REQUESTS FOR INFORMATION

Date

Name/Title
Business/Organization
Address
City, State Zip Code

Dear Sir/Madam:

Could you please send us your current catalog and price list of the video recorders advertised in this month's issue of *Professional Video Equipment News*? We are operating a video production facility and are particularly interested in Models AA5 and AA8.

Please, reply as soon as possible as we would like to make a purchasing decision early next month.

Sincerely yours,

Signature

Name

Date

Name/Title
Business/Organization
Address
City, State Zip Code

Dear Sir/Madam:

We have seen your advertisement in the March issue of *Business Catering Management* and would be grateful if you could send us details about your catering services for medium-sized companies.

A prompt reply would be appreciated.

Sincerely,

Signature

Name

Date

Name/Title
Business/Organization
Address
City, State Zip Code

Dear Name:

Please send us two copies of the color brochure on your new Samson Color Copier Model 33H advertised on page 15 in your "Office Supplies" catalog No. 93.

Thank you for your prompt response to this inquiry.

Sincerely,

Signature

Name

Date

Name/Title
Business/Organization
Address
City, State Zip Code

Dear Name:

Could you please send me information about the international sales training program as advertised in the April issue of *International Sales Training Magazine*? Thank you very much.

Sincerely,

Signature

Name

Date

Name/Title
Business/Organization
Address
City, State Zip Code

Dear Name:

We are interested in having a stand in next year's Consumer Electronics Exhibition in Boston and would be grateful if you could mail us a copy of your detailed Exhibition Folder.

Sincerely yours,

Signature

Name

Date

Name/Title
Business/Organization
Address
City, State Zip Code

Dear Name:

Your company has been highly recommended to us by the Alex Thallier Company in Paris, France. We are a small company specializing in cordless telephone equipment and have received numerous inquiries from our business customers for a cordless phone that delivers sound quality comparable to that of a corded telephone. We want to expand our range of equipment and would like you to send us full details of your cordless phone models as well as the latest sales catalogue and your most competitive dealer prices. Please, also include information about packing and shipping (CIF Boston) and the minimum quantity for a trial order.

We look forward to hearing from you soon.

Sincerely,

Signature

Name

Date

Name/Title
Business/Organization
Address
City, State Zip Code

Dear Name:

A business associate of ours, Berend Kasius of the Hilbers Company in Albany, New York, mentioned your name and showed us your company's brochure. We own and operate six medium-sized hotels in the Rochester area and are looking for a reliable fire prevention/sprinkler system for these properties. Could you mail us your latest sales catalogue and price list? Thank you very much.

Sincerely,

Signature

Name

Date

Name/Title
Business/Organization
Address
City, State Zip Code

Dear Name:

When we attended the International Electronics Trade Fair in London last month, we visited your stand and saw a very interesting demonstration of your automatic high-security garage doors. The ability to drive straight in and out of your garage from the comfort of your car, as well as your emphasis on theft protection, appealed to us. We believe that there is a ready market for this in the United States.

Our company is a wholly owned subsidiary of the international Zetax Corporation, well-known in the security and theft prevention industry.

Would you please send us your current sales literature and price list? Of course, we will be glad to provide the usual credit and trade references if we decide to order from your company.

Sincerely yours,

Signature

Name

Date

Name/Title
Business/Organization
Address
City, State Zip Code

Dear Name:

One of our business associates—Mr. Ben Nevins of Gorham Brothers in Hong Kong—informed us that your company is a major manufacturer of pure cotton-striped or solid polo shirts and terry jumpsuits in all sizes for young women. We would like you to send us detailed information and your export price list, as well as several samples of the shirts and jumpsuits.

Thank you very much!

Sincerely,

Signature

Name

Date

Name/Title
Business/Organization
Address
City, State Zip Code

Dear Name:

We are interested in ordering 175 new electronic memory-read typewriters for our new direct-mail facility at Reddington, Utah. Could you please send us an estimate? The enclosed specification sheet provides the necessary details.

Sincerely yours,

Signature

Name

Date

Name/Title
Business/Organization
Address
City, State Zip Code

Dear Name:

We have heard from the German Consulate in Chicago that you are a leading producer of self-adjusting, all-weather sunglasses in Germany. Since there seems to be a growing interest in and demand for such high-quality ambermatic sunglasses in the United States, we would like to know the frame styles that are now available for both men and women.

We are importers of optical products, including glasses, sunglasses, binoculars, and loupes.

Please, send us your illustrated catalog, export price list, and terms of business. As a rule our domestic and international suppliers allow us to settle by monthly statements. We can supply you, of course, with business and bank references. We look forward to your reply.

Sincerely,

Signature

Name

Date

Name/Title
Business/Organization
Address
City, State Zip Code

Dear Name:

We would be grateful if you would send us patterns and prices for your floral-print, quilted comforters and geometric-design bed spreads (sizes: Twin, Full, Queen, and King). Please, also inform us whether you could supply these goods from stock, because we need them before the Christmas season starts.

Sincerely,

Signature

Name

Date

Name/Title
Business/Organization
Address
City, State Zip Code

Dear Name:

We are the U.S. buying agents for a direct mail organization in Japan offering quality merchandise to consumers at bargain prices. Products, which carry an unconditional money-back guarantee, include tools, do-it-yourself aids, automotive supplies, plus a whole range of hobby and sporting supplies.

Would you please send us your latest price lists and illustrated catalogs for all the products you stock, including detailed information on your discount system for substantial orders?

We look forward to hearing from you soon.

Sincerely,

Signature

Name

USEFUL SENTENCES FOR LETTERS OF INQUIRY AND REQUESTS FOR INFORMATION

We were given your name by the XYZ Company in Billings, Montana.

We have been given your name by our business associates, Messrs. Carlson & Sons in Twin Falls, Idaho, who inform us that they have been doing business with your company since 1988.

Your company was recommended to us by Ms. Andrea Jensen of the Heyerdahl Company in Providence, Rhode Island.

The Belgian Consulate General in New York advised us that your company is looking for an import agent in Belgium to represent you.

We have learned from the Muller Company in Frankfort, Maine, that you are the manufacturer of the Selekta answering machine with built-in telephone and fax.

Mr. Frank Norris of the Butler Company in Woodlawn, Oregon, advised me that your company is interested in supplying sporting clubs and fitness centers with competitively priced, high-energy soft drinks and candy.

Your company has been highly recommended to us by Stewart, Jones & Company in Melbourne, Florida, with whom we have done business during the past twenty years.

We are a major retail store chain and are inviting estimates for the supply and installation of new universal product code cash registers in all of our 12 outlets in the Chicago metropolitan area.

We are writing to several industrial coffee machine manufacturers to invite estimates for the installation and maintenance of automatic coffee machines in our headquarters in Williamsburg, Virginia, as well as at our two production facilities in the Philadelphia area, in accordance with the attached specification list.

We are interested in importing Dutch cheese (in particular Edam, Gouda and Zaanlander) and would like to receive a copy of your latest sales brochure, export price list, and export terms.

Please let me know what quantities your company can supply from stock and your earliest date of delivery. In addition, I would like to know if your company is prepared to grant a ten-percent discount.

Please send us details about your Document Binding machine as advertised in the Sunday edition of *The Newark Gazette*.

We have studied the specifications of your electronic typewriters (Model 227BB) and would like a quote from you for the supply of 200 of these typewriters.

Since we intend to place a substantial order for your new line of BMX lightweight binoculars and monoculars, we would like to know whether you are prepared to grant special quantity discounts for orders in excess of $10,000.

If your products and terms of business are as competitive as we have heard from our associates, Berrbaum Company in Denver, we would be interested to discuss a long-term contract with your company.

Provided you can offer competitive prices and guarantee delivery within five weeks from receipt of our order, we intend to place orders with your company throughout the year.

We believe that there is a promising market in the Pacific Northwest for your company's high-quality products, provided they are competitively priced.

If the price is right and your goods are up to sample, they should readily sell in the Italian market.

Would it be possible for us to have a dozen sets of your imported knit sweatshirts for young women (BO157—White, Pink, Melon, and Indigo Blue; Misses sizes: small, medium, and large) on approval before we place a firm order? We intend to test the response to and demand for these colorful knits in our stores in Gainesville, Morristown, and Dugan.

Please let us know on what terms you can deliver the video recorders.

Please reply as soon as possible because we would like to make a decision early next month.

Please send us your latest catalog and full details of your export prices, discounts, and terms of payment.

Please let me have your quotation as soon as possible.

We would appreciate a prompt reply quoting export trade and delivery prices to Martinsville, West Virginia.

Replies to Letters of Inquiry

Date

Name/Title
Business/Organization
Address
City, State Zip Code

Dear Name:

Thank you very much for your request of April 16 for samples of our new ABC fabrics. We have asked our agents in San Diego, Arthur Roth Company, to supply you with a copy of our current sales catalog and price list and a full line of samples.

We appreciate your interest and thank you for writing to us.

Sincerely yours,

Signature

Name

Date

Name/Title
Business/Organization
Address
City, State Zip Code

Dear Name:

Thank you for your recent communication.

Regrettably, we cannot supply the wooden picnic basket (Model 4A). This item is out of stock and we do not have a firm date for further supplies. However, if we receive more stock in the near future, we will contact you.

Yours sincerely,

Signature

Name

Date

Name/Title
Business/Organization
Address
City, State Zip Code

Dear Name:

Thank you for your interest in our sales management training program. Per our telephone conversation of yesterday, I am enclosing detailed information about this program.

If you have any questions, please do not hesitate to contact me.

Sincerely,

Signature

Name

Date

Name/Title
Business/Organization
Address
City, State Zip Code

Dear Name:

Thank you for your inquiry. I hope that the enclosed information about our institute's direct-mail marketing course will be of use to you. Just give me a call at (000) 000-0000 and I will be happy to answer any questions you may have.

Sincerely yours,

Signature

Name

Date

Name/Title
Business/Organization
Address
City, State Zip Code

Dear Name:

Thank you for your request for additional information on the Misell Carpet Machine, which we have been producing since 1994. This professional vacuum cleaner removes deep-down dirt.

Misell Company has an excellent reputation for high-quality products, reliability, and service. Our products are designed and manufactured in the United States.

I have enclosed a special folder on the Misell Carpet Machine and a catalog that describes our other professional floor care products, including the Silent Power cannister and the Full-Power Upright Vacuum Cleaner. Please call me at (000) 000-0000 if you have any questions.

Sincerely yours,

Signature

Name

Date

Name/Title
Business/Organization
Address
City, State Zip Code

Dear Name:

Thank you for your fax of February 19. Enclosed is our current summer sales catalog for the complete range of Fairfax products you asked for, together with full details of our liberal terms of business. As you can see on page 3 of our price list, we allow you a special discount off all net prices for orders of the value you stated in your fax. Delivery will be within four weeks of receipt of your order. However, to take full advantage of these special summer sales offers, we advise you to place your order promptly. We expect considerable response to our summer sale and supplies are limited.

If you have any further questions, please contact us. We look forward to hearing from you as soon as possible.

Sincerely,

Signature

Name

Date

Name/Title
Business/Organization
Address
City, State Zip Code

Dear Name:

Thank you for your telex of December 2 in which you asked for detailed information about our new range of Sou'western Rain Hats, styled after the classic foul weather hat worn by Scottish fishermen for more than a century. We now have designed these rain hats in contemporary fabrics and colors and they can be supplied from stock.

Our export prices in the enclosed catalog and price list are quoted for delivery in Tokyo. Payment is to be made by irrevocable letter of credit.

We look forward to hearing from you soon. If you need any further information, please contact us.

Sincerely yours,

Signature

Name

Date
Name/Title
Business/Organization
Address
City, State Zip Code

Dear Name:

Thank you for expressing an interest in Elyxx/Automated Simulations. In response to your request for further information on our product line of computer games, we enclose our latest catalog and price lists.

We are in the process of expanding our distribution channels internationally as the demand for high-quality computer games increases. Our games are unique and positioned for your market. Take a few minutes and review the enclosures, and you will see why so many top retailers have added the Elyxx computer games to their product mix.

Please contact us if you have any questions regarding the product line or material enclosed. We look forward to hearing from you in the near future.

Sincerely,

Signature

Name

Date

Name/Title
Business/Organization
Address
City, State Zip Code

Dear Name:

We are pleased to enclose the Master Film Classic Video catalog you requested in your letter of April 2. Also included is a catalog of titles available on the Master Famous Films label. You may order these titles using either the Film Classic or Famous Films order form.

Please note that postage rates listed in both catalogs apply to USA destinations only. Parcel postage to countries within the European Union is $5 per tape; outside the European Union $7 per tape.

Kind regards,

Signature

Name

Date

Name/Title
Business/Organization
Address
City, State Zip Code

Dear Name:

Thank you for inquiring about Graphica Corporation and our products. The enclosed literature details the capabilities of our computer graphics systems. We understand the need for efficient information management and let it guide the research and development of our integrated software and hardware products.

If you have additional questions after reading our literature, please call our company's regional office in your area. Our sales or technical representatives would be happy to discuss pricing or arrange a demonstration at your office. A list of regional offices and telephone numbers is enclosed for your convenience.

We appreciate your interest in Graphica Corporation.

Sincerely,

Signature

Name

Date

Name/Title
Business/Organization
Address
City, State Zip Code

Dear Name:

Thank you for your fax of April 23 requesting dealer information about our company's newest Grand Mobile Homes.

With over 4,000 Grand Mobile Homes sold and in service in the southwestern United States, our unique concept has been proven popular. Built with the latest technology and newest materials and with simplicity of maintenance in mind, our rugged and durable Grand Mobile Homes offer flexibility available in no other mobile home on the market today.

The enclosed brochures as well as the detailed technical and dealership information show you why our Grand Mobile Homes have become an outstanding sales success during the past three years. After you have reviewed our information package, please feel free to contact us for further information. We also want to invite you to visit our manufacturing facilities in Sun Valley, Arizona. We would be pleased to show you how our Grand Mobile Homes can meet your requirements of mobile homes in southern Florida, efficiently and economically.

Sincerely,

Signature

Name

Date

Name/Title
Business/Organization
Address
City, State Zip Code

Dear Name:

In reply to your letter of September 12, we are pleased to enclose a copy of our most recent sales catalog which features the complete range of our new corduroy sports jackets for men. These handsome and versatile jackets—in beige, navy, chocolate, or rust—can be worn from the office to informal dinners to weekend activities in great style and comfort. The medium-wale corduroy is made from a long-wearing blend of long staple cotton and polyester and is soft and easy to wear. The models that you are interested in are presented on pages 9 to 15.

Mr. Robert Dillon, our regional sales manager, will telephone your office next week in order to arrange a meeting. He will be able to provide you with complete details of our other new sportswear lines.

Sincerely,

Signature

Name

FOLLOW-UP LETTERS

Date

Name/Title
Business/Organization
Address
City, State Zip Code

Dear Name:

You have probably received the brochures you requested about our sales management training program. However, since these booklets only provide general information about this program, I suggest that we get together for a brief personal discussion. In this way, I can answer your questions and tell you how this training program can benefit you and your company.

I will get in touch with you early next week to determine your interest in this program.

Sincerely,

Signature

Name

Date

Name/Title
Business/Organization
Address
City, State Zip Code

Dear Name:

We wondered whether you received our sales catalog and export price lists you requested in your fax of October 10.

We would be pleased to discuss the possibility of having our products distributed in your country. We will call you to set up a meeting.

We hope that we will be able to meet soon, either in New York or in Chicago.

Sincerely yours,

Signature

Name

Date

Name/Title
Business/Organization
Address
City, State Zip Code

Dear Name:

The catalog and price list mailed to you last week provided descriptions of our professional video recorders. However, you may have some specific questions on these new models. For that reason, I would welcome the opportunity to answer your questions and, if necessary, advise you on how these new models can best suit your company's requirements.

I would be happy to arrange a brief demonstration for you and key members of your staff at a mutually agreeable time. There is, of course, no cost or obligation. Please, contact me so that I can reserve a date for you.

Sincerely,

Signature

Name

Date

Name/Title
Business/Organization
Address
City, State Zip Code

Dear Name:

During last month's Catering Trade Exhibition in Miami, you visited our stand and showed a considerable interest in our Sabatini carbon steel knives. They are the sharpest knives you can buy and also the easiest knives to resharpen, according to our kitchen tests and conversations with professional cooks and meat cutters. Sabatini carbon cutlery has been manufactured in Italy for more than a century.

We enclose our newest brochure and suggest that the special set of four steel knives (see page 9) would be of particular interest to you. We are sure that you will find our prices very competitive and our export service outstanding.

We look forward to doing business with you.

Sincerely,

Signature

Name

Date

Name/Title
Business/Organization
Address
City, State Zip Code

Dear Name:

It was a pleasure meeting you last Thursday. Thank you for letting me show you and your key staff members how our company can handle your company's specific needs. I am pleased to send you the booklet you requested on our audiovisual services. I will call you early next week to see whether you have any questions.

Sincerely yours,

Signature

Name

USEFUL SENTENCES FOR REPLIES TO LETTERS OF INQUIRY AND FOLLOW-UP LETTERS

Please find enclosed our color brochure and export price list, which will give you a good idea of the range of our best-selling brass-look curtain rods.

I enclose our latest catalog and export price list which will provide you with detailed information about our newest range of smooth leather gloves and crocodile-look belts. Our company allows a trade discount of 25 percent off the quoted list prices to wholesalers in North America.

Please find enclosed a copy of our latest catalog and price list quoting prices for delivery in Montreal. The prices quoted are subject to change, however, because the international market for pure cotton is rather unstable at the moment. Of course, we will inform you by fax or telephone if there is an increase in our quoted prices.

We believe we have covered every point of your inquiry in our recent follow-up letter. Since the Christmas season will soon start, we must therefore ask you to answer our letter before the end of this month to guarantee stock availability.

If your company requires the goods urgently, we will send them by United Carrier airfreight from London, although this would of course involve higher freight charges.

Any orders you place with our company will have our prompt attention, because we can supply from stock. Goods that are delivered from stock are usually sent within four or five days of receipt of order.

We are confident of an enthusiastic response from the Latin American market. I look forward to discussing this with you in Rio de Janeiro later this month, when I hope we may also be able to explore your production line-up for next year.

The samples you requested in your letter of June 21 will be sent to you today as a separate airfreight package.

Please let us know if you would like to have a demonstration of our document-binding machine at your office next week.

If you would like more information or have any questions on any of our products, please do not hesitate to get in touch with me.

Our international sales manager, Ms. Louise Truffaut, will be in San Diego next month and will be pleased to visit your office to discuss the contents of our follow-up letter of April 9.

I am sorry to say that our company no longer manufactures the Model 3GF tool storage box that you are interested in. However, I can suggest an excellent alternative, Model 4GG, which also carries a five-year guarantee.

The brochures you ordered are being printed now. We will ship them on December 3.

Requests for our color brochure concerning our SLR-35 mm automatic camera outfit have been so overwhelming that we temporarily are out of copies. We are reprinting and will soon mail one out to you.

Our usual terms of payment are cash on delivery (C.O.D.).

Our usual terms of payment are 30 days net.

Our usual terms of payment are sixty days from the date of delivery.

Our quotations are subject to 2 percent discount for cash.

Our terms are 30 percent discount, with 3 percent for settlement within fifteen days of date of invoice.

This is a special introductory offer and is therefore not subject to our usual discount schedule. If you accept our quotation of November 5, please advise us by fax or telex.

We are enclosing our current catalog and price list quoting F.O.B. prices Tokyo and urge you to order as soon as possible, because there is a great demand for the new Models ZA2 and ZB3. Our quoted price includes special export packing and airfreight delivery.

We very much regret the delay in sending your merchandise and assure you that future orders will be handled promptly.

We are offering your company a special discount for our video recording equipment based upon the following sliding-scale: On purchases exceeding an annual total of $2,500 but not exceeding $5,000: 2 percent; $5,000 but not exceeding $15,000: 4 percent; $15,000 but not exceeding $35,000: 5 percent; and $35,000 and above: 6 percent.

We hope that this initial order is only the beginning of a long and pleasant business relationship.

## CHAPTER 3

Letters of Complaint, Adjustment, and Apology

Letters of complaint about delays, wrong shipments, damaged goods, missing parts, defective merchandise, billing errors, late deliveries, faulty equipment, community problems, rude employees, or warranties (to name just a few problems) are usually written by dissatisfied, indignant or angry customers seeking redress. In writing such letters you must provide a clear description or explanation of what is wrong with the delivery, product or service. If an appliance is faulty, also provide exact information about the model and serial number; order and delivery dates; and invoice or account numbers. Also describe the inconvenience that this has caused you and the steps you expect the company to undertake to solve the problems promptly or else refund the purchase price. The language and tone in a letter of complaint should be firm, reasonable, and courteous. Avoid sarcasm or rudeness and do not use words such as "infuriated," "enraged," or "disgusted." The use of such angry terms will probably irritate and antagonize the recipient of your letter of complaint. Since almost any company values its customers, you can expect that it will replace defective products or correct the errors without delay.

The writing of courteous and reasonable adjustment letters to respond to letters of complaint must be done with care, tact, and restraint in order to keep the customer happy. Assuming that the complaint is justified, a letter of adjustment should acknowledge the complaint, offer an apology, and explain what the company is doing about the complaint. Also point out that the fault or the error seldom occurs. If you cannot deal with a genuine complaint promptly, always acknowledge this fact as soon as possible. At the same time, explain that you will provide a full reply at a later date. If you believe that a complaint is unreasonable or unjustified, a polite but firm answer must be given. In the event that no justification exists for an error, a problem or an unpleasant situation, a straightforward admission of that fact often has a disarming effect upon the recipient of such a letter.

A sincere letter of apology for bad behavior, an oversight, an error, a discourtesy, or a mistake—plus the valuable words "I am sorry"—often go a long way to smooth relations with a disgruntled customer.

LETTERS OF COMPLAINT

(Complaint about a delivery)

Date

Name/Title
Business/Organization
Address
City, State Zip Code

Dear Name:

We are sorry to inform you that your delivery of 28 four-drawer chests (Model H95—white finish) on February 19 has given us cause for serious complaint. They were delivered in substandard condition and cannot be fixed. We have been doing business with your company for the past four years and have always been satisfied until today. For that reason, please let us know as soon as possible what your company intends to do to rectify this situation.

Sincerely,

Signature

Name

(Complaint about missing articles in a shipment)

Date

Name/Title
Business/Organization
Address
City, State Zip Code

Dear Name:

On checking the waterproof parkas with taffeta lining (Models 666L and 999XL; our Order No. 7778) we received this morning, we find that 32 parkas listed on your packing lists as well as on your invoices have not been included in this shipment. For that reason, we enclose a list of the missing articles. Please check with your packers before we make a formal claim.

Sincerely,

Signature

Name

(Complaint about a wrong item shipped)

Date

Name/Title
Business/Organization
Address
City, State Zip Code

Dear Name:

On June 14, I ordered an answering machine with a built-in telephone (Article No. 172AM-TE) from your Summer Sales Catalog. On opening the parcel, I found that it did not contain the ordered item. Instead it contained an entirely different machine. I am therefore returning the item for replacement.

Sincerely,

Signature

Name

(Complaint about merchandise that does not match the samples)

Date

Name/Title
Business/Organization
Address
City, State Zip Code

Dear Name:

We are sorry to have to inform you that the bulk of the acrylic loungewear (button-front robe with V-neck; our order no. SSLW-V2) that was delivered is not up to the samples which we received on March 15.

On comparing the loungewear received with the samples, we were unpleasantly surprised to discover that the models are not the same high quality. We can only assume that a mistake was made and that the loungewear we ordered has been wrongly delivered.

We cannot accept this delivery because we pride ourselves on the fact that our stores carry only the very best quality in ladies' fashions. For that reason, we must ask for replacement of this entire collection. Please let us know what you wish to do with this order.

Sincerely,

Signature

Name

(Complaint about a color photocopying machine)

Date

Name/Title
Business/Organization
Address
City, State Zip Code

Dear Name:

I am writing for the third time to complain about the color photocopying machine you installed in our office only three months ago. This machine has not met our staff's high expectations. Contrary to the description in your sales and instruction booklets, the colors (at least of our color copier) are not "real." In addition, your service representative who has examined this machine on various occasions has not been able to correct this continuing serious problem.

We shall expect you to deal with this problem without further delay.

Sincerely,

Signature

Name

(Complaint about damaged merchandise)

Date

Name/Title
Business/Organization
Address
City, State Zip Code

Dear Name:

The seven-piece wood-and-glass dining set (Order No. 13899) I ordered on April 2 was delivered yesterday. Since I was away on business that day, my neighbor (who has a key to my apartment) accepted the packaged set and signed for it without question. However, when I unpacked the oak-finished table myself with great care, I discovered that one glass insert of the table's three glass inserts was badly scratched. I can only assume that this damage must be due to careless handling at some stage prior to packing. I cannot accept the table in this state and want to receive a replacement as soon as possible.

Sincerely,

Signature

Name

(Complaint about a damaged office machine)

Date

Name/Title
Business/Organization
Address
City, State Zip Code

Dear Name:

Two weeks ago we ordered a Highspeed Bookkeeping Office Machine Model X-10, which was delivered this morning. However, when we opened the box, we discovered that the machine (with serial number ADD-595001-X) was damaged. As a matter of fact, it looked like a used model that has served as a demonstration sample. It is obvious, of course, that we cannot accept this. We have been doing business with your company during the past six years, but we now feel cheated. Your company, which prides itself on first-class equipment and service, has some explaining to do. Meanwhile, we expect you to pick up this machine.

Sincerely yours,

Signature

Name

(Complaint to a manufacturer's district manager about a car dealership)

Date

Name/Title
Business/Organization
Address
City, State Zip Code

Dear Name:

On April 13, I purchased a brand-new, four-door Excellenta Model GLX automobile from the Frank Smith Car Dealership in Anytown, Pennsylvania. Right from the beginning, I have experienced serious stalling problems with this car, even while driving the automobile on the highway. Moreover, the Frank Smith service department seems to be unable to solve this very annoying and extremely dangerous problem. My wife does not even want to drive this car, because she is truly scared that this new automobile will accidentally stop running. Nine trips (!) to the service department have failed to solve or correct this stalling problem.

I am sure that you will agree that this is a ridiculous situation. My direct question to you is: what are you going to do about this very serious as well as dangerous situation? If you, in your capacity as the manufacturer's district manager, cannot solve this situation in a satisfactory way within ten days, I will address my complaint directly to both the president of your company and the Automobile Industry Safety Board.

Sincerely,

Signature

Name

USEFUL SENTENCES FOR LETTERS OF COMPLAINT

I am writing to complain, not only about the very poor service we received from your company this week, but also about the discourteous behavior of your new sales representative, Arthur Jones.

I want to lodge a complaint about the very discourteous treatment that my wife and I experienced in your department store on Friday afternoon, May 29.

My wife and I would like to register a serious complaint about one of your store's salesmen.

We refuse to pay for merchandise that was never delivered to our company.

I am returning the damaged goods to your office for a full refund.

We are returning the defective products for credit at your expense.

We are returning the entire order of 55 tennis rackets and would like to be refunded for their full purchase price of $2286.37 plus shipping expenses of $198.11.

In our opinion, the damage seems to have been caused by inadequate packaging.

I would like to clear up this unpleasant situation without delay. For that reason, I expect a prompt reply.

This mistake must be corrected as soon as possible, because we are far from satisfied with the service your company offers.

We are confident that we can resolve this serious complaint without having resort to the Small Claims Court.

Our order No. 88KLS was placed on condition that we receive the blue jeans before November 15. Unless your company can fulfill our monthly orders efficiently in the future, we will have to consider other reliable sources of supply.

I am seriously disappointed to find that the quality of the tricycles for young children (Model EK3-RR) you supplied does not correspond with that of the sample tricycle submitted to us in February.

Thank you for your promptness in dealing with our complaint. However, we absolutely deny your allegation that our company is at fault in this matter. Therefore, we demand a formal and thorough investigation of our claim.

Your recent action not to replace the faulty floor-to-floor belt conveyor constitutes a flagrant breach of contract.

Things have now reached the point that I want action within forty-eight hours or I will place the whole matter in the hands of my lawyer.

RESPONDING TO LETTERS OF COMPLAINT

(Reply and apology for problems with an oven)

Date

Name/Title
Business/Organization
Address
City, State Zip Code

Dear Name:

Thank you for telling us about your problems with the electric oven that you purchased in our store on January 14. Since this oven is covered by our unconditional refund policy, we can either provide you with a new oven or else give you a full refund. Please, let us know your decision.

We value your patronage and are very sorry for the inconvenience the problems with the oven have caused you.

Sincerely yours,

Signature

Name

(Reply and apology for damaged glassware)

Date

Name/Title
Business/Organization
Address
City, State Zip Code

Dear Name:

We are sorry to hear that you were not satisfied with the shipment of wine glasses we sent you by Associated Parcel Service last week, because we always check our shipments with great care. However, we have already arranged for two new complete sets of wine glasses to be sent to your company by air express. Please return the damaged glassware to us. We very much regret this inconvenience.

Thank you for your cooperation.

Sincerely,

Signature

Name

(Reply and apology for defective coffee machine)

Date

Name/Title
Business/Organization
Address
City, State Zip Code

Dear Name:

Thank you for your letter of July 30. Of course, we are deeply concerned when one of our customers is not satisfied with one of our products. Our company takes great pride in trying to produce only top products. Unfortunately, we sometimes fail.

If you return the defective cappuccino coffee machine to the dealer who sold it to you, he will replace it with a new one. However, if you prefer, we are also willing to refund the purchase price to you.

We are sorry to have inconvenienced you and offer our apologies.

Sincerely,

Signature

Name

(Reply and apology for damaged CD-player)

Date

Name/Title
Business/Organization
Address
City, State Zip Code

Dear Name:

We are sorry your automobile radio-compact disc player arrived in a damaged condition. As described in your letter, the damage apparently happened during shipment. A replacement will be delivered to your home on Wednesday morning, April 17. Our driver, who delivers the replacement, is authorized to pick up the damaged radio-CD player. We regret your inconvenience and thank you for your understanding and cooperation in this unfortunate matter. We value your business.

Sincerely,

Signature

Name

(Reply and apology for a billing error)

Date

Name/Title
Business/Organization
Address
City, State Zip Code

Dear Name:

I am in receipt of your letter of April 9 and regret the error on your bimonthly invoice. When this invoice was made up, two items had been duplicated on invoice 778, with the result that your company was overcharged $1311.29. I have deducted this amount from your invoice and will mail you a new one for the correct amount of $11,430.88.

Thank you for bringing our billing error to our attention. Again, I apologize for the inconvenience this has caused you.

Sincerely,

Signature

Name

(Reply and apology for a billing error)

Date

Name/Title
Business/Organization
Address
City, State Zip Code

Dear Name:

Thank you for calling the billing error in your last weekly statement to our attention. This error was caused by a new clerk in our accounting department. We have corrected your statement and a new statement is enclosed. Please accept our sincere apologies for the inconvenience caused you. We look forward to our continued good business relations.

Sincerely,

Signature

Name

(Reply and apology for a delay in delivery)

Date

Name/Title
Business/Organization
Address
City, State Zip Code

Dear Name:

We are in receipt of your fax of November 28 and regret the delay in delivery of your order No. SSTX-32AA for floor lamps and pole lamps. When we received your order in late October, our supplier was out of stock. However, we are pleased to advise you that your order will be filled by December 8. We apologize for any inconvenience caused by this delay. Thank you very much for your patience and cooperation in this matter.

Sincerely,

Signature

Name

(Reply and apology for a damaged desk)

Date

Name/Title
Business/Organization
Address
City, State Zip Code

Dear Name:

We are sorry to learn about the damage to the four-drawer desk that you purchased at our store in Philadelphia on September 26. Our delivery-person informed us that the damage probably occurred during the shipment from the furniture manufacturer to our warehouse in Wilmington, Delaware.

Meanwhile, we have ordered an exact replacement from the manufacturer and expect that delivery will take place within one month. As soon as the desk arrives, we will telephone you immediately and will arrange a convenient delivery time.

We regret the inconvenience this has caused you.

Sincerely,

Signature

Name

Useful Sentences for Acknowledging and Responding to Letters of Complaint

Thank you for your letter of February 28 bringing this problem to our attention.

We thank you for bringing this matter to our attention.

Thank you for writing us as candidly as you did about the defect in your new vacuum cleaner.

We can understand your annoyance at not having received the color television set you ordered on September 15.

We are sorry that the Model 233 Expresso Machine you purchased on April 12 has not lived up to your expectations. We are prepared to exchange this model or else give you a full refund.

We greatly regret your unsatisfactory experience with our direct mail order products. You have every right to be upset about the fact that the clock radio did not work.

We are sorry to learn that you are not completely satisfied with the performance of our multipurpose manual lift, Model 34-10-16A. We are prepared to exchange the faulty parts.

We are very sorry that our work was unsatisfactory and did not meet your company's expectations, especially since we take great pride in our work. We can, however, assure you that we will do our utmost to correct this situation as quickly as possible. Please, accept our sincere apologies for the inconveniences this has caused you.

We sincerely regret to inform you that the replacement of your two damaged tablecloths will be delayed by approximately five weeks due to a fire at our manufacturer's plant in Chicago.

I suggest you discuss this problem with your local dealer for a replacement or a possible refund.

We will make every effort to ensure that this problem will not happen again.

Enclosed you will find our credit note for $371.40 representing a complete refund on the faulty merchandise you returned to our warehouse last month.

Therefore, we are anxious to settle this claim to your complete satisfaction. Don't you agree this is an equitable way to settle this matter? We do see your point of view, but we are also sure that you will consider ours.

We appreciate your patronage and are, of course, always willing to help a customer with a problem.

Thank you once again for your concern and understanding and for bringing this serious matter to our attention.

Your company will receive immediate credit for all shipping charges. If this is not satisfactory, please let me know.

Please return the damaged chair to our warehouse in Deakinsville. They will replace the chair and ship a new one to your office address. Thank you very much for your understanding and cooperation. If we can be of further service, please let us know.

The replacement of the faulty vacuum cleaner is on the way and should be in your possession within one week. Please, accept our apologies for the inconvenience.

We will correct the discount error on your pro-forma invoice immediately. It is unusual for this type of error to arise and we apologize for any inconvenience this may have caused you.

LETTERS OF APOLOGY

Date

Name/Title
Business/Organization
Address
City, State Zip Code

Dear Name:

Thank you for your letter of June 17 pointing out the error in our invoice No. A-531 dated January 9. We would like to apologize for this billing error and we are sorry for any inconvenience that our error has caused you. We try our best, but occasionally errors do slip by our accounting department. Therefore, we have canceled the old invoice and now enclose a revised invoice for the correct amount.

We would like to thank you once again for bringing this matter to our attention.

Sincerely,

Signature

Name

Date

Name/Title
Business/Organization
Address
City, State Zip Code

Dear Name:

I apologize most sincerely for any discourtesy by our employee, Roberta Foster, last Saturday afternoon. None was intended. Because of this unfortunate incident, we would like to offer you as a token of good faith, a gift certificate for $100 of merchandise valid at any of our five department stores in Bergen County. Please be assured that we have taken steps to prevent a recurrence of such inexcusable rudeness by our sales staff.

Sincerely,

Signature

Name

Date

Name/Title
Business/Organization
Address
City, State Zip Code

Dear Tenant:

Our local council will be doing some electrical work in our office building between Monday, March 21, and Wednesday, March 23.

During this time there may be some short interruptions to electrical supply.

Please accept our apologies for any inconvenience that this may cause.

Name
Title

Useful Sentences for Letters of Apology

Please accept our sincere apologies for the error in your bill of December 16. We have corrected the situation and are very sorry for any inconvenience.

We are sorry for the error in your bill and thank you for calling it to our attention.

We really must apologize for our serious oversight in failing to credit your payment of $568.13 to your account. Your check was credited to the wrong account due to an error in our computer records.

Please accept our company's sincere apologies for the inconvenience that the delay in processing your claim of September 12 has caused you.

Thank you for your letter of July 2 regarding your well-justified complaint about the serious defect in your new HJF Laserprinter. We do apologize and are pleased to have the opportunity to put things right.

Please accept our profound apologies for this mistake, which could not have happened to a more valued customer.

We are extremely embarrassed about our sales representative's behavior last week and we understand why you are angry. We have taken steps to ensure that this will not happen again.

I apologize for my thoughtlessness and hope that this situation can be rectified to your company's satisfaction.

We trust that no lasting or substantial harm was done and apologize most sincerely for any confusion this error has caused your company.

We apologize and sincerely hope that reinvoicing you will resolve the issue to your satisfaction.

Please forgive my delay in responding to your urgent fax of October 17 about the poor printing of your company's sales catalog. An unexpected business trip to Europe kept me away from the office for four days.

Please accept our sincere apologies if this late reply to your letter of December 19 has caused you any problems.

We owe you an apology for not answering your e-mail letter sooner.

## CHAPTER 4

Letters of Congratulation and Appreciation

People always appreciate personal letters of congratulation and appreciation and thank-you letters or notes, especially if they are handwritten. However, such informal letters must be warm, friendly, sincere, and must avoid excessive flattery, because otherwise they defeat their purpose. Always send such letters or notes as soon as possible.

Congratulatory and thank-you letters to employees must reflect genuine sincerity and should be reserved for outstanding performances, achievements, or for a difficult or time-consuming job well done. These letters must also briefly describe that person's specific performance, contribution, or achievement that deserves praise. Always send a copy of a letter of congratulation or appreciation as well as thank-you letters to that person's boss. Letters of congratulation and appreciation and thank-you letters to good friends, for example, thanking for hospitality, assistance, advice, service, favor, or a gift, should of course always be friendly, informal, and personal depending on the degree of friendship.

Letters of Congratulation

(Congratulatory letter on promotion)

Date

Name/Title
Business/Organization
Address
City, State Zip Code

Dear Name:

My congratulations to you on your recent promotion to national sales manager. I know that you have worked hard for Newton Corporation and therefore I am delighted that you have been promoted to this new and challenging position.

Your company is very fortunate to have benefited from your expertise as well as loyalty during the past nine years.

Cordially,

Signature

Name

(Congratulating a top salesperson)

Date

Name/Title
Business/Organization
Address
City, State Zip Code

Dear Name:

Congratulations to you on establishing a new sales volume record last year. I know you worked hard to achieve this and it is great to see that you were able to attain your goal.

We need people like you, Richard. Keep up the good work!

Sincerely,

Signature

Name

(Congratulating a top salesperson)

Date

Name/Title
Business/Organization
Address
City, State Zip Code

Dear Name:

My congratulations to you on being the Number One Salesperson in the Southwest Sales Group during the past quarter. You outsold all other salespersons during that quarter in both volume and gross margins. An outstanding achievement. If this continues, you will be in line for promotion to Assistant Regional Sales Manager next year.

Keep up the good work for the next quarter!

Sincerely,

Signature

Name

(Congratulating a top sales team)

Date

Name/Title
Business/Organization
Address
City, State Zip Code

Dear Name:

Congratulations! Murray Sofas and Chairs is, once again, leading the Northeast zone sales standing report for both the month of July and calendar year to date.

Please pass along my thanks to your sales team for an extraordinary comeback effort during the month of July.

Best regards,

Signature

Name

(Congratulations on being elected president of an association)

Date

Name/Title
Business/Organization
Address
City, State Zip Code

Dear Name:

Congratulations on your election to the presidency of the United Association of Engineers. You can be proud of this election, because it is a well-deserved recognition of your outstanding work as well as long-time commitment to the activities of the Association. I am also certain that the members appreciated the excellent job you did last year as director of the Association's international activities program.

My best wishes for success in your new position.

Sincerely yours,

Signature

Name

Letters of Appreciation

(Letter of appreciation)

Date

Name/Title
Business/Organization
Address
City, State Zip Code

Dear Name:

On behalf of the management and staff of St. Joseph's Relief Services, we want to express our deepest appreciation for your hard work during our recent fund-raising activities. Your untiring energy and labor made this fund-raising drive the most successful one since our foundation began six years ago. Thank you very much!

Sincerely,

Signature

Name

(Letter of appreciation)

Date

Name/Title
Business/Organization
Address
City, State Zip Code

Dear Name:

On behalf of the Board of Directors and Officers of the Heyerdahl Corporation, I would like to express sincere appreciation and congratulations to Davis Construction Company for successfully completing the reconstruction of our headquarters building in Woodtown, which was devastated by fire last year.

Your company has distinguished itself as a leader in the construction industry by performing what appeared to be an almost impossible task. Working under difficult conditions and accelerated construction schedules, your company completed the building on June 1, as scheduled.

This accomplishment is a tribute to the fine group of professional engineers and skilled craftsmen you assembled on site, and to the individual skill and dedication of your project manager, David Wallace.

Sincerely yours,

Signature

Name

(Letter of appreciation)

Date

Name/Title
Business/Organization
Address
City, State Zip Code

Dear Name:

Please accept my sincere appreciation for all the assistance you gave me in planning our recent customer seminar at the Cambridge Hotel. Being a novice at planning this type of event, I am certain its success was directly related to your suggestions and directions.

All the people who attended were extremely pleased with their accommodations as well as the friendliness and attentiveness of your entire staff. Please extend my appreciation to the staff and, in particular, to Lisa and Wendy.

Sincerely,

Signature

Name

(Letter of appreciation)

Date

Name/Title
Business/Organization
Address
City, State Zip Code

Dear Name:

I would like to take this opportunity to express my appreciation to the staff of your conference center for the prompt and courteous service that we received during our NBD sales meeting on March 9. We were quite pleased with your facility and with the friendly and helpful service we experienced.

I am sure we will be at your conference center again in the future.

Sincerely yours,

Signature

Name

(Letter of appreciation)

Date

Name/Title
Business/Organization
Address
City, State Zip Code

Dear Name:

Often, in our industry, when an innovative plan or project is successfully brought to completion, we tend to remember the problems and the disputes rather than the pleasure of accomplishment. Happily, this is decidedly not the case with the completion and implementation of our new marketing and advertising plan thanks to you and your dedicated and creative team.

Leonard Finch joins me in extending our particular appreciation to Fred Brown, Anne Fairmont, Warren Silverberg, and, of course, to Ruth Rodney and Michael Ingram.

All the best,

Signature

Name

Thank-You Letters

(Thank-you letter)

Date

Name/Title
Business/Organization
Address
City, State Zip Code

Dear Name:

Thank you for the excellent job on our recent two-day sales conference. You and your entire staff were so supportive and always available for our last minute changes. It was a real pleasure working with such a helpful and committed group of professionals.

I look forward to future successful meetings at the Summit Conference Center.

Sincerely yours,

Signature

Name

(Thank-you letter)

Date

Name/Title
Business/Organization
Address
City, State Zip Code

Dear Name:

Thank you for taking the time to complete our guest comment card during your stay with us on May 15 to 18th.

We were certainly pleased to have you as our guest here in the hotel and welcome the comments that you provided. You may be assured that the air conditioning unit in room 815 has been repaired and adjusted to provide a consistent cool airflow. I have also taken the liberty of forwarding your kind mention of William Dodd, our Front Office Clerk, whom you found to be of great assistance during your stay.

We thank you and we do look forward to welcoming you back to the Chesterfield Hotel during your next trip to Atlanta.

Sincerely,

Signature

Name

Useful Sentences for Congratulation, Appreciation, and Thank-You Letters

We were delighted to learn of your promotion.

On behalf of the Cooperville Bank, I offer you our sincere congratulations on your recent appointment to the Cooperville City Council.

I want to compliment you on your outstanding work as a market researcher.

We do appreciate your assistance in solving this difficult problem.

We view your accomplishment as outstanding!

Best wishes from all of us at Chesterfield.

Congratulations on surpassing your annual sales volume record.

We just heard the good news about your promotion to regional sales manager—Congratulations and best wishes!

I am offering you my sincerest congratulations on your appointment as a member of the board of directors of the Williamson Company. I am certain that Williamson will benefit from your organizational skills and business experience.

My congratulations to you and your sales force for having surpassed last year's sales level.

It is because of high achievers like you that our company has attained such success for the past five years.

Your impressive sales ability as well as your loyalty and devotion to our company have been noted.

Your department's all-out efforts to achieve record sales are apparent to all of us.

Your sales team's efforts have secured once again a significant increase in annual sales volume.

I will have a meeting with our national sales manager next week and I will tell her about the important contribution your sales team made during last month's sales drive.

Just a note to tell you how much we appreciate the salesmanship and hard work you did during our sales drive last month. Without you, we could not have done it. Thank you once again for a great job.

We want to express to you and your staff our deep gratitude and appreciation for your company's generous sponsorship of the Annual Arts Festival.

Judging by your award-winning advertising work for the Hamlin Corporation in Pittsburgh, we are indeed fortunate that your agency is handling our client's international sales efforts.

Thank you once again for the courtesy and kindness extended to us when Mr. Jones and I visited your printing plant last week.

Thank you very much for your excellent suggestions on how to reorganize our mailroom operations.

Thank you very much for your hospitality during our visit to Houston. My wife and I very much enjoyed meeting your family and hope to be able to return your hospitality next year.

We enjoyed your hospitality and hope you will give us a chance to reciprocate the next time you are visiting Boston.

In conclusion, we would like to express once again our deep appreciation for your cooperation.

## CHAPTER 5

BUSINESS ANNOUNCEMENTS

Business announcements are letters or printed notices that inform a select group of regular customers about a range of subjects; for example, an upcoming sales or promotion campaign, the introduction of a new product line, new products or services, incentive programs, price reductions or price increases, the opening of a new factory, office, or branch, a move to a new office location, executive changes or appointments, or the introduction of a new sales representative. Many special announcements are often followed by a personal call from a sales representative.

(Formal printed announcement of the opening of a new business)

Marla Hill and Sidney Johnson

Attorneys at Law

Announce the Opening of Law Offices

Tuesday, February 10, 19__

00 Jackson Avenue   Tel. (000) 000-7910
Centralia, Virginia 00000   Fax: (000) 000-7911

(Formal printed announcement of the opening of an office)

Dr. Anthony Carlton

is pleased to announce

the opening of his office

for the practice of geriatric medicine

000 First Street
Anytown, South Dakota 00000

tel. (000) 000-6655

(Formal printed announcement of the opening of an office)

Anne F. Sanders, M.D.

Announces the opening of her office
for the general practice of medicine

0000 East 68th Street
Columbus, FL 00000

For Appointments: Office Hours
Tel. (000) 000-0000   8:30 A.M. to 5:30 P.M.
                                                                 Monday through Friday

---

(Formal printed announcement of the opening of new offices)

Gerald M. Winter & Partners

Certified Public Accountants

is pleased to announce the opening

of their new offices for the

practice of international tax consulting

ABC Business Center
000 West Appleton Street   Telephone (000) 000-0000
Boston, MA 00000   Fax (000) 000-0000

(Printed letter announcing the opening of a new restaurant)

Dear Cedartown Resident:

We are happy to announce that on Saturday, March 15, at 6.00 P.M., the Fin & Claw Seafood Restaurant will open its doors in the Cedartown Shopping Center. To welcome customers to our new seafood restaurant, we offer special reductions of 25 percent on all items on our luncheon and dinner menu during our Grand Opening weekend.

The Fin & Claw Seafood Restaurant features the most extensive selection of seafood dishes in town.

The Management
Fin & Claw Seafood Restaurant

Reservations for Luncheon and Dinner: tel. (000) 000-0000

(Formal printed announcement of a move to a new location)

ABC, Inc.
Announces that its office
has been moved to:

Peacock Office Building
0000 Peach Street
Atlanta, GA 00000

Tel. (000) 000-0000
Fax: (000) 000-0000

(Letter notifying clients of a move to a new location)

XYZ Company
000 Broad Street
Newton, IL 00000
Tel. (000) 000-0000

Dear Client:

Please note that on July 1, we will move our
offices to a new location:

XYZ Company
000 18th Street
Dearton, IL 00000

Our new telephone and fax numbers:

Tel. (000) 000-0000
Fax (000) 000-0000

Your cooperation in changing your records accordingly will be appreciated.

Sincerely yours,

Signature

Name

(Notice of a change of address on company's stationery)

Dear Name:

The rapid growth of our photocopying service has prompted us to move to a new and larger premises. Effective October 15, our address will be:

00 Fairview Avenue
Maplewood, CT 00000
Tel. (000) 000-0000
Fax: (000) 000-0000

(Letter notifying clients of a move to a new location)

BBB Corporation
0000 Grant Street
Westwood, NJ 00000
Tel. (000) 000-0000
Fax: (000) 000-0000

Dear Client:

On March 15, our office will be moving from
0000 Grant Street, Westwood, NJ 00000
to our new address:

000 Perkins Avenue
Centerpoint, NJ 00000
Tel. (000) 000-0000

Please change your records accordingly. Thank you.

Sincerely,

Signature

Name

(Letter notifying clients of a new association and a move to a new location)

Dear Client:

It gives us great pleasure to inform you that on July 1 we have entered into a close association with ABC Company, Certified Public Accountants, 00 Tapper Street, Centertown, Virginia 00000. We have formed a new company that now practices as ABC & VZZ Associates. As a result we will be moving to larger premises and, effective September 1, our new address will be:

00 Berkshire Court
Centertown, VA 00000

Tel. (000) 000-0000
Fax: (000) 000-0000

The enlarged base that this association provides will enable us to offer improved services to our clients, but at the same time retain the close personal contact and interest in our clients' affairs.

We also take this opportunity to inform you that Mrs. Rina Agricola, C.P.A., who is already known to many clients, became a partner of the new company on July 15.

Sincerely yours,

Signature

Name

(Formal printed announcement of an executive appointment)

We are pleased to announce
and welcome to our law firm
Harold C. Westwood
as a partner of

Jones & Beretta

00 Longwood Avenue
Hamilton, Rhode Island 00000

Tel. (000) 000-0000

(Formal printed announcement of an executive appointment)

NCC Communications, Inc.
is pleased to announce that

Margaret O'Sullivan

has joined the company as
executive vice president

000 Central Avenue
Magnolia, AL 00000
Tel. (000) 000-0000
Fax: (000) 000-0000

(Announcing a new product to customers)

Dear Customer:

Benson & Baker Company is proud to announce our newest product: the Pennsylvania Dutch Farmer Stainless Cookware Set. It combines copper-clad bottoms for outstanding responsiveness to heat, with attractive stainless steel for unsurpassed durability. The transparent temperature glass lids have our full ten-year warranty.

The Pennsylvania Dutch Farmer Stainless Cookware Set is beautifully functional and built to last. The nine-piece set includes the covered oven, steamer insert, covered saucepans, and open skillets.

Our introductory price through September 30 is $___; after September 30, $___.

(Announcing a new product line)

Mirra Living Home

is pleased to announce

a New Line of Curtains and Draperies

Available in both ready-made
and made-to-measure sizes

Shopping Mall
Route 000

Dawson, New Mexico 00000
Tel. (000) 000-0000

Monday–Saturday: 9 A.M.–9 P.M.   Sunday: Noon–5 P.M.

(A letter announcing the acquisition of a new distribution company)

Dear Valued Customer:

Because you are a valued customer, we want to share some interesting news with you. Our company has signed a letter of intent with the XYZ Corporation in Chicago to acquire the XYZ Distribution Company in Miami, Florida. Completion of the sale is subject to various conditions and is expected to occur by year end.

The new organization will retain its own name. The management team of the new company will consist of Herald B. Fisher, currently executive vice president of the XYZ Corporation. Mr. Fisher has been directly involved with the XYZ Distribution Company for the past two years.

We will now have the distribution resources necessary for continued growth and viability in providing the services and products demanded by our customers. In addition, we strongly believe that this acquisition will benefit our existing relationship with your company.

We appreciate your continuing support and business and look forward to the opportunities that lie ahead.

Sincerely,

Signature

Name

(A letter announcing a price increase)

Dear Customer:

Due to an unexpected price increase from our manufacturer in Italy, we are forced to raise the dealer's prices of all our imported sueded pigskin leather women's shoes (all sizes and all colors) by 4.7 percent, effective September 1. Orders entered *before* that date will be invoiced at our old price levels.

We sincerely regret the need for increased prices. However, we know you will understand that this across-the-board increase, which is caused by inflation as well as higher production and labor costs, is beyond our control.

We do appreciate your business and look forward to a continuing association with your company.

Sincerely,

Signature

Name

(A letter announcing a price increase)

Dear Valued Customer:

On May 1, a 2.3 percent price increase will become effective on all our multi-purpose manual lifts as a result of increased production and labor costs.

Orders entered before April 1, with shipment dates prior to May 1, will be invoiced at the old price levels. However, orders entered after April 1 will be invoiced at the increased price levels. We feel that, despite this modest price increase, your company will still be able to sell our products at very competitive prices.

Please contact our sales department if you have any questions.

Sincerely yours,

Signature

Name

(A letter announcing a price increase)

Dear Customer:

Due to an increase in our labor and production costs, we are forced to make a small increase in the price of our future line of classic dress shirts, blazers, slacks, and V-neck sweaters for men (slim, regular and husky sizes). The new prices, shown on the enclosed price list, will go into effect on September 1.

Sincerely yours,

Signature

Name

(A letter announcing a price reduction)

Dear Customer:

We have just signed a new contract with our manufacturer and are glad to pass the savings on to you. Therefore, we are pleased to announce a *price reduction* of 9 percent on the dealer's prices of our entire line of Glenmore household floor and carpet cleaners, including our heavy-duty three-speed shampoo/polisher machines.

We feel that these price decreases will enable you to sell even more Glenmore cleaning and polishing units at very competitive prices.

Thank you very much for your business.

Sincerely,

Signature

Name

(Hotel announcing a towel-saver program)

Dear Guest:

To help protect our environment, The Manchester Hotel Chain has implemented a Towel Saver Program. In doing this we hope to reduce the amount of laundry detergent being released into our waterways. Imagine the tons of towels that are unnecessarily washed each day in all hotels worldwide, and then picture the enormous quantities of laundry detergent that are polluting our water.

Please make your choice:

* towels in the bathtub or showers mean:
  Please Change.

* towels back on the towel rack mean:
  I will use them once again.

Help us preserve our environment. Thank you for your support!

The Manchester Hotels

(Notice about an electronic security system in use in a store)

Dear Customer:

Theft causes losses, and losses push up the costs of operating a store. Increased costs also mean increased prices.

In order to discourage and prevent theft, the management of this store has installed an electronic security system. Products are invisibly marked. Should any item be removed from the store without passing through the checkout, an alarm will sound.

This system is designed in the interests of our customers. Thank you for your cooperation and continued support.

The Management

## CHAPTER 6

BUSINESS AND PRIVATE INVITATIONS

Both informal and formal invitations are often made by telephone. There are, however, many occasions where a letter or printed card is the most appropriate way to invite people. Informal business invitations (for example, inviting a person to a dinner or an award presentation) are usually written on business letterhead. Companies also frequently use sales letters in which customers or prospective buyers are invited to stop by for a demonstration at a trade show or to attend an "open house," such as for the opening of a new store or office. Since such invitations are sent in a mass mailing, no replies are requested or expected. Everybody is welcome.

Invitations to a formal affair or reception can be sent either in the form of a printed or engraved card or a letter (on business letterhead or personal stationery). A formal reply is expected. Often a card (with a stamped self-addressed envelope) is enclosed with a text.

Example:

> I will _____ will not _____ attend the dinner party in honor of John Wilkins
> on Friday, September 14, Name _____

A formal invitation should always include the R.S.V.P. (or RSVP) notation, which is used on an invitation to indicate that the favor of a reply is requested. This French abbreviation stands for *Répondez s'il vous plaît* (please reply).

Formal printed invitation cards are always written in the first person.

Example:

> Mr. and Mrs. Albert Jennings request the pleasure of the company
> of _____

or

> The Directors and Officers of the ABCD Company request the pleasure
> of the company of _____

Social invitations to a married man who holds a title are addressed to the man and his wife.

Example:

Mr. and Mrs. William Taylor; Dr. and Mrs. Brian Sullivan; Senator and Mrs. Fred O'Malley; Lord and Lady Collins.

When the wife holds a title, the name of her husband is still written first on the invitation.

Example:

Mr. Donald and Senator Marie Wilson; Mr. Walter and Dr. Anita Potter.

(Inviting a speaker to address an audience)

Date

Name/Title
Business/Organization
Address
City, State Zip Code

Dear Name:

The Executive Council would like to invite you to speak about the new developments in the European satellite broadcasting industry at our annual General Meeting of the Society of Marketing Directors to be held in Chicago on October 24. About 200 members will be present at this annual meeting.

Several members have recommended you highly. Your recent article in *International Broadcasting Industry* also addresses this very interesting topic. We usually ask our speakers to prepare a 30-minute address, followed by a 10-minute question and answer period.

Our society is prepared to pay all your expenses including overnight accommodation and a modest honorarium of $ _____.

We do hope that you will consider this invitation and join us on October 24. Please, let us know as soon as possible if you will accept this speaking engagement so that we can finalize our program for that evening at the Roosevelt Room of the American Heritage Hotel in Chicago.

Sincerely,

Signature

Name

(Accepting an invitation to address an audience)

Date

Name/Title
Business/Organization
Address
City, State Zip Code

Dear Name:

Thank you very much for your invitation to address the General Meeting of the Society of Marketing Directors at the American Heritage Hotel in Chicago on October 24 on the subject of new developments in the European satellite broadcasting industry. I am pleased to accept your invitation.

According to your request, I plan to take about 30 minutes for the main part of my speaking engagement followed by a question-and-answer period of about 10 minutes. Meanwhile, I am looking forward to receiving additional information about the annual meeting.

Sincerely yours,

Signature

Name

(Declining an invitation to address an audience)

Date

Name/Title
Business/Organization
Address
City, State Zip Code

Dear Name:

Thank you very much for your kind invitation to address the members of your Society of Marketing Directors at their annual meeting in Chicago on October 24. Unfortunately, I cannot attend this meeting owing to a prior speaking engagement on that same date. However, I will be happy to address your organization on another occasion.

As an alternate, I suggest that you contact James Novak of ABC Advertising in Pittsburgh. He recently addressed the members of the Broadcasting Executives Association with a speech about new developments in the satellite industry in the European Union. Thank you again for your invitation. Best of luck with your annual meeting.

Sincerely,

Signature

Name

(Declining an invitation to address an audience)

Date

Name/Title
Business/Organization
Address
City, State Zip Code

Dear Name:

Your letter requesting Ms. Mary Andrews to speak before the Young Managers Club on September 18 arrived the day after she had left on an extended business trip to Europe. Ms. Andrews will not be back before September 15. Therefore, it will be impossible for her to address the members of your club.

I know, however, that Ms. Andrews will appreciate your kind invitation. I am sure she will be in touch with you when she returns from Europe.

Sincerely,

Signature

Name

(An informal invitation in the form of a letter; reply expected)

Date

Name/Title
Business/Organization
Address
City, State Zip Code

Dear Name:

We are pleased to announce that we have moved our offices to a spacious new building at a new location. For that reason, we cordially invite you to see our new facility and to attend an Open House at 175 Fifth Avenue on Thursday, May 10, from 4:00 P.M. until 7:00 P.M.

We certainly hope you can join us on that day. Please let us know if you can, so that we can finalize our program.

Sincerely,

Signature

Name

(Sales-oriented invitation in the form of a letter; no reply expected)

Date

Name/Title
Business/Organization
Address
City, State Zip Code

Dear Client:

We will introduce our newest Laser Printer Model CC 8 during the upcoming Computer Hardware Exhibition in San Francisco from April 3 to April 6. Since you probably will attend this major trade exhibition, we would like to invite you to stop by our demonstration booth number 189 so that we might introduce you to and demonstrate this brand new model.

We are looking forward to having the opportunity to meet you.

Sincerely,

Signature

Name

(Sales-oriented invitation in the form of a letter; no reply expected)

Date

Name/Title
Business/Organization
Address
City, State Zip Code

Dear Sir/Madam:

The compact disc is the ultimate in recorded listening pleasure. . . . Now, portable CD boxes let you take the crisp sound along wherever you go! Colin Ronan Electronics Corporation invites you to the Electronics Trade Exhibition to view its full range of new CD boom boxes at its company display at:

Booth 374, Convention Center
New York City   January 18–23

Our sales representatives and product specialists will be on hand to answer any questions you may have.

We are looking forward to seeing you in New York City.

Sincerely,

Signature

Name

(Formal printed invitation card; no reply expected)

The Executive Board of The Brinkman Art Museum of Philadelphia
Cordially invites you to a Special Preview of the Exhibition of works
by French printmaker Albert Renault

6:00 to 8:30 P.M.   January 9, 1999

Refreshments

(Formal printed invitation card; reply expected)

XYZ ASSOCIATES
00 Fitzharding Square
Manchester, VT 00000

INVITATION

I will/will not* be able to attend the

New England Tourism and Travel Corporation Roadshow at the ABC Hotel in Chicago

Wednesday, October 2, at 6:00

Name:
Company:

* Please delete as appropriate

R.S.V.P.
Franca Lester

Tel. (000) 000-0000

(Formal printed invitation; reply expected)

THE BOARD OF DIRECTORS
of
ABYZ CORPORATION

invites you to attend a dinner party

in honor of

JOHN B. WILKINS

President and Chief Executive Officer

to be held at the ABC Hotel, Atlanta

on Friday evening, September 14

at 7:00 P.M.

RSVP
(000) 000-0000

(Formal printed invitation; reply expected)

THE BRENTWOOD CITY TRADE COMMISSION

requests the pleasure of your company

at a dinner dance in honor of

Dr. Janet Davidson

on Friday, April 9, 7:30 P.M.

The Ballroom of the Williams Hotel

RSVP

(000) 000-0000

(Formal printed invitation; reply expected)

THE EXECUTIVE BOARD OF VITEX CORPORATION

cordially invites you to

a welcoming cocktail party

to meet

Mrs. Paula Taylor, President, International Division

on Wednesday, November 2

from 6:30–8:30 P.M.

at the Anderson Room of the ABC Hotel, Denver

Please reply
(000) 000-0000

(Formal printed invitation; reply expected)

The Management Team
of the XYZ Corporation

in honor of

William R. Chesterfield

requests the pleasure of the company of

Mr. and Mrs. Charles Drake

at a dinner dance

on Saturday, September 12

at seven o'clock

Alexandria Hotel—San Diego

RSVP
(000) 000-0000

(Accepting a formal invitation)

Date

Name/Title
Business/Organization
Address
City, State Zip Code

Dear Name:

Mr. and Mrs. Charles Drake thank the Management Team of the Winchester Corporation for the invitation to attend the dinner dance honoring William R. Chesterfield on September 12, at which they will be happy to attend.

Yours sincerely,

Signature

Name

(Accepting a formal invitation)

Date

Name/Title
Business/Organization
Address
City, State Zip Code

Dear Name:

Dr. and Mrs. John McDonald are pleased to accept the Winchester Corporation's kind invitation to attend the dinner dance at the Alexandria Hotel on Saturday, September 12.

Yours sincerely,

Signature

Name

(Declining a formal invitation)

Date

Name/Title
Business/Organization
Address
City, State Zip Code

Dear Name:

Mr. and Mrs. Alex Longman thank the Management Team of the Winchester Corporation for the kind invitation to attend the dinner dance honoring William R. Chesterfield on September 12, but regret that they are unable to attend due to a prior commitment.

Sincerely,

Signature

Name

(Declining a formal invitation)

Date

Name/Title
Business/Organization
Address
City, State Zip Code

Dear Name:

Mr. and Mrs. Frank Hitching sincerely regret that owing to a previous engagement they are unable to accept the kind invitation of the Winchester Corporation for the dinner dance to be held on Saturday, September 12.

Sincerely,

Signature

Name

Useful Sentences for Invitations

We hope that you and your wife will be able to join us on March 17 and look forward to seeing you then.

Thank you for your kind invitation to the dinner dance on December 9, which my wife and I will be happy to attend.

Thank you very much for your kind invitation for dinner at the Bailey Restaurant on June 2. My wife and I are delighted to accept.

I would be delighted to accept your kind dinner invitation, but my wife and I have already made arrangements to attend a wedding reception on that date.

We regret that we already have another engagement at this time and will not be able to attend.

My wife and I regret that owing to a prior engagement we will not be able to be present at the reception on August 10.

I regret that owing to a prior commitment I am unable to accept your kind invitation for dinner on April 18.

Thank you for your kind invitation to the dinner dance on November 29. I much regret, however, that owing to a prior engagement, my wife and I will not be able to attend.

I regret that I am not able to accept your kind invitation for the buffet reception on January 14. My business schedule calls for me to be in Europe during the entire month of January.

## CHAPTER 7

MISCELLANEOUS BUSINESS LETTERS

This chapter contains letters dealing with a variety of topics. For example, letters asking for or making an appointment; acknowledging receipt of letters during a person's absence from the office; requesting, acknowledging, or refusing a donation; and confirming reservations of a meeting room and other facilities. Also letters dealing with club membership; requests to participate in surveys; requests for an agency, change of address notice, a letter demanding a retraction in a newspaper, welcome notices, and a letter thanking for hospitality.

ASKING FOR OR MAKING AN APPOINTMENT

Date

Name/Title
Business/Organization
Address
City, State Zip Code

Dear Name:

Ms. Diane Bond, national production manager of our sales catalog division, will be in Boston on Thursday, January 28 and would like to tour your web offset printing plant in nearby Cambridge during that afternoon.

Would it be convenient for you or your assistant to meet her on this date? I will get in touch with you by telephone early next week to make an appointment.

Sincerely,

Signature

Name

Date

Name/Title
Business/Organization
Address
City, State Zip Code

Dear Name:

I will be in Manchester on Tuesday, June 7, until Thursday, June 9, and would like to meet you at your office to discuss the brochure layout requirements that we briefly talked about at the recent Technical Trade Exposition in New York. Please, let me know when you could see me. I can come to your office at any time during the above mentioned period.

I will telephone your secretary next week to schedule an appointment. I am looking forward to meeting you.

Sincerely,

Signature

Name

Date

Name/Title
Business/Organization
Address
City, State Zip Code

Dear Name:

As per our telephone conversation yesterday, I have checked the availability of my French colleague in September. We would indeed be happy to meet with you in San Francisco on Thursday, September 7, at whatever time would be convenient for you.

I am looking forward to our meeting.

Sincerely,

Signature

Name

Date

Name/Title
Business/Organization
Address
City, State Zip Code

Dear Name:

Thank you for your letter of November 6 asking for an appointment with Ms. Louise Rainer. Unfortunately, she is away from the office and is not expected back until the end of this month. Ms. Rainer will contact you upon her return and I am sure she will be pleased to meet with you.

Sincerely,

Signature

Name

Acknowledging Receipt of a Letter During a Person's Absence

Date

Name/Title
Business/Organization
Address
City, State Zip Code

Dear Name:

Thank you for your letter of February 5, addressed to Mr. Ronald Santori, concerning the proposed distribution center. Mr. Santori is out of town, but I will see that your proposal is called to his immediate attention as soon as he returns to the office next Tuesday.

Sincerely,

Signature

Name

Date

Name/Title
Business/Organization
Address
City, State Zip Code

Dear Name:

In Ms. Silverman's absence, I am answering your request for information about our Model XX5 Laserprinter. I enclose a brochure describing its many new features.

I hope this information will be of some help to you until Mrs. Silverman returns to the office early next week. She will be in touch with you then to answer any further questions you may have about this new model which we have in stock.

Sincerely,

Signature

Name

Date

Name/Title
Business/Organization
Address
City, State Zip Code

Dear Name:

Mr. Peter Auerbach is away on business in Canada now and plans to return to Atlanta the second week of June. I will bring your letter about the sales conference to his attention at that time. I am certain that Mr. Auerbach will contact you promptly.

Please accept my apologies for this unavoidable delay.

Sincerely,

Signature

Name

Date

Name/Title
Business/Organization
Address
City, State Zip Code

Dear Name:

This letter will acknowledge your letter of May 3 addressed to Ms. Anne Colfax. Ms. Colfax is ill and is not expected to return to the office until the end of this month. Just as soon as I am in touch with her, I will mention your letter.

Sincerely,

Signature

Name

LETTERS REQUESTING, ACKNOWLEDGING, OR REFUSING DONATIONS

Letters requesting, acknowledging, or refusing donations should be brief and courteous. Provide a brief explanation in the event that you do not want to give a donation although this is, of course, not obligatory.

Date

Name/Title
Business/Organization
Address
City, State Zip Code

Dear Name:

The local chapter of the National Annual Welfare Fund is starting its annual fund-raising drive this month. We hope that your company will contribute to this very worthy charitable cause.

Thank you very much for your support.

Sincerely yours,

Signature

Name

Date

Name/Title
Business/Organization
Address
City, State Zip Code

Dear Name:

We are pleased to enclose our company check for $1,000 as our annual contribution to the fund-raising drive for the local chapter of the National Annual Welfare Fund.

We wish you well in your drive this year.

Sincerely,

Signature

Name

Date

Name/Title
Business/Organization
Address
City, State Zip Code

Dear Name:

In response to your letter asking for support for the March of Dollars Benefit Program, we are enclosing a check for $1,500.

Sincerely,

Signature

Name

Date

Name/Title
Business/Organization
Address
City, State Zip Code

Dear Name:

Please accept our gratitude for your company's contribution of $2,500 to the annual drive of the United Charitable Fund. We would like to thank you and your employees for your generosity.

Thank you for your continued support of the fund.

Sincerely yours,

Signature

Name

Date

Name/Title
Business/Organization
Address
City, State Zip Code

Dear Name:

Although we firmly believe in the principles behind your fund-raising drive, we regret that we are unable to contribute to the American Animal Welfare Fund this year—our available budget for contributions is tied up at this time of the year.

However, we do hope that next year we will be once again in a position to contribute to this worthy cause.

In the meantime, we wish you success in your endeavor on behalf of the fund.

Sincerely,

Signature

Name

Date

Name/Title
Business/Organization
Address
City, State Zip Code

Dear Name:

We have sent your request for financial support for the summer sports activities program of the Junior Sports Club to the chairman of our company's contributions committee. We expect that the committee will contact you early next month.

Sincerely,

Signature

Name

RESERVATIONS OF MEETING ROOM AND OTHER FACILITIES

Reservations of a meeting room and other facilities in a hotel or conference center are always made and confirmed in writing in order to avoid any misunderstandings or omissions.

Date

Name/Title
Business/Organization
Address
City, State Zip Code

Dear Name:

As discussed on the telephone, we want to reserve the use of a small conference room where dinner can also be served for 23 people for the evening of Thursday, June 7 from 6:00 P.M. until 11:00 P.M.

We also want to reserve your three-course steak dinner ($24.95) for every participant, as well as optional bar service.

Please, confirm this reservation by return mail or fax.

Sincerely,

Signature

Name

Date

Name/Title
Business/Organization
Address
City, State Zip Code

Dear Name:

I enjoyed talking to you on Tuesday. The Dorset Hotel does have the facilities that our company needs to schedule its annual shareholders' meeting on April 2, with check-in time scheduled for 9:30 A.M.

I hereby confirm that we have booked the Wessex Room, which can comfortably seat 100 people; the Flamingo Suite (spacious seating for at least 15 people) for press meetings; and the Washington Dining Room (seating capacity for more than 100 people) where drinks and luncheon will be served after the shareholders' meeting.

We also need the following audiovisual and other equipment and services:

- In the Wessex Room:
  - Public address system
  - One VHS videocassette player
  - Four television monitors
  - One overhead projector and screen
  - Coffee and tea service

- In the Flamingo Suite:
  - One flip chart
  - Coffee, alcoholic and non-alcoholic beverages

- In the Washington Dining Room:
  - Public address system
  - One motion picture projector (16 mm)
  - One motion picture screen
  - Alcoholic and non-alcoholic beverages
  - Luncheon (including wine service)

I will telephone you on March 29 about the arrangements as outlined above. Please send me your written confirmation.

Sincerely,

Signature

Name

LETTERS DEALING WITH CLUB MEMBERSHIP

The following letters deal with an invitation as well as a request to become a member of a club, a proposal for club membership, a letter of resignation, and invitations to members to attend certain functions.

(A request to propose a person for club membership)

Date

Name/Title
Business/Organization
Address
City, State Zip Code

Dear Name:

Your name has been suggested to me by Alfred Drake as a person who is actively interested in community affairs in our town. For that reason, I would like to request your permission to propose your name for membership at the Centreville Civic Club at the next monthly meeting scheduled for Monday, October 4. Please let me know as soon as possible if you are willing to become a member.

Sincerely,

Bill Rogers
Chairman
Centreville Civic Club

(An invitation to consider membership in a club)

Date

Name/Title
Business/Organization
Address
City, State Zip Code

Dear Name:

On behalf of the Carl Wallace Board of Directors in Tiltonville, I would like to invite you to consider a membership in the Tiltonville Businessman's Club.

Proceeds from membership directly benefit the Foundation's mission, which is to help higher education pursuits at the vocational/college level and assist with selected funding needs for various local, state, and regional organizations and projects with an agricultural emphasis.

Established in 1978, the Tiltonville Businessman's Club facilities offer an atmosphere where friends, family, and business associates can enjoy dining and socializing. In addition, the support you give through a membership is directly related to the ongoing commitment to preserve and enhance our communities and the interests they serve.

Join us in our support of this region's leading industry . . . agriculture.

Sincerely,

William J. Rochester
Chairman
Tiltonville Businessman's Club

(A proposal to consider a person for club membership)

Date

Name/Title
Business/Organization
Address
City, State Zip Code

Dear Name:

I would like to propose Mr. Carl Lewes for membership in the Alpha Omega Society.

Mr. Lewes, who has been very active in community and sports affairs in various parts of the country, recently moved to our town from Dallas, Texas.

I am certain Mr. Lewes would be a real addition and credit to our membership.

Sincerely yours,

Signature

Name

(Installation of a new club member)

Date

Name/Title
Business/Organization
Address
City, State Zip Code

Dear Name:

Thank you very much for recommending me to the Alpha Omega Society. I was chosen as one of the members and attended the colorful installation ceremony at the Windgate Hotel last week.

Sincerely,

Signature

Name

(Request to become a member of a professional organization)

Date

Name/Title
Business/Organization
Address
City, State Zip Code

Dear Name:

I believe that, based upon my professional qualifications and business experience, I meet the criteria for membership in the U.S. Association of Certified Travel Agents. For that reason, I would like to receive a membership application form for your organization.

Thank you very much for your attention to this request.

Sincerely,

Signature

Name

(Resignation of club membership)

Date

Name/Title
Business/Organization
Address
City, State Zip Code

Dear Name:

It is with considerable regret that I must tender my resignation as vice president of the Halifax Admiralty Club. I have not yet fully recovered completely from a recent illness and my business travel schedule for this coming year is such that I would not be able to participate vigorously in the Club's activities. However, I sincerely hope that in a year or two, my health and business affairs will permit me to become active once again in the Club.

Sincerely,

Signature

Name

(Invitation to members of a professional organization to attend a dinner meeting)

Dear Member:

Our bimonthly dinner meeting scheduled for February 25 should be extremely interesting to all members. Our speaker:

> William Sokoloff
> Production Manager
> ABC Photograph Books

He will discuss: A Photo-Journalistic Approach to Book Publishing.

In 1993, ABC Photograph Books became a separate division of ABC Publishing Company. Mr. Sokoloff has been in charge of production since 1994. He will cover the wide range of working with photo-journalists and the problems involved in producing high-quality color photo books.

See you at the Mandarin Hotel on Wednesday, February 25, at 7:30 P.M.

Gerald Gleason
President
Graphic Arts Association

(Announcing a special guest speaker for an annual conference)

Dear Member:

During our annual conference of the League for City School Teachers on April 17, we will have a special guest—Dr. Alicia Hobson, Superintendent of Schools, Auburn City—to speak to us about America's educational system and where it might be in the future.

Meeting the needs of our rapidly expanding educational system, Dr. Hobson has been both teacher and administrator for more than 31 years at all levels of public education. Her personal experience in the classroom, her position as head of a large public school system, and her involvement as a trustee of The Center for Interracial Urban Education make her eminently qualified to speak about the future needs of our public schools.

We hope to see you in the Auburn City Conference Center on Thursday, April 17 at 9:00 A.M.

Alexander Scanlon, Jr.
Chairman, Annual Conference Committee
League for City School Teachers

MISCELLANEOUS LETTERS

(A letter with an unsolicited offer)

Date

Name/Title
Business/Organization
Address
City, State Zip Code

Dear Name:

We have seen your name and advertisements in various British trade periodicals and note that you are a major importer of quality garment and shoe racks and accessories, which provide additional hanging space for clothing, shoes, ties, and other personal items. Since 1973, our company is the export agent for the well-known Woodson Quality Racks in Devonport, Idaho, and we are confident that we can offer your company a great variety of high-quality garment and shoe racks at very competitive prices.

We enclose a copy of our most recent sales catalog and price list and hope you will be encouraged to place a trial order with us.

Sincerely,

Signature

Name

(An American manufacturer offering merchandise on consignment)

Date

Name/Title
Business/Organization
Address
City, State Zip Code

Dear Name:

We are a large American manufacturer specializing in cutlery. As we are particularly keen to promote our high-quality stainless-steel cutlery in Southeast Asia, we are writing to ask if your company would be prepared to allow us to send a representative selection of this cutlery on consignment. In return, we would allow a commission of 11 percent calculated on gross profits. No risks are involved, because we will fully reimburse your company for the return of any goods that are not sold within one year. We enclose our catalog and price list for your inspection.

We look forward to hearing from you.

Sincerely,

Signature

Name

(An American retail chain requesting a sole agency)

Date

Name/Title
Business/Organization
Address
City, State Zip Code

Dear Name:

We are a small retail chain with ten sales outlets in the San Diego metropolitan area. Our company specializes in all types of beds (ranging from brass beds, daybeds, French-style and country-style beds, to electric adjustable beds) as well as mattresses (single, twin, queen, and king size and so forth).

There is an increasing demand in our sales area for all types of high quality beds and mattresses. For that reason, we are looking for a well-known British manufacturer of these items who is willing to offer us a sole agency to retail their beds and mattresses in the San Diego metropolitan area, which includes a large number of suburbs and other communities. Our company is already the sole agent for a major French manufacturer of beds and mattresses in the above-mentioned sales territory.

Awaiting your answer to this letter with great interest, we remain,

Sincerely,

Signature

Name

(An American manufacturer looking for an agent in the Netherlands)

Date

Name/Title
Business/Organization
Address
City, State Zip Code

Dear Name:

We are keen to expand exports of our comfortable recliner chairs to the Netherlands and are looking for an agent who can represent us in that country. You were highly recommended to us by Ms. Elske Doets of the Netherlands-USA Chamber of Commerce and Industry in New York. She told us that you might be interested to act as the sole Dutch sales agent for our luxury recliner chairs featuring a hardwood frame and steel springs.

Our company already has sole agents in Germany, Denmark, and Sweden, who represent us for a ten percent commission on net list prices, plus advertising support. These sole agents were offered an initial 18-month trial period and are only required to hold a representative selection of sample chairs.

We enclose a copy of our latest sales catalog and price list and a draft contract for your inspection. If you are interested in accepting our company's agency, our sales manager, Richard Wallace, would be pleased to visit you in Amsterdam in late April and discuss the terms of such an agency. If you have any further questions, please contact me by fax or telephone. I look forward to hearing from you.

Sincerely,

Signature

Name

(A letter about possible collaboration in a business venture)

Date

Name/Title
Business/Organization
Address
City, State Zip Code

Dear Name:

I was pleased to learn from Dick Lane of your interest in expanding your professional vacuum cleaner business in Vermont and Maine. Therefore, I would welcome an opportunity of discussing with you how we might collaborate in such a way that your objectives could be advanced and implemented.

I look forward to an early meeting.

Sincerely,

Signature

Name

(Request to participate in a survey)

Date

Name/Title
Business/Organization
Address
City, State Zip Code

Dear Sir/Madam:

We are carrying out a survey about the use of business computers in the state of Texas on behalf of the 179 local chapters of the Texas Always Better Business Organization.

The enclosed survey is being conducted among a small, randomly selected sample of medium-sized companies (up to 100 employees). Your participation is very important to our organization. We value your professional opinion. Please feel free, when completing the questionnaire to include any additional comments you may wish to make.

An independent market research company has been hired to tabulate and analyze your answers in the enclosed questionnaire. Please be assured that all your answers will be kept strictly confidential and anonymous and will never be associated with your name or used to sell you anything. Your answers will only be used to prepare a statistical summary of the survey results.

A reply envelope is enclosed and we would very much appreciate your completing and returning the questionnaire to us.

Thank you very much for your kind help and cooperation with this project.

Sincerely,

Geraldine Scott
Project Director

(Request to participate in a customer research survey)

CUSTOMER SERVICE QUESTIONNAIRE

Dear Customer:

From time to time, we seek the opinion of our customers. We are always trying to improve the quality of our products and services and the information that you are able to supply will assist us to serve you better. Your answers will be kept in strict confidence and will only be used for statistical analysis.

This questionnaire forms part of our Customer Care Program and we would appreciate your help by completing the enclosed form. Please complete this questionnaire in block letters and place a "x" in the appropriate boxes. You can return the questionnaire by mail in the pre-addressed envelope or by fax (000) 000-0000.

Thank you for taking the time to help us.

Sincerely,

Roger M. Hunt
Manager
Market Research Department

(Letter demanding a retraction in a newspaper)

Dear Editor:

We noticed a serious error in the tourism section of the *Daily Tribune* of September 29. The article "Brave Hearts" about the Native American reservations in Montana, states that our company—John's Trek Tours—only specializes in organizing tours of the Rocky Mountain region. This is incorrect and misleading, because we also offer (since 1991) organized riding and camping tours on Native American tribal lands in Arizona and Utah.

We would appreciate a correction in the next edition of the *Daily Tribune*. Thank you.

Sincerely,

Signature

Name

(Letter thanking for hospitality)

Date

Name/Title
Business/Organization
Address
City, State Zip Code

Dear Richard,

Thank you for the kindness and hospitality I enjoyed at your home. Mary is a marvelous cook!

I sincerely hope that we may develop some mutually profitable software projects. It would indeed be advantageous to meet your Chicago representative. Please extend my best wishes to Gerald Weeren. I will write to him in some detail about the production details we discussed.

Do not forget the standing invitation to visit our home on your next trip to Cleveland.

With kind regards,

Sincerely,

Signature

Name

(Welcome letter)

Date

Name/Title
Business/Organization
Address
City, State Zip Code

Dear Mr. and Mrs. Dickson,

It is certainly a pleasure to welcome you to the Park Hotel.

We are delighted to have you as our guests and I am confident that our services will meet with your satisfaction.

If I may be of any assistance during your stay, please do not hesitate to contact me.

Sincerely,

Alexander D. Higgins
General Manager

(Change-of-address notice to a magazine subscription department)

Date

Name/Title
Business/Organization
Address
City, State Zip Code

Dear Sir/Madam:

I am writing to inform you that as of September 1, I will be moving from my current address on 00 Lincoln Boulevard, Wildwood, VA 00000, to 000 Casper Avenue, Baltimore, MD 00000. Please change your records accordingly as of that date. Thank you.

Sincerely,

Signature

Name

(An example of a Guest Comment Card and Questionnaire)

ABC RESTAURANT AND BAR

Dear Customer:

This is a Customer Comment Card. With your help we hope to continue to provide a high standard of food and service.

Day _____   Date _____   Time Visited _____

How often do you visit us?   First time   _____
    Twice a week or more _____   Once a week _____
    Once or twice a month _____   Once a year _____

What was your opinion of:	Poor	Good	Very Good
Liquor Service	____	____	____
Food Service	____	____	____
Staff Friendliness	____	____	____

Your Meal

Soup/Entrée	____	____	____
Main Meal	____	____	____
Dessert	____	____	____

Please comment on above _____
_____
_____

Any further suggestions or improvements? _____
_____
_____

Thank you very much for your comments. When completed, please place your Customer Comment Card in container provided.

## CHAPTER 8

MINUTES

Minutes are a written record of the proceedings, decisions, motions, amendments, and resolutions transacted at a formal or informal meeting. Minutes should be written in the third person and past tense. If you need detailed information about the commonly accepted procedures for conducting meetings of all types and sizes, as well as procedures for motions, it is wise to consult a copy of the well-known manual *Robert's Rules of Order Newly Revised*, written by Henry Martyn Robert. Robert, a United States parliamentarian, based his handbook on procedures followed in the U.S. Congress and the British Parliament. It is used by many companies, organizations, and clubs in the United States and Canada to conduct meetings. A glossary of terms used in meetings is provided at the end of this chapter.

SAMPLE MINUTES

(Agenda for the meeting of a board of directors)

XYZ COMPANY

Meeting of the Board of Directors to be held
on Wednesday, April 3, 1999 at 10:15 A.M. in
the Company Boardroom.

AGENDA

1. Apologies for absence.
2. Minutes of the meeting held on March 2, 1999.
3. Points arising from minutes as read.
4. Report by the Chairman (a copy of the report is attached to this agenda).
5. Resolution.
6. Date of next meeting.
7. To transact any other business that may come before the meeting.

(Minutes of the monthly meeting of a board of directors)

Minutes of the Board of Directors of the XYZ Company held on Wednesday, April 3, 1999, at 10:15 A.M. in the company boardroom. Chairman John Brown presided.

PRESENT: Edward Bendex, Kenneth Morgan, Sharon Moretti, Ronald Jaslow, Otto Tadros, Peter Asselmeyer, and Laura Tish (recording secretary).

APOLOGIES: Apologies for absence were received from Rina Dollinger and Alfred Kessel.

MINUTES: The minutes of the March 2, 1999, meeting were read by the secretary and approved.

REPORT BY CHAIRMAN: The Chairman reported that he had met Mr. Nathan Rosenberg concerning XYZ's interests in computer software development and the services Mr. Rosenberg is prepared to extend to aid XYZ in developing these interests. For the information of the Chairman, Mr. Rosenberg outlined the growth of the software industry from the time he launched ABC Software Company in 1987 until today.

MOTION: Chairman Brown proposed a motion, seconded by Sharon Moretti, that an ad hoc committee of directors should be instituted to study Mr. Rosenberg's involvement in greater detail. The board agreed to vote on this motion at the next meeting.

RESOLUTION: A resolution authorizing the company's transfer agent to issue new shares was unanimously adopted by all members.

NEXT MEETING: It was agreed that the next meeting will be held on May 2, 1999, at 10:30 A.M., in the company boardroom.

There being no further business, the meeting closed at 11:45 A.M.

(Minutes of the regular monthly meeting of a board of directors)

BZN & COMPANY

Minutes of the regular monthly meeting of the Board of Directors held on October 15, 1999 at 1:30 P.M. in the conference room.

Present:　　　　　　　　　　Christina Zeller (chairperson)
　　　　　　　　　　　　　　Ron Cedino
　　　　　　　　　　　　　　Thomas Kilroy
　　　　　　　　　　　　　　Charles Levitsky
　　　　　　　　　　　　　　Ellen Novak
　　　　　　　　　　　　　　Nicholas Raines
　　　　　　　　　　　　　　Robert Vogler

Apology for absence

An apology for absence was received from Michael Ferris.

Minutes

The minutes of the meeting of September 14, 1999 were read by Robert Vogler and approved. The following amendment was made in the Minutes of August 16, 1999. The sentence which refers to the management consulting services to be provided by Driscoll & Associates should be changed to read "Although the descriptions of the services we are prepared to accept are intended to be exploratory only, BZN & Company shall be pleased to receive a proposal, including your fee, for the first phase and an indication of fees for phase two."

Report

Thomas Kilroy summarized his detailed discussions with Jay Jefferson, Chief Executive Officer of Hudson Audiovisual Productions ("Hudson") and BZN's interests in audiovisual instructional materials. The classroom use of audiovisual instructional materials in the United States, Canada, the United Kingdom, and other countries of the European Union has been a major educational trend and has had phenomenal growth. A trend that educators in North America and Western Europe are predicting is likely to continue.

Since there are many ways that Hudson can help BZN develop an international audiovisual program for use in English-speaking countries and with translation for other parts of the world, Mr. Kilroy made the following proposal, seconded by Nichols Raines, to authorize a feasibility study to cover the following:

a) The present educational audiovisual marketplace in the United States, Canada, and the United Kingdom, and its potential for expansion.

b) Present companies operating in this marketplace and their share.

c) Growth patterns of different types of audiovisual materials and their potential for continued growth and change.

Report

Thomas Kilroy gave a summary of a study on the feasibility of acquiring an audiovisual instructional materials company in North America and the United Kingdom. Results indicate more investigation is needed.

—To select the companies that seem to offer the best opportunities to BZN and to investigate the possibility of acquiring them.

—To inquire about the terms of sales from the owners of the companies selected by BZN and report these terms to BZN.

Date of the next meeting

The proposal for a feasibility study about the audiovisual industry will be discussed at the next meeting of the Board of Directors, to be held on November 12, 1999 at 9:30 A.M. in the Conference Room.

The meeting adjourned at 4:25 P.M.

Respectfully submitted,

Robert Vogel, Recording Secretary

GLOSSARY OF TERMS USED IN MEETINGS

ad hoc committee: a committee formed for a specific purpose (for example, a committee to investigate the feasibility of a certain action).

adjourn: to suspend or defer the proceedings of a meeting *(adjournment)* until a later stated time or date.

agenda: a schedule or list of things to be considered and discussed at a meeting.

amendment: a minor change or revision in the wording of a motion.

ballot: a sheet of paper *(voting slip)* used to cast a vote, especially a secret one.

carried: a term used when the number of affirmative ("yes") votes outweighs the number of negative ("no") votes.

casting vote: a final vote cast by the chairperson to resolve a deadlock when an equal number of votes are cast for and against a motion.

chairperson: a nonsexist descriptive term for the person—man or woman—who takes the chair (leads) at a meeting; chairman; chairwoman.

closure: a motion to bring to an end a discussion on a matter before a meeting.

committee: a group of people selected from a larger group to discuss, investigate, or report on a particular subject; see *ad hoc committee*.

constitution: a set of written rules adopted by the members of an organization that prescribes the nature and functions of an organization to govern it.

deadlock: a standstill that arises when equal numbers of votes are cast for and against a motion.

lie on the table: documents, proposals, or motions that are postponed or put aside for consideration at a later date.

motion: a formal proposal put forward at a meeting for consideration, debate, and decision and then put to a vote. A motion must be moved by a member and seconded (supported) by another member ("the seconder") before the chairperson allows a vote on it. A motion by a majority vote that has been accepted by an organization or a club becomes a resolution.

motion of dissent: a motion against a particular ruling or decision.

move a motion: to make a formal proposal at a meeting.

mover: the person who initiates, proposes or requests ("moves") a motion.

notice of a motion: a notice given at a meeting of a motion that will be discussed at the next meeting.

out of order: not in accordance with recognized parliamentary rules, proceedings, or procedures.

point of honor: a matter that affects a person's honor or reputation.

point of order: a question as to whether the present proceedings or procedures at a meeting are allowed or in order. Plural: points of order.

proxy: a person authorized to act for another person at a meeting; *to vote by proxy; to stand proxy for.* Also the written authorization to act or vote on behalf of another who cannot attend a meeting *(proxy vote).*

quorum: the minimum number or proportion of members of an organization or committee, usually a majority, who must be present at a meeting for the valid transaction of business.

rebuttal: the act of rebutting: to refute, especially by offering or presenting opposing convincing evidence to oppose an argument.

rescission: the act of rescinding a motion; the repeal or annulment of a motion.

resolution: see *motion.*

seconder: see *motion.*

secret ballot: see *ballot.*

show of hands: a popular method of voting to raise one hand in favor of or against a motion.

unanimous: sharing the same views or opinions; chararacterized by complete agreement or assent; for example, *a unanimous vote.*

verbatim notes: minutes that record exactly everything that is said (word for word) at a meeting are referred to as being made *verbatim.* Recording secretaries usually take verbatim notes of motions, amendments, and resolutions.

vote down: to defend by a vote.

vote in: to elect or establish by vote.

vote out: to defeat by a vote.

voting slip: see *ballot.*

## CHAPTER 9

BUSINESS REPORTS AND PROPOSALS

Business reports are written factual accounts that objectively, accurately, and clearly communicate and document information about one or more aspects of a given business. The formats of business reports may vary from brief and informal reports to highly detailed formal reports with an appendix providing additional information, statistical data, diagrams, graphs, maps, tables, bar charts, line charts, pie charts, flow charts, organization charts, and even a bibliography. Business reports can also be classified as internal reports (for use within the company itself) and as external reports (sent to persons in other companies).

Informal reports are usually short and may consist of one to five or six pages. For that reason, such reports are often written in the form of a letter or memo. In contrast with informal reports, formal reports are often written in impersonal terms. Pronouns such as "I" and "you" are frequently not used. However, expressions such as "I am convinced," "In my opinion," or "In my view" are acceptable provided they are used sparingly. Personal biases should be kept in check and emotionally charged language must be avoided. However, be sure that the information in informal and formal business reports is accurate, reliable, and specific; contains all the relevant facts and figures; and also reflects and exercises good judgment. Moreover, it must put the facts in perspective and present plenty of valid evidence to develop recommendations to support the writer's conclusions.

Formal business reports are longer and more detailed than brief informal reports. The proper format, style, length, and organization of a business report (also referred to as a "study") depends on the person or persons who originate this document, why it is prepared, what subject it covers, and who the recipients or end-users of the report are. In this chapter, examples are provided of a letter of transmittal, several proposals for a business report, and an executive summary of a business report. In this manner, the reader will get a good idea about the type of information such informal and formal business reports contain and the manner in which they are presented. A list of useful sentences concludes the chapter.

A formal business report is an important management tool and should have a logical structure consisting of the following (optional) components:

A. *Title Page*—This page includes the full title of the report; the name and title of the person who authorized the report; the name and title of the person who prepared the report; and the date on which the report was submitted.

B. *Letter of Transmittal*—This letter is addressed to the person(s) who authorized the report and states that the report is ready.

C. *Table of Contents*—The heading and subheadings that are used in the text of the report are frequently used as the basis for the table of contents. In addition, the beginning page number for each heading or subheading is given.

D. *Executive Summary or Synopsis*—An Executive Summary provides in an abbreviated form all the relevant "highlights" (in particular the conclusions and recommendations) of a report. An Executive Summary provides more information than a synopsis, which gives only a brief descriptive outline or general view of the report.

E. *Introduction*—The introduction of a formal business report generally states the authorization for the report; the purpose of the report; the scope of the report (what the report covers or does not cover); and a brief description of the sources (for example, personal interviews, field research, questionnaires, secondary sources, etc.) that have been used for the report. A list of definitions that are used in the report may also be included, although these definitions may also be explained in footnotes in the text itself.

F. *Main Body of the Report*—The main body of the report consists of all chapters or sections that make up the report.

G. *Conclusions*—Conclusions sum up the results, outcome, decisions, or judgment reached after the writing of the report. A frequently used introductory sentence is the following: "The findings of this study lead to the following conclusions."

H. *Recommendations*—Recommendations describe a course of action on the basis of the facts as presented in the study. A frequently used introductory sentence is the following: "Based on the conclusions of this study, the following recommendations are made."

I. *Appendix*—An appendix (plural: appendixes or appendices) is a collection of supplementary material (for example, charts, diagrams, and statistical, numerical, and financial information) at the end of a formal report.

J. *Bibliography*—A bibliography is an alphabetical listing of sources of information in print on a specific subject—usually in the form of books, reference works, magazine or newspaper articles, government documents, and so forth—that have been consulted during the preparation of the study.

(A consultant's letter accompanying a proposal for a feasibility study)

Date

Name/Title
Business/Organization
Address
City, State Zip Code

Dear Name:

Attached is the business proposal for a feasibility study you requested at our meeting in Orlando last month. I am sure you will agree that it covers all the relevant points we discussed at that time. I believe that such a feasibility study would offer your company the tools to make a balanced decision on the value of the Zandstra Apartment Project in southern Florida.

It goes without saying that our firm would also be pleased to advise your company during the implementation of these plans as outlined in our proposal.

Please let me know your reaction to our proposal so that we may plan our time schedules accordingly. If you have any questions or comments I will be happy to answer them.

Sincerely,

Signature

Name

(An American consultant's proposal for a business report to study the potential for expansion and opportunity in the United States for a French company)

XYZ Management Consultants
Boston

January 7, 1999

Mr. Pierre Renoir
President
Renoir Business Information Services S.A.
91 Boulevard Arlette Vierny
75000 Paris
France

Dear Mr. Renoir:

Following our meeting of November 29 and your request for consulting support, I am pleased to submit a proposal for a business report to define a corporate strategy for Renoir Business Information Services ("Renoir") in the United States. The following chapters contain:

- a summary of the underlying developments that have led to the need of a detailed business report;

- our understanding of the basic issues that Renoir faces; and our suggestions as to the approach and work plan to be followed in addressing these issues;

- a delineation of subjects and areas to be included in the study; and an outline of items we will deliver to you as a result of our work;

- a description of the assignment, together with an indication of expected timing and budget.

BACKGROUND

Renoir, one of the larger and technically more advanced business information systems and service companies in France, has developed various applications of new electronic information technologies. Renoir is also active in the United Kingdom. There its focus has been on business information systems through a combination of two partial acquisitions, collectively referred to as "Renoir Business Information Services UK."

Extension of business information systems and services into the United States has been avoided until now, because of the advanced development stage of these markets. However, recent developments led Renoir management to believe that the time for U.S. expansion may have come. In particular, European business information users are becoming more sophisticated and demanding. Partly because of this, large French suppliers like Axion Business Services and Rathers European Information Company are also actively expanding their product lines and customer base in the United States, and a number of smaller companies are trying to enter this market with either multinational databases or with new software tools. Accordingly, you are requesting our company to undertake this business study to understand the potential for expansion and opportunities in the United States of America.

ISSUES

In taking the cornerstones for an American strategy in business information services, Renoir management faces two sets of issues: what is the nature of the opportunities and how can Renoir benefit from them?

1. In which market areas of business information systems and services will there be a gap between demand and supply?

   - What is the demand outlook by segment?

   - Which competitors can be expected to meet this demand, what are the key factors of success, and what opportunities are available for different suppliers? For example, multinational and national competitors; small local competitors; competitors that provide information as a sideline (e.g. banks); and public service companies.

- What is the required scale for business information services and will this call for an international approach or permit a local effort? Will barriers emerge that can protect attractive segments?

- How will the technological evolution impact these opportunities as it changes required scales, timings, and as it breaks down barriers protecting niche markets?

- What is the "window" of these opportunities: that is, timing and area of development for the United States?

2. How can Renoir benefit from these opportunities?

- Which function can Renoir best perform in each selected segment: for example, database supplier, information source, enhancer, software distributor or supplier?

- Which synergies exist with Renoir's existing business in France and the United Kingdom in terms of overall personnel and financial and other resources?

- What is the potential of Renoir's European business information activities in terms of business size and volume; market positions by segment and countries; and growth and profitability?

- What concrete steps should Renoir take to enter the U.S. market: for instance, partnerships, priorities, organizations and resource development needs or actions and timing?

APPROACH

In view of the range and complexity of the issues stated above, we believe it is advisable to conduct this business report in three phases. In Phase I, we will focus on the first set of issues over a relatively broad area of business segments, at a rather superficial level. At the end of this phase, we will select segments that are promising enough to warrant detailed study in Phase II, which should answer the remaining issues. The following statements regarding scope and deliverables are all directed at Phase I only. This leaves us the flexibility to fit the project to our improved understanding and evolving needs as we enter Phase II.

During the first days of Phase I, we will rapidly familiarize ourselves with the characteristics of Renoir. This will be followed by a basic segmentation of business information systems in the United States. Subsequent external analyses and interviews will all be directed at improving the definition of these segments and at describing them in terms of, among other things, demand, growth, supply, and competitive patterns. This combination of analysis and information gathering will result in a selection of promising opportunities, by segment, to be analyzed in detail in Phase II.

In the strategy development of Phase II, our work will become much more interactive. First, we will have to review Renoir's available resources in some detail. Subsequently, the business development hypotheses that we have created together with Renoir management will have to be tested in the outside marketplace. These activities will produce a set of proposals on how to penetrate these markets.

Phase III consists of the actual implementation of the plan, including approaching business partners, setting up organizations and resources and preparing for commercial operations. This work should be done by Renoir management, with XYZ Consultants providing a support role as necessary.

As a result of Phase I, we will deliver to Renoir a segmentation of the business information systems and services that are pertinent to this business report; a demand overview for each segment; and a preliminary review of the supply and competitive outlook. An indication of the areas of opportunity for Renoir that warrant further research in Phase II will also be delivered, together with a detailed work and resource plan for Phase II.

TIMING AND BUDGET

If the decision deadline of September 1999 that you have set for this ambitious business study is to be met, we will have to start in the first days of February. Our schedule aims at finishing Phase I at the end of May and Phase II at August 15.

For the effort of our team in Phase I, we propose that you authorize a budget of $____, amount that we will not exceed without your written permission. Expenses for travel, report reproduction, and project administration will be charged in addition, but are not expected to exceed __ percent of the professional fee.

GENERAL PROVISIONS

Our work for Renoir will be on a best effort basis. We sincerely hope that the results will meet the objectives sought by your company. We have assigned to this business report professional personnel who have the required skills, experience, competence, and foreign language capabilities. In any event, our liability for damages direct or consequential resulting from this work will be limited to the amount paid to us.

Any change in this agreement shall be confirmed in writing and signed by authorized representatives of both parties. Since you have already verbally authorized us to proceed on this study, we look forward to receiving a signed copy of this proposal in confirmation.

We appreciate the opportunity to work with your company on this challenging assignment.

Sincerely yours,

Charles Goldwater
President
XYZ Management Consultants

Letter in duplicate

Approved for XYZ Consultants   Accepted for Renoir

By _____   By _____

Title _____   Title _____

Date _____   Date _____

_____

(Letter of transmittal of an Executive Summary of a business report)

American Book Publishers (ABP)
Toronto

Date

Name/Title
Business/Organization
Address
City, State Zip Code

Dear Name:

The enclosed Executive Summary presents our department's study and analysis of the college and professional book publishing market in the United States, and an evaluation of two acquisition candidates for our company. The study is in accordance with our proposal of April 22. The complete text of the report will be available early next month.

To meet the objectives of this project, we have completed a number of tasks. These have included:

- A conceptual review of the college and professional publishing business.

- Interviews in the United States with professors and other college personnel, college bookstores, general trade bookstores, book distributors, publishers, and others.

- A statistical study of the industry.

- A study of the new title output and publishing backlists of the two candidates.

- Analysis and summarization of these inputs.

- Written report and Executive Summary of the findings.

We have organized the report into six sections, as follows:

I.   Executive Summary (enclosed)

II.   An Overview of the Publishing Industry. In this section we provide an overview of the college and professional publishing market in the United States as a background for discussion of the two candidates. We review the following: structure of the industry including size and growth, profitability, segmentation of the markets, important characteristics, and concentration of participants.

III. The Requirements to be Successful in Publishing. The overview material and other analysis has been used to identify the key requirements for success. These are discussed in this section and include: the importance of scale of operation, the importance of discipline dominance, the importance of developing business thrust around related disciplines, and the requirements for success in each major market. These requirements are developed as a basis for comparing the two acquisition candidates.

IV. Comparative Analysis. In this section a number of key factors in the performance of each of the two candidates have been compared among themselves and against industry performance. They are: sales growth vs. markets, profit margins, profit growth and stability, new titles introductions, backlist strength, and stock performance. In addition, operating ratio comparisons requested by ABP including sales/net current assets, operating income/sales, net profit/equity, sales/inventory, profit before taxes/tangible net worth, profit before taxes/total assets, sales/equity, current assets/current liabilities, equity/total capitalization, and dividends/net profits.

V.   Review of the Two Candidates and Summary. In this section, we summarize the performance of the two candidates, from the following two standpoints: (a) The operating performance of each company. This review includes present position in the college/professional markets, profit character, and publishing strengths; and (b) How each candidate meets the key requirements for success, including all the factors as outlined in Section 3 of this letter.

VI. Appendix. The Appendix provides the following charts and tables: structure of college and professional publishing in the United States, distribution channels, estimated publishing industry sales by college and professional book markets, comparative market segments of the candidates, mergers and acquisitions, analysis of publishing catalogs, books in print, financial situation, and management of the candidates.

Sincerely yours,

Anthony B. Hyde
Director
Research & Analysis Department

(Executive summary of a business report)

American Book Publishers (ABP)
Toronto

EXECUTIVE SUMMARY

A Study of the College and Professional Book Publishing Industry in the United States and an Acquisition Evaluation of Two Companies in this Publishing Sector

BACKGROUND

American Book Publishers (ABP) is an English-language publisher in Canada, with a range of activities covering various areas of publishing. The Company specializes in textbooks and trade books, which are sold and distributed in Canada and parts of the United States of America. ABP management recognizes that there are distinct limits to further expansion in its present markets and is considering a move outside of Canada as its major strategic thrust for the future. The Company's present operations are quite profitable and the resulting cash flow is sizable, hence a major move into market areas is entirely feasible.

As part of its consideration of a major thrust into the English-language publishing markets, ABP has been giving consideration to a move to the United States through the acquisition of a major company in the college and professional book publishing field. These two areas are recognized as having potential future growth significantly above the average of all book publishing. Although ABP is not a major factor in college and professional publishing in its home markets, this field is recognized as being closely allied to present businesses and hence a logical new area for business development in publishing. An acquisition of a sizable and attractive company in this business in the United States could be a strong base for future expansion in this country, as well as other international markets.

First, several important points should be made concerning the college and professional publishing field.

1. *The growth of college and professional book publishing has been strongly impacted by the population demographics.*

   Historical birth rates in the United States, particularly the lower birth rates of the late 1970s, have and will continue to affect negatively total college enrollments, and hence, book purchases. On the other hand, the professional ranks are increasing and will have a positive effect on professional book sales. Within college and professional markets, there are distinct differences in growth prospects among disciplines.

2. *The profits of college and professional book publishing have consistently run above average for all U.S. business.*

Book publishing for these two markets has been a dependable profit generator, and has returned net profit margins in the six or seven percent range versus five percent for all manufacturing. At the same time, return on total assets, typically near eight percent, has been a percentage point above all manufacturing. This provides a solid and dependable result (at least for the larger companies) and should continue for the future.

3. *Concentration of business in a coherent pattern, with concentration by discipline and/or market area, provides substantial strength to the individual publishing company.*

In the college and professional book publishing field, the strongest and most profitable publishing companies are those that have developed a pattern of business directed toward a particular business focus. This focus can be by discipline or by level of educational need.

> *Discipline.* It has been found that all college and professional publishing can be conceptualized as a matrix of disciplines with related disciplines forming a coherent interrelated group. Hence, the engineering and science cluster as a similar interrelated group, as do business subjects and medicine. Companies that have been able to concentrate and grow in a related group of disciplines have developed much greater strength.

> *Levels.* Level of the market, that is, college introductory courses or advanced and professional at several levels, provides another focus of concentration. Individual companies have developed strength of position by developing excellence in a market level even across discipline lines.

4. *There is advantage to size of operation; however, the extent of this advantage varies widely across the college and professional book publishing field.*

As in most businesses, sheer size of operation can provide competitive advantage from efficiencies of operation and market strength, which can strengthen the position of a particular participant. However, in publishing, this strength from size differs among markets. Size provides considerable strength in the college book publishing business but only moderate advantages in the professional sector. In the college market, the need for broad distribution, the higher volumes of books, and greater customer response to publisher name, provide substantial advantage to the larger publisher. On the other hand, the professional market, with access to the market through direct mail and wholesalers, and where a title itself can sell the book, provides an environment where a small but effective publisher can often compete with the larger publisher.

CANDIDATE ASSESSMENT

As a result of this study, the Research Staff of ABP has identified two acquisition candidates:

- Julius Haines, Inc.
- Oradell Montoya Publishing Company

Each company has a pre-eminent position in a major area of publishing and each has aggressively maintained and expanded that position in recent years.

1. *Julius Haines Company has a strong business position in the engineering and scientific book publishing field.*

   Key issues in considering this company are as follows.

   One of the top two or three publishers in the engineering and scientific field. Julius Haines, through a large and high-quality backlist of more than 350 titles, a prodigious new title output, in-depth editorial and author resources, and a strong field sales force maintains an extraordinarily strong position in this field.

   Extremely well run in most management functions. This company has excellent marketing relative to the needs of engineering and scientific publishing, effective editorial and marketing skills, and good controls on planning and fulfillment.

   Not positioned in a growth market. The engineering and scientific field has only moderate growth prospects for the future, and the company's efforts to move into nonscientific areas have been only moderately effective, showing a difficulty in entering new disciplines.

   Questionable internal capabilities to move to growth markets. While the company has adequate operational strengths in marketing, editorial, and general management, there are few indications that internally it could convert its business toward more attractive markets in the near future.

   Possible continued growth by acquisitions. In the past ten years the company has acquired three smaller companies that have been effectively integrated and have accounted for much of the company's growth in the engineering and scientific fields. These skills in integrating acquisitions could be used in the future.

   The company may need additional cash over the intermediate term. Although Julius Haines is a very strong publisher, trends in the business and the company's own growth plan may place it in a strained position regarding future "undedicated" cash flow.

2. *Oradell Montoya Publishing Company has a strong position in the medical field, which management appears to be willing to maintain rather than expand.*

   The key issues in considering this company are as follows.

   Concentrated position in the medical publishing field. Oradell Montoya over the years has developed a number of standard textbooks for the medical field which have long life and considerable strength in this growing field. However, the company has generated only a limited number of new titles in such major areas as nursing and medical research.

Strong penchant for conservative management. Low title generation, heavy use of distributor for marketing, and conservative financial policies all indicate a very conservative management willing to maintain an unaggressive business posture.

Availability of company for acquisition questionable. Company ownership is tied up in family trust, which would make acquisition of the company difficult at best.

A detailed analysis of the two candidates will be found in Section V of the full-text report which will be submitted to you as soon as it is available.

(Sample of the "highlights" of a business report provided free of charge to a variety of clients)

ABC Advertising and Marketing Research
Seattle

May 18, 1999

Dear Client:

We are pleased to present the Highlights of our most recent survey entitled "Viewers' Reactions to Basic Cable Television and Pay-Cable Television in the Pacific Northwest." This study was conducted by mail using our own Consumer Panel. The Panel consists of 3,200 households—four separate panels of 800 households each—with each panel being representative of American households as a whole in terms of geographic region, market size within region, income within region, and age within income.

In two of these panels, the survey was conducted among the female head of household (1,771 questionnaires delivered to qualifying households), while in the other two panels responses were obtained from the husbands of married panel members (1,065 questionnaires delivered only to households with husband present). Of the 2,836 delivered questionnaires, 2,162 usable returns were received—a completion rate of 76 percent. Over half of the respondents (52 percent) live in homes passed by cable television. Of this 52 percent, 55 percent subscribe to basic cable and 48 percent subscribe to a pay-cable service.

In order to accurately measure consumers' reactions, it was important to conduct this study among a highly representative sample of American households. We selected our company's own Consumer Panel as the sampling frame of this study due to its ability to meet these strict sampling requirements.

The representative nature of the Panel is evidenced by the fact that data from the study are in strong agreement with current industry estimates in the United States regarding several general measures. These measures include:

	Study Findings	Industry Estimates
Cable Television Availability (Homes passed)	72%	74%
Cable Television Subscription	85%	81%
Pay-Cable Subscription	48%	46%

This high degree of consistency on these general measures strongly suggests that the study findings as a whole are highly projectable to total American households. It should be pointed out that men and women showed very similar attitudes and behavior toward the new technologies. Consequently, the findings in this study are presented in total. In general, younger, more affluent and better educated consumers have higher interests in the various new television products and services described in this study.

Question areas included in the study were:

- Awareness, penetration, and perception of basic cable television and pay-cable television

- Reasons for subscribing or not subscribing to basic cable television

- Reasons for subscribing or not subscribing to pay-cable television

- Subscriber satisfaction

- Attitudes toward advertising on basic cable and pay-cable services

- Attitudes toward new two-way interactive cable television systems and enhanced services including, for example, connecting the home to burglar or fire alarm systems; requesting shopping information such as prices for products at various stores; banking from home; making ticket reservations for concerts, theater, and sports events; shopping at home by ordering products shown on cable television ("teleshopping"); and participating in opinion polls.

HIGHLIGHTS

The first section of our study highlights the major findings and the implications we see for marketing and advertising the various products and services comprising the new communication technologies. The remainder of our report provides more detailed coverage of methodology and findings.

BASIC CABLE TELEVISION

Cable Television Faces a Subscription Rate Barrier:

- Eighty-five percent of households in the United States where cable television is available subscribe to the service

- Subscription interest is parallel where cable is not available—81 percent of these households would like to subscribe

- Most cable television rejectors—people who have access to cable but do not subscribe—have little or no interest in subscribing in the future (78 percent)

Without product or marketing changes, the cable television subscriber rate will not go much beyond the present level.

Emphasizing Program Diversity Is the Way to Break Through the Barrier

Cable rejectors give one main reason for not subscribing:

- Cost—not wanting to pay money to watch television (49 percent) and feeling that cable television is too expensive (48 percent).

Emphasizing Program Diversity Is the Way to Break Consumer Resistance

- Among newer cable subscribers, the most important reasons for subscribing are to get more channels (63 percent), more movies (55 percent), and different kinds of programs (53 percent).

These facts clearly show that as cable television comes available in new areas, subscribers will be looking for program diversity. Furthermore, because reasons for subscribing to cable have changed dramatically in recent years, people who previously rejected cable television may now be much more interested in the tremendous diversity that cable has to offer.

PAY-CABLE TELEVISION

Pay-Cable Television Is Fast Becoming an Integral Part of the Cable Television Package

- Seventy percent of recent cable purchasers (less than 18 months ago) subscribe to pay-cable television while only 25 percent of long-term subscribers (five years or more) also buy pay-cable.

- In the last few years, pay-cable has more than doubled in importance as a reason for subscribing to basic cable television.

Price Is and Will Continue to Be a Serious Obstacle of Pay-Cable Growth

- Price is currently the most important reason for not subscribing to pay-cable television, and it is growing in importance—58 percent of recent pay-cable rejectors do not subscribe because the service is too expensive, while 41 percent of rejectors five or more years ago did so for that reason.

Advertising Will Play a Vital Role in the Success of Pay-Cable Television

Greater use of advertising on cable television can successfully be used to overcome price resistance—the most serious obstacle to the growth of cable television services.

- Cable subscribers would welcome advertising on pay-cable television if it lowered the cost of the service. 64 percent of current pay-cable subscribers have interest in such a service. Even 45 percent of pay-cable rejectors would like to subscribe at a lower cost made possible by advertising.

TWO-WAY INTERACTIVE CABLE TELEVISION

Viewers will passively accept help and information from television, but companies should not expect them to actively participate in it. The possibilities for new uses for cable television become very diverse when the concept of sending as well as receiving information by television—referred to as two-way interactive cable television—is introduced. A number of new cable systems have this two-way interactive capacity allowing both home-to-station and station-to-home communication. However, our study indicates that consumers are much more interested in passive services offered by new two-way interactive cable television systems than one requiring active participation.

- Fifty percent of the population wants fire and burglar alarms connected to a two-way interactive cable system.

- Thirty-six percent would like shopping information such as prices for products at various stores.

- Only 12 percent of people would like to shop at home over their television and only 15 percent want to take part in opinion polls.

The new two-way interactive cable services will only become popular when consumers are really convinced that they offer distinct advantages over the present way of doing things.

Specific objections people have to these new interactive systems are that they want to see things in person before buying (61 percent); like to go out shopping (36 percent); and might be tempted to buy things they do not need (32 percent).

More specific general objections are that the new television systems are just not needed (56 percent); people want to relax while watching television (29 percent); and two-way interactive systems would be an invasion of privacy (30 percent).

Useful Sentences for Proposals and Business Reports

Attached is the detailed proposal you requested at our meeting last month. I am sure you will agree that it covers all the points we discussed.

The enclosed business report represents a comprehensive plan to put your distribution department back on firm ground.

We have set forth in this memorandum, in broad outline, information we believe to be responsive to the requests made of us during our meetings in Los Angeles with Albert Mollander and his staff.

We have sought to establish, in a preliminary way, the various possible bases of relationships between our company and MID's New Activities Unit. We are prepared to elaborate on any of the concepts set forth, to discuss in greater detail any aspects of the proposed relationship and to move forward with the New Activities Unit in the implementation of all or any portion of the suggested activities.

We suggest, for the services involved in our company's ongoing program of seeking products and services suitable for the needs of LeRoy & Jones Company, a monthly consulting fee of $_____ for an initial period of six months. At the end of that period, the results of our company can be assessed and the decision taken as to a renewal of the arrangement. This fee is considerably lower than normal for our operation and is intended only as a recovery of a portion of payroll costs. (Travel and out-of-pocket expenses would be additional to the monthly fee).

If products or services selected by your company as a result of our efforts are marketed in Canada, we would like to negotiate a percentage of sales or some similar form of compensation. It is in this area that we are hopeful the relationship will be most rewarding for both companies.

If your company's marketing department elects to utilize our facilities for the preparation of layout, copy, and art in order to implement its marketing activities, we would make such facilities available at our regular annual contract rate of $____ per hour for services of staff members involved in the preparation of such materials.

It goes without saying that we would be pleased to serve your company in the implementation of the recommendations in the enclosed business report. I am enclosing a partial list of clients who have used our company's specialized consultancy services.

In an effort to convey to you an understanding of the day-to-day work in which our company is engaged, it would be useful to review a typical program we are working on with a major American company. We ask you to bear in mind, however, that in many instances, we are bound by strictures of confidentiality, and are therefore not in a position to spell out programmatic details or even to reveal company names.

At the suggestion of Mr. Max Hedges, I am summarizing in this memorandum a report of our conversation with Mr. Hedges concerning your company's interest in telemarketing services and the services that we are prepared to extend to aid your company in developing these interests.

If, as a result of our company's consulting efforts, Calembus Enterprises consummates a purchase or a joint venture with a marketing company that we have referred to Calembus, our fee in such cases, is based on the generally accepted 5-4-3-2-1 formula. (Five percent of the first million dollars of purchase price or investment; four percent of the second million; three percent of the third million; two percent of the fourth million; one percent of the fifth million and any excess.)

In suggesting a two-phase feasibility study, we are fully aware, however, that the plans you and your associates may have for expanding your technical division in Mexico may lie in different directions than the ones we suggest. If you will advise us about the plans you have under consideration, we would welcome the opportunity to describe the services we are prepared to offer to assist you in carrying them out.

Although the descriptions of the marketing and distribution services we can offer your company are intended to be exploratory only, we will be pleased to submit a detailed proposal, together with a fee schedule.

There is little doubt, in our view, that there are a large number of American producers of goods and services who are interested in and would welcome the opportunity for international expansion of their activities in the countries of the European Union, and especially in collaboration with a company such as Sullivan. We believe that this interest has broad negotiating possibilities, which might be expressed in such terms as: (a) No-risk or "consignment" shipments of specific products; (b) Absorbing or sharing in promotional and marketing costs; (c) Exclusive licensing for specific geographical areas; (d) Translation and publication rights for textual services such as foreign language courses; and (e) Joint ventures and/or numerous forms of partnership.

## CHAPTER 10

PLACING AND ACKNOWLEDGING ORDERS

Letters for placing and acknowledging orders should be brief, accurate, and to the point. In many cases, companies use printed prenumbered order forms. A cover letter is often sent with a printed prenumbered order form. In turn, sellers also use printed acknowledgments.

When placing an order by letter or fax, the following details must be mentioned: reference to price quotations, discounts, price lists or catalog numbers; quantity; quality, models, patterns, or colors; packing, special markings, and shipping instructions; warehousing; delivery; documents (e.g. invoices, pro-forma invoices, customs documents, bill of lading, insurance); and confirmation of the terms of payment.

An order should be acknowledged as soon as it has been received. When an order is canceled it must always be done in writing. The reason for the cancellation must also be stated briefly.

This chapter covers the following topics:

- Cover letters for placing an order.

- Letters for acknowledging an order.

- Letters canceling an order.

COVER LETTERS FOR PLACING AN ORDER

Date

Name/Title
Business/Organization
Address
City, State Zip Code

Dear Name:

We acknowledge receipt of your samples and quotation of October 3. Please find enclosed our order No. GW/RK 1193-DdeO, for 450 Martinex 100 percent cotton thermal blankets for twin- and full-size beds.

We would remind you that, as stipulated in our letter of August 29, the blankets must be delivered to our warehouse in Salt Lake City before October 15, because our special Winter Sales Week will start on Monday morning, October 27.

Sincerely,

Signature

Name

Date

Name/Title
Business/Organization
Address
City, State Zip Code

Dear Name:

We are happy to enclose our trial order No. SidB-8822, for 325 Burda Ladies' Car Coats, size medium, navy blue color; at $98.75 per coat, subject to six percent quantity discount. Please sign the duplicate of the enclosed order form and return it to us as your acknowledgment.

As stated in your quotation of April 8, we may expect immediate shipment from stock.

We are looking forward to your acknowledgment.

Sincerely yours,

Signature

Name

Date

Name/Title
Business/Organization
Address
City, State Zip Code

Dear Name:

Enclosed you will find our order No. X776 for 550 Brass Finish Table Lamps Model 33D. In accordance with your terms of payment we have instructed International United Commerce Bank to open a credit for $18,710.40 in our favor at their branch office in Newark, New Jersey. This branch office will accept your draft on them for the amount of your invoice.

Sincerely,

Signature

Name

Date

Name/Title
Business/Organization
Address
City, State Zip Code

Dear Name:

We thank you for your quotation of July 3 for the supply of vacuum bottles and find your terms acceptable. We are pleased to enclose our order, No. 993 for 1,500 unbreakable stainless steel vacuum bottles (Cat. No. 330C 1-quart Bottle) at $19.75 per bottle.

We would appreciate delivery within one month and look forward to your acknowledgment.

Sincerely,

Signature

Name

Date

Name/Title
Business/Organization
Address
City, State Zip Code

Dear Name:

Thank you for responding so quickly to our telephone inquiry of June 26 about your "Rough Country" insulated leather sports boots for men (spring catalog: Model X9-ZZ).

We believe that these guaranteed waterproof boots will sell well in Norway and therefore we enclose our order form No. 02985B for a substantial trial order. We accept the terms in your quotation of June 28 and also confirm that payment will be made by irrevocable letter of credit.

Please acknowledge this order and also confirm that you will make delivery to Dallas, Texas, before September 15.

Sincerely yours,

Signature

Name

USEFUL SENTENCES FOR LETTERS PLACING AN ORDER

Please find enclosed our official order form No. 338A for fifty (50) Model B Regina compact disc players.

This fax will confirm our order—placed by telephone this morning with your representative, Janet Gaynor—for 100 Annis pocket thermometers Model F4.

We hereby confirm our telephone order for 25 sets of your special Quartz Clock (see page six of your summer catalog) at $89.50 per clock, minus two percent cash discount.

We would like to emphasize that this is a trial order. If the quality of your merchandise is up to sample, we expect to place substantial orders at regular intervals.

As agreed in our telephone conversation of August 12, we will pay half the amount of this order against your invoice when the goods are delivered at our warehouse in Fayetteville, Maryland, and the remainder within 30 days, deducting three percent discount.

We place this trial order on the clear understanding that delivery to our warehouse in San Diego, California, has to take place before May 1. Therefore, we reserve the right to cancel this order and refuse delivery after this date.

You will find detailed instructions regarding marking and packing on the attached sheet.

When packing, please wrap each part separately in soft material.

Please, limit the overall length of any one crate to two yards.

LETTERS FOR ACKNOWLEDGING AN ORDER

Date

Name/Title
Business/Organization
Address
City, State Zip Code

Dear Name:

We acknowledge receipt of your trial order No. MvZ-903 for 275 wrist watches (Model X92), which we received today. Your order is now being processed for immediate dispatch and will be ready for airfreight shipment for delivery to Heathrow Airport London early next week. As requested, we will enclose a packing note with the goods.

We are sure you will be pleased with this new line of wrist watches and look forward to working with your company again soon.

Sincerely,

Signature

Name

Date

Name/Title
Business/Organization
Address
City, State Zip Code

Dear Name:

We welcome you as a new customer and appreciate very much your order of May 6, which will be shipped on the 24th by air express. As agreed upon, this order as well as future orders will be shipped to you on our most favorable credit terms.

We are packing our latest window display cards with this order. Within the next few days you will hear from our sales promotion department, a service that is conducted exclusively for our customers. Please feel free to make use of this service at any time without any obligation or charge.

We are looking forward to pleasant business relations with your company.

Sincerely yours,

Signature

Name

Date

Name/Title
Business/Organization
Address
City, State Zip Code

Dear Name:

Thank you for your order (SB-8802) for three general purpose lightweight hand trucks. We are currently processing this order, which we expect to have ready for shipment by Ameri-Express Services within two weeks. Our shipping department will notify you in advance.

Thank you for doing business with us.

Sincerely,

Signature

Name

Date

Name/Title
Business/Organization
Address
City, State Zip Code

Dear Name:

Thank you for your order No. C 876-DD for 125 Do-It-Yourself Paint Machines. However, we are unable at this time to fulfill this order due to a fire in our manufacturing plant in New Orleans three days ago. We intend to resume production next week and expect to deliver your order early next month.

We apologize for the delay and hope it will not cause you serious inconvenience.

Sincerely,

Signature

Name

Date

Name/Title
Business/Organization
Address
City, State Zip Code

Dear Name:

In our circular letter of September 15 (a copy of which is enclosed with this letter), we advised our customers of price increases in our entire Speedy Sport Bicycle line which would become effective on October 1. For that reason, we regret that we cannot accept your order No. ACC-18 of October 10 which uses the expired price list.

Please advise us whether you want to confirm this order in accordance with our current price list.

We look forward to hearing from you soon.

Sincerely,

Signature

Name

Date

Name/Title
Business/Organization
Address
City, State Zip Code

Dear Name:

Thank you for your order No. 396CF. Much as we would like to accept your order and to do business with your company, we are unable to accept your order at the price you requested of $107.25 per ten units. As indicated in our fax of November 14, we stated that $117.50 was our lowest price per ten units. Our profit margins, which are already the lowest in the industry, simply do not warrant a further reduction in our quoted price. It stands to reason that we will be pleased to fulfill your order 396CF if you will confirm our price of $117.50 per ten units.

Sincerely,

Signature

Name

Date

Name/Title
Business/Organization
Address
City, State Zip Code

Dear Name:

Thank you for your order No. 00530 of January 19 for 600 Bambo Quartz Travel Clocks Model 18A at $19.95 per unit. We have these clocks in stock and will be able to deliver them before the date—March 6—you requested.

However, we are sorry that we cannot supply your order on the credit terms you requested and for that reason request prepayment. Enclosed you will find our pro-forma invoice. We would be obliged if you would arrange payment for this invoice by either irrevocable letter of credit or banker's draft as soon as possible in order that we can ship the goods F.O.B. Buenos Aires.

Sincerely,

Signature

Name

Date

Name/Title
Business/Organization
Address
City, State Zip Code

Dear Name:

We have received your most recent order (#98-ZAZ/Bob) and we thank you. Unfortunately, we are temporarily out of stock of cordless infra-red headphones. We expect to receive a new supply shortly and we will send your order as soon as possible.

Thank you so much for your patience during this delay.

Sincerely yours,

Signature

Name

_____

Useful Sentences for Letters Acknowledging Orders

Your order No. 8502 for 100 anti-theft auto locks is being processed and will be ready for shipment on October 13.

Thank you for your order No. 00833, which has been completed and transported to the Port of Newark, New Jersey, where it will be loaded onto the *S.S. Denver*. The freighter sails for Hamburg on April 11 and arrives on April 20.

We are pleased to inform you that your order (GWRK/229) is being processed and will be dispatched by airfreight to Naples on July 2.

Your order (No. 88QE) will be dispatched immediately upon receipt of your remittance of DM 5,700.69 as per the attached pro-forma invoice.

We enclose our pro-forma invoice for $21,875.40. Please inform us what arrangements you have made for payment. On receipt of your remittance we will forward your order immediately f.o.b. Sumter, Mississippi.

We enclose our pro-forma invoice. Your order will be ready for immediate shipment to Canmore, North Dakota, when we receive your remittance.

Thank you for your order (D-3302) for 1,000 panel alarm clocks. Unfortunately, this new product has been so popular that our stock has been temporarily depleted. However, in view of your urgent need, we are giving your order priority when a new shipment arrives at the end of this month.

We are pleased to receive your Order No. AA-9947 for 1,500 chain-saw sharpeners. However, we regret that we cannot supply these items immediately owing to a strike of truck drivers in Illinois.

We are very sorry to have to advise you that we are unable to accept your order #8311 for 575 tricycles until further notice, because our manufacturing facilities in Thailand are fully occupied with long-term contract orders.

We are sorry for the inconvenience this delay has caused you. Of course, we will inform you as soon as we are able to send the merchandise.

We are unable to give you a firm date for delivery until the necessary documents are received.

We are sorry that we cannot supply your order on the credit terms you requested in your fax of March 3.

We have been very pleased to serve you and hope to establish a pleasant business connection with your company.

We hope that this initial order will lead to further business.

We appreciate your business and look forward to serving you again soon.

Canceling an Order

Date

Name/Title
Business/Organization
Address
City, State Zip Code

Dear Name:

We are sorry to inform you that we must cancel our order No. GRA:1874 of June 9 due to the inexcusable delay in the shipment of the goods, which we still have not yet received.

Sincerely,

Signature

Name

Date

Name/Title
Business/Organization
Address
City, State Zip Code

Dear Name:

We are sure you will understand that your very long delay in delivery puts our company in an embarrassing position. For that reason, we can see no alternative but to cancel our order #RKTR-741 dated March 28. In addition, we will hold your company liable for all losses caused by this inexcusable delay.

Sincerely,

Signature

Name

Special Markings

Special directions or markings are often put on boxes, cases, cartons, crates, drums, or containers. Here are some examples of special markings:

Fragile
Handle With Care
Do Not Drop
Glass
Lift Here
This Side Up
Top
Keep Dry
Use No Hooks
Do Not Stow on Dock
Stow Away From Heat

## CHAPTER 11

CREDIT LETTERS

Since few business transactions are settled in cash at the time, modern society rests largely on credit or on trust and confidence. Credit is a promise of future payment in money or in kind given in exchange for present money, goods, or services. Almost all businesses offer commercial credit or consumer credit privileges to their customers because it increases their sales. This wide use of credit helps to maintain a balance between production, distribution, and consumption of goods.

The majority of commercial sales are made on credit, allowing payment to be delayed at least 30 days. When a business extends credit to its customers, it realizes that some customers will be unable or unwilling to pay for their credit purchases. Credit managers must therefore decide which companies will be allowed to buy on credit and what maximum amount of credit purchases will be allowed each customer. Today, credit management is so important to the financial health of companies that in almost every country a number of professional information services are in business to help rate customers for creditworthiness. For example, the Dun & Bradstreet Corporation, with headquarters in the United States, offers extensive business and credit information services in the United States as well as in many countries around the globe that enables a company to check on a business customer's credit rating and help them steer clear of bad debts. In addition, credit information can often also be obtained from regional or local credit-reporting agencies.

Many large retailers, retail chains, and department stores conduct their own consumer credit departments where consumers can apply for a charge account by filling out an application form. These retailers believe there is a great deal of store loyalty generated through consumer credit services. Consumers also show up more regularly where they have credit accounts and tend to spend more than cash customers. Today, hundreds of millions of consumers rely on credit because it allows them to buy what they want, when they want it, and to pay for it from future earnings. Retailers sell to consumers on credit and buy on credit from their suppliers who, in return, order on credit from the companies who manufacture the merchandise.

Commercial credit letters should be written with care and should also be short and to the point. For that reason, five types of letters are provided in this chapter covering the following topics:

- Letters requesting commercial credit.

- Letters responding to a request for commercial credit.

- Letters requesting creditworthiness information from credit references given by commercial credit applicants.

- Letters written by credit references in response to requests for creditworthiness information.

- Letters accepting or turning down applications for commercial credit.

REQUEST FOR A LINE OF COMMERCIAL CREDIT

Date

Name/Title
Business/Organization
Address
City, State Zip Code

Dear Name:

For the past six months, we have been purchasing household appliances from your company on a C.O.D. basis. However, we would now like to open a line of credit. Please, let us know your usual credit terms and also what credit references and other business information you require to open such an account.

We hope your company will be willing to comply with our request.

Sincerely,

Signature

Name

_____

Date

Name/Title
Business/Organization
Address
City, State Zip Code

Dear Name:

As we have done business with your company for more than 18 months on the basis of payment on invoice, we would now like to request you to grant us open credit terms with monthly settlement.

You may check our credit rating with Mr. William Hamilton, Branch Manager of the Bank of Indiana, 000 Orchard Street, Belleville, Indiana 00000.

For information concerning our company's promptness in paying invoices, we refer you to the following credit references:

- Wells Export Company, 000 Oxford Street, Phillipsville, PA 00000.

- Nathan Kane, Inc., 000 West 42nd Street, Nathan, MA 00000.

- Paxton & Asscher Company, 000 Brentwood Place, Chicago, IL 00000.

If you would require additional information, we will be glad to supply it.

Sincerely,

Signature

Name

Date

Name/Title
Business/Organization
Address
City, State Zip Code

Dear Name:

We would like to order nine Samsom Laser Printers, Model HJ 933, at $1,339 per printer, as listed in your January Dealer Catalog. Also, we request that you open an account with 30-day credit terms for us, starting with the order listed above.

Our company, Computeronica Consultants, was established ten months ago. It sells computer hardware and software to small businesses located in and around Dayton, Ohio. We also act as computer systems advisers to these companies. Computeronica Consultants has enjoyed a steady improvement in business since our opening.

The following companies will furnish you with credit information about our financial responsibility and promptness in paying our bills:

- Kaiser Electronics, Inc.
  00 Franklin Avenue, Palo Villas, CA 00000.

- Edward Mills & Company
  000 Broad Street, Cambridge, VT 00000.

- Ruta Computer Sales, Inc.
  00 Wilson Plaza, Westwood, NJ 00000.

Our bank is The International American Bank Branch Office (Mr. John Brown, Vice President), 000 Wallington Avenue, Edgewater, NJ 00000.

You are, of course, welcome to call us if you need additional names of credit references or require more information for granting credit.

Since your Samsom Laser Printers are of the high quality and attractive price range sought by our small business customers, we expect to place many more orders for them. This initial order could therefore mark the beginning of a profitable relationship.

Sincerely,

Signature

Name

LETTERS RESPONDING TO A REQUEST FOR COMMERCIAL CREDIT

Date

Name/Title
Business/Organization
Address
City, State Zip Code

Dear Name:

Thank you very much for your purchase order #CC-373. So that we may extend our normal credit terms of 30 days, please provide us with the following information:

- Your company's most recent financial statements

- Names of three suppliers with whom your company is presently doing business

- Name of your bank

Thank you for your cooperation.

Sincerely,

Signature

Name

Date

Name/Title
Business/Organization
Address
City, State Zip Code

Dear Name:

Thank you for your inquiry regarding opening an account with our company. Please, fill in the enclosed financial information form and provide us with two or more trade references as well as one bank reference. Of course, all information will be kept in the strictest confidence. We appreciate your business and anticipate a long relationship with your company.

Thank you very much for your cooperation.

Sincerely,

Signature

Name

Date

Name/Title
Business/Organization
Address
City, State Zip Code

Dear Name:

Thank you for your letter of February 12 with your detailed request for an increase in your commercial credit. Your company's present financial condition only partially meets our credit requirements at this time. For that reason, we are unable to grant your request to increase your current credit limit. However, this limit can be raised as your financial condition and business improves during the second half of this year.

Sincerely yours,

Signature

Name

Useful Sentences for Letters Responding to a Request for Commercial Credit

Thank you very much for your letter of April 8. We are always glad to open accounts with new customers. We therefore request you to send us the names of three department stores with which your company already has accounts at present.

Our company policy requires that credit applicants complete the enclosed credit application before we can consider opening a line of commercial credit.

I have enclosed our company's standard credit form for you to complete and would appreciate it if you would return it to me as soon as possible. If you should require additional information about the form, I will be pleased to provide it.

If your company can supply us with two additional credit references as well as current financial statements, we will be pleased to reconsider your commercial credit application.

Letters Requesting Creditworthiness Information from Credit References

Date

Name/Title
Business/Organization
Address
City, State Zip Code

Dear Name:

Mr. Colin Wilson, President of ABC Company, has asked us to extend credit to his company. He has given your name and company as a credit reference.

We would like your opinion of ABC Company's business reputation, promptness of payment, and financial responsibility. Of course, any information you furnish will be treated with the utmost confidence. If we can ever be of similar service to your company, please call on us.

Thank you very much for your cooperation.

Sincerely,

Signature

Name

Date

Name/Title
Business/Organization
Address
City, State Zip Code

Dear Name:

Jacqueline Turner, president of XYZ Company, has given us your bank as reference to establish credit with our company. We would like to know this company's banking history with you. Any information you could provide us about XYZ's local and regional reputation, its recent loans, its record of repayments, and its average bank balance would be most helpful.

Any information you furnish will, of course, be treated with the strictest confidence. Should we ever be able to return this favor, be assured we will be happy to do so.

We would appreciate hearing from you as soon as possible.

Sincerely,

Signature

Name

Date

Name/Title
Business/Organization
Address
City, State Zip Code

Dear Name:

We have been contacted by the Superior Transmission Company in Dayton, Ohio, who wish to place a large order (in excess of $50,000) for electronic equipment. Superior Transmission has requested 90-days credit from us, although this would be their first order from our company. The company has listed your name as a credit reference. For that reason, we are writing to you to enquire whether we would be justified extending the company the credit terms they request. We will, of course, keep any information we receive from you about the company's financial standing in the strictest confidence.

Thank you very much for your cooperation.

Sincerely,

Signature

Name

Date

Name/Title
Business/Organization
Address
City, State Zip Code

Dear Name:

We have received a large order for photographic equipment from the XYZ PhotoResource Company in Detroit, Michigan. Joanna Andersen, president of XYZ PhotoResource, has given us your name as a credit reference. Therefore, we would be grateful if you could provide us with information about the company's financial standing and creditworthiness. We would appreciate your prompt reply.

Your remarks will be treated with the utmost confidence.

Sincerely,

Signature

Name

Date

Name/Title
Business/Organization
Address
City, State Zip Code

Dear Name:

We have received a request for credit privileges from the Ventura Stationery Company in Plainfield, New Hampshire. Your company was listed as a credit reference.

We would appreciate your answers to the following questions:

- Length of credit relationship with this company.

- Have your credit relations been satisfactory in the past?

- What is the extent to which your company has granted credit to Ventura Stationery Company?

- What information can you give us about the company's promptness in meeting its financial obligations?

We will, of course, keep any information and remarks we receive in strictest confidence. Thank you very much for your cooperation.

Sincerely,

Signature

Name

Date

Name/Title
Business/Organization
Address
City, State Zip Code

Dear Name:

The Alexander Halifax Company, Inc., 0000 West 52nd Street, New York, N.Y. 00000, has applied to our company for an open credit account. Ms. Clara Bow, Chief Financial Officer, has given us your name as the bank in which her company deposits its funds. In order to determine the company's credit rating, we would like to know your bank's answers to the following questions:

How long has the Alexander Halifax Company account been with your bank?

Is its bank balance fairly steady?

If not, is it subject to drastic fluctuations?

What credit terms do you extend the company?

Has the company ever borrowed funds from your bank?

Has your bank ever denied loans to the company?

All facts and remarks will, of course, be held in strictest confidence.

Thank you very much for your cooperation.

Sincerely,

Signature

Name

Useful Sentences for Letters Requesting Information from Credit References

Butler Company in Tolex, Ohio, has listed the name of your company as a financial reference. This company wishes to establish an account with us with estimated purchases in the low five figures monthly.

Mr. John Durham, proprietor of the Durham Fresh Bakery Company in Bergentown, New Mexico, has applied for an account with our company and listed you as a credit reference.

Could you please furnish us with information about the Grunder Company, in particular about the promptness and regularity with which management meets their financial obligations? You have our assurance that your reply will be held in strict confidence.

We would appreciate receiving any information you can give us about the general reputation and creditworthiness of the Miller Corporation that will help us to make a quick decision about that company's credit application.

We would like to receive information about whether the Berkshire Hills Company in Pineville, Michigan, is considered to be strong financially and whether we would be justified in delivering to this company goods on 60-day credit in excess of $25,000 at any one time.

We would appreciate receiving your confidential information regarding the Rosenbaum Company's credit rating as soon as possible.

We would appreciate a brief statement concerning your company's length of credit relationship with Murphy Jansen Company and that company's promptness in meeting financial obligations.

Our credit department is now reviewing Hinton Company's application and we would appreciate receiving the following information regarding your company's experience as one of Hinton's creditors.

LETTERS WRITTEN BY CREDIT REFERENCES IN RESPONSE TO REQUESTS FOR CREDITWORTHINESS INFORMATION

Date

Name/Title
Business/Organization
Address
City, State Zip Code

Dear Name:

We are happy to endorse the Allied Graphics Company—with corporate headquarters at Hooverville, Florida—as a good credit risk. This company is well known to us, since we have had business dealings with them during the past twelve years. As far as we can ascertain the company appears to be in good financial condition and their record of payment has been completely satisfactory. Therefore, you should have no hesitancy about extending credit to the company up to the amount of $15,000 a month.

Sincerely,

Signature

Name

Date

Name/Title
Business/Organization
Address
City, State Zip Code

Dear Name:

In reference to your inquiry of May 11, as to the financial standing of the Cedexa Company in Middletown, South Carolina, we are pleased to inform you that this company enjoys an excellent reputation and has been in business since 1982. We have dealt with Cedexa for the past eight years and they have been very prompt in meeting all their finanical obligations during that entire period. Most of their monthly purchases have been in the low five-digit figures.

We believe that your company would be justified in working with Cedexa on the credit terms they propose.

Sincerely,

Signature

Name

Date

Name/Title
Business/Organization
Address
City, State Zip Code

Dear Name:

I acknowledge receipt of your letter of November 21. However, I regret that I am unable to give you a satisfactory reference for the Jacques Lamberte Company in Carrollton, Kansas. During the past two years that I have been doing business with Lamberte Company, my experiences have been unsatisfactory. Payments are never made promptly and the company accounts are always in arrears for two or more months.

I trust that this information, which is given to you in strictest confidence, will be helpful to you.

Sincerely,

Signature

Name

USEFUL SENTENCES FOR LETTERS RESPONDING TO REQUESTS FOR CREDIT INFORMATION

We are pleased to send you, in the strictest confidence, the credit information you requested concerning the Gerrards Company in Brookhaven, Georgia.

Based on our entirely satisfactory relationship with the Eberhardt Company, we believe the company is creditworthy and reliable. All payments have been made promptly. The amount of credit you envision to extend to Eberhardt has already been granted since last year by our company.

The Janowski Company has never failed to meet their obligations with promptness. Therefore, we have no reservation in recommending this company and think a credit restricted to $8,500 in any one month a fair risk.

The Bartoks Company is respected throughout the industry and also has a well-deserved reputation of being a company of the highest integrity and reliability.

We are able to testify to the sound management and finances of the Evergreen Corporation. Business dealings have been conducted satisfactorily during the past six years and their bills have always been settled promptly.

On the basis of our experience of doing business with Mr. Sidney B. Skelton, we believe him to be creditworthy.

Our limited business experience with the Dandorf Davis Carburetor Service in Summersfield, Connecticut, would not really warrant us to give you a sound evaluation of their financial standing and creditworthiness. For that reason, we would rather not express an opinion on this company.

It is our company's standard policy not to provide written information about the financial standing of our customers. However, if you would telephone Ms. Ann Summers of our credit department, she would be able to provide you with general credit information about the BXX Company.

We regret we are unable to provide the credit information you requested concerning the Alfred Zimmerman Corporation, because we have never had any business dealings with this company.

We have some reservations in recommending the Ronsodon Business Forms Company in Bartlestown for your company's normal credit terms of 30 days net.

Since the accounts of the Centertown Store with our company are frequently from 45 to 60 days in arrears, we cannot recommend this store without certain reservations.

Under no circumstances could we recommend Larry Benn's Florist Shop for credit, because all their outstanding bills with us have become overdue. We advise you to act with caution.

We are sorry that we are unable to give the confidential credit information that you requested in your letter of July 12 about the Zoltanax Corporation. However, we suggest you contact our business associate, Mr. Anthony Higgins, who may be able to help you.

We trust that you will treat this information about the Gulicks Company with the utmost discretion.

I hope that this strictly confidential information will be of service to your company.

I do not have sufficient information about the Ogill Company. Consequently, I feel that I am not in a position to advise your company on this delicate matter.

I have not known Mr. John A. Oldfield long enough and therefore I do not feel qualified to give a fair and balanced opinion on the way he conducts his company's financial affairs.

LETTERS ACCEPTING OR TURNING DOWN APPLICANTS FOR COMMERCIAL CREDIT

Date

Name/Title
Business/Organization
Address
City, State Zip Code

Dear Name:

We are very pleased to welcome you as a new customer with open account terms to a credit limit of $12,500. We have shipped your order immediately and hope this will be the beginning of a long and prosperous relationship with your company.

If at any time, you wish to raise this above-mentioned credit line, we will of course be pleased to consider your company's financial statements once again.

Sincerely,

Signature

Name

Date

Name/Title
Business/Organization
Address
City, State Zip Code

Dear Name:

We are pleased to inform you that your bank as well as all your credit references have replied to our request for credit information. In view of the facts received, we will allow you a credit line of $25,000. Of course, the amount you may purchase over this limit for cash is unlimited.

We trust that you will make full use of this credit account and look forward to a long and profitable business relationship with your company.

Sincerely,

Signature

Name

Date

Name/Title
Business/Organization
Address
City, State Zip Code

Dear Name:

Thank you for your order #8366 of August 4. Unfortunately, our records show we have an insufficient basis for extending our regular credit terms to your company at present. However, we will be glad to arrange immediate shipment and send your order on a cash on delivery basis. We hope that perhaps conditions will change with your next order and will allow us to grant your company our customary credit terms.

We are truly sorry for the delay and await your instructions regarding your purchase order.

Sincerely,

Signature

Name

Date

Name/Title
Business/Organization
Address
City, State Zip Code

Dear Name:

We have received information from various credit sources indicating that your company might have occasional difficulties meeting our standard credit terms. For that reason, we regret that we are unable to extend you credit at the present time. Of course, we are aware that temporary problems frequently are resolved in due course. We will therefore review your application once again in July.

Sincerely,

Signature

Name

Date

Name/Title
Business/Organization
Address
City, State Zip Code

Dear Name:

Thank you for your recent application for 30-day terms of credit. We appreciate your desire to establish credit with our company. However, based upon the present financial standing of your company as well as reports from various credit references, we find we are unable to extend you credit at the present time. We are sorry to make this decision, but we are sure that you understand our situation.

Perhaps we can review another credit application from your company early next year.

Sincerely,

Signature

Name

Date

Name/Title
Business/Organization
Address
City, State Zip Code

Dear Name:

Thank you for your order of January 15 for 12 terrain bikes and 15 recreation bicycles in the amount of $4,964, in which you request credit terms of 60 days. Unfortunately, our credit investigation indicates that the extent of your current financial obligations would make your company a bad credit risk. Under the circumstances, additional credit might be difficult to handle for you and therefore we feel it necessary to defer credit privileges at this time.

Of course, Mr. Taylor, we fully understand that financial problems can be temporary. For that reason, we hope that your company's financial condition and credit rating will improve in the near future. We will be pleased to reconsider your request for credit should your financial obligations be reduced. In the meantime, however, we do value your company's business and will be happy to serve you on a cash on delivery or certified check basis. We do offer a two percent discount on cash orders.

Sincerely,

Signature

Name

Date

Name/Title
Business/Organization
Address
City, State Zip Code

Dear Name:

Although we would like to extend credit to your company, a careful and impartial review of the bank reference and the four credit references you gave to us indicates that you are experiencing considerable financial difficulties in making prompt payments. For that reason, we believe it would not be in your company's best interests to grant credit at the present time. We do hope that this situation may soon change. Perhaps you would like to apply for credit privileges again in another six months.

Sincerely,

Signature

Name

Date

Name/Title
Business/Organization
Address
City, State Zip Code

Dear Name:

We regret that we are unable to approve your credit application of June 18 at this moment. Your application, in conjunction with the limited credit history that we received from the ATCC credit reporting bureau in Portland, Maine, did not meet our company's standard credit-granting criteria. However, we will review your application again at the end of this year. Of course, you are always welcome to buy from our company on a certified check or C.O.D. basis.

Sincerely,

Signature

Name

Useful Sentences for Letters Granting or Refusing Credit

It is a great pleasure to welcome you as a credit customer, for your request for credit has been approved.

I am pleased to tell you that your application for credit has been approved.

We are pleased to welcome you as a preferred customer. The bank and credit references you submitted to us have been checked and we want to compliment you, because your company has an excellent credit record. We have therefore set your credit limit at $25,000 in any one month.

It is our pleasure to welcome your company as a credit customer of the Kleinman Corporation.

Because of your company's excellent credit rating, we now have $20,000 available for you, subject to normal credit requirements.

Please let us know whether your company needs a higher credit limit. We are sure that we can work together and set up a schedule for gradually increasing your line of credit that will be of mutual benefit.

We will review your company's credit limit, which has now been set at $15,000 after one year.

We are sorry to inform you that due to your current financial obligations your application for a regular charge account with Woods Department Store has been turned down.

We are sorry that we are unable to approve your loan application at this time.

We regret that we have to decline your request for a six-month extension of your personal loan.

On the basis of the information we have received from various credit references, we are unable to grant your company the credit requested in your application of September 15. However, should you feel that at some future date your company's circumstances regarding a request for credit have changed, we hope that you will submit a new credit application.

We have carefully reviewed your company's credit application. Since we have noticed a pattern of very slow payment as well as nonpayment in your credit history, we are sorry to report that we cannot extend credit to you.

Based upon your current financial responsibilities and obligations, we believe that additional credit will be difficult for your company to handle at the present time. However, when your financial situation has changed, we will be pleased to have you reapply for credit. In the meantime, we hope to serve you on a cash basis.

## CHAPTER 12

COLLECTION LETTERS

When a company grants credit to another company, it is assumed that the debtor will pay his or her bills on time. However, collecting money from delinquent companies and consumers who do not pay their bills on time is often a major problem. Some companies handle their own delinquent accounts, while others prefer to use the services of professional debt-collection agencies. The techniques used to collect past-due accounts must be firm but flexible. Collection techniques involve a series of firmly written reminders and collection letters to inform customers that their accounts are overdue. Frequently only one or two reminder letters are sufficient to settle a delinquent account.

In addition to collection letters, other debt-collection techniques are used; for example, telephone calls to urge payment and personal visits to offices or homes in order to stress the necessity of paying past-due accounts. As the past-due period lengthens, each collection letter should be more insistent and stern than the previous letter and with increasing degrees of urgency, demand prompt payment of the account. The final collection letters will state that the customer's past-due account will be referred to an attorney or professional debt-collection agency for forced collection (which will harm the customer's creditworthiness in the future); and, finally, legal action, although this is a last resort. If a customer responds to a collection letter and offers a valid reason for delaying payment or promises partial payment of the outstanding balance, the mailing of other collection letters should be stopped.

Since collection letters are often written as a series, we have divided the following model letters into four series:

Series 1—Friendly reminder collection letters
Series 2—Firm reminder collection letters
Series 3—Urgent reminder collection letters
Series 4—Final ("Ultimatum") collection letters

SERIES 1—FRIENDLY REMINDER COLLECTION LETTERS

Date

Name/Title
Business/Organization
Address
City, State Zip Code

Dear Name:

Just a friendly reminder that we would very much appreciate your payment of $125.50 for a copy of our annual Computer Hardware Directory that you purchased on February 19. If your check is already in the mail, you should disregard this letter. If it is not, please take a moment to mail your check today.

Thank you very much for your cooperation.

Sincerely,

Signature

Name

Date

Name/Title
Business/Organization
Address
City, State Zip Code

Dear Name:

This is just a friendly reminder that your payment of $769.14 will be very much appreciated. This amount is still outstanding in our books. Please check your records.

Sincerely,

Signature

Name

Date

Name/Title
Business/Organization
Address
City, State Zip Code

Dear Name:

In checking our records, we find there is still a balance of $1175.80 due to us for the purchase of a personal computer on October 2. Has the payment been overlooked?

If your check is already in the mail, please disregard this notice. However, if you cannot send us your check, please inform us when we may expect payment of this balance.

Sincerely,

Signature

Name

Date

Name/Title
Business/Organization
Address
City, State Zip Code

Dear Name:

This is just a reminder to inform you that your account is overdue. Please, send us a check for $1,605.38 by return mail. If you have sent us payment recently, it may have crossed this reminder in the mail. In that case, please ignore this letter.

Thank you for your cooperation.

Sincerely,

Signature

Name

Date

Name/Title
Business/Organization
Address
City, State Zip Code

Dear Name:

An examination of our records indicate that the following two amounts—for a total of $1,605.38—are due from your company:

- Invoice A 8763 dated June 18, 1999 for $962.10

- Invoice A 8911 dated July 14, 1999 for $643.28

If the above listed amounts are in order, we would appreciate receiving your check for $1,605.38 immediately.

Please, inform us in the event there is a valid reason why this balance cannot be paid immediately. If payment has already been made, you should disregard this reminder.

Sincerely,

Signature

Name

Date

Name/Title
Business/Organization
Address
City, State Zip Code

Dear Name:

It is some time since we dispatched your order (No. 922) and payment has not yet been received. The details are shown on the enclosed statement.

Our terms of business require prompt payment.

Could you please pay the amount due now? If you have already paid, and this letter has crossed your payment in the mail, please accept our thanks. If you have any query regarding this account, please complete the enclosed form and return it to us.

Sincerely yours,

Signature

Name

Date

Name/Title
Business/Organization
Address
City, State Zip Code

Dear Name:

We are sorry to inform you that your check No. 224, dated on June 7, and drawn to our company in the amount of $374.67 is not good. The Bank of Atlanta returned this check today with the notation "Insufficient Funds."

It is with reluctance that we now make this formal approach and request you to send us immediately a certified check for $374.67. We insist on your prompt attention to this matter.

Sincerely,

Signature

Name

Useful Sentences for Friendly Reminder Collection Letters

Series 1

Just a friendly reminder . . . A past due amount is shown on the enclosed statement. May we have your remittance by return mail? Thank you.

Please note that your account, as shown on the attached statement, is past due. Your prompt remittance will be appreciated.

This letter is sent to you as a reminder of your account with us. Our invoice of May 7, amounting to $436.89, is now due for payment. We will be pleased to receive your check for this amount.

This is a friendly reminder, which is mailed to you because we believe that you may have overlooked our invoice in the amount of $2,430.00, which is now more than six weeks overdue.

In looking over our records, we find that your account shows an unpaid balance of $113.92. It is now past our 30-day terms and your remittance will be very much appreciated.

Our records show that your balance of $407.10 is still unpaid.

As of February 15, we still had not received your December payment of $225.41.

If your check is already on the way to us, please accept our sincere apologies for an unnecessary reminder.

SERIES 2—FIRM REMINDER COLLECTION LETTERS

Date

Name/Title
Business/Organization
Address
City, State Zip Code

Dear Name:

We still have not received payment for the balance of $1,822.58, despite the reminder we sent you on September 2.

Please send us a check for this amount by return mail or inform us immediately about the reason this payment is delayed.

Thank you for your cooperation.

Sincerely,

Signature

Name

Date

Name/Title
Business/Organization
Address
City, State Zip Code

Dear Name:

In looking over our records, we noticed that your account shows an unpaid balance of $711.45. Oversights, of course, do happen and therefore we are bringing this matter to your immediate attention.

We are sure you will cooperate in keeping your account within the agreed terms: payment upon receipt of the monthly statement. A postage-paid envelope has been enclosed for your convenience.

Your prompt remittance will be appreciated.

Sincerely,

Signature

Name

Date

Name/Title
Business/Organization
Address
City, State Zip Code

Dear Name:

Our records indicate that we have had no remittance from your company in response to our reminder letter of May 21. The amount due is $221.87 and we would appreciate your remittance. Thank you for your prompt attention.

Sincerely,

Signature

Name

Date

Name/Title
Business/Organization
Address
City, State Zip Code

Dear Name:

A review of your account shows that you have not yet settled your outstanding balance of $331.95, which has been on our books for the past two months. It becomes necessary for us to remind you once again to pay this amount. We really must have a remittance by return mail.

Sincerely,

Signature

Name

Date

Name/Title
Business/Organization
Address
City, State Zip Code

Dear Name:

According to our records, your account for our invoice #891 of September 7, amounting to $282.73, is unpaid and past due. We wrote you about this account on July 23, but we received no answer. We wish again to call your attention to the need for immediate payment of this overdue invoice.

Sincerely,

Signature

Name

USEFUL SENTENCES FOR FIRM REMINDER COLLECTION LETTERS

Series 2

We are disappointed that our letter and statements to you have brought no reply.

May we call your attention to your loan payment, which is now 30 days past due? The amount is $562.19. Prompt payment will be appreciated.

We have not yet received your remittance and we must therefore call your immediate attention to your past due account of $43,156.33. Please send us a check.

We have not yet received a remittance of $277.08, which is due on your account. Please send us a check for this amount.

May we draw your attention to the amount of $2,973.14, which according to our records remains as yet unpaid?

Please let me hear from you as soon as possible if there is a problem I should know about. In that case, please call me at (000) 000-0000 to discuss your situation.

We would appreciate hearing from you as soon as possible so we can arrange a mutually agreeable payment schedule.

We want to help your company fulfill its financial obligations. Are there any unusual circumstances or problems that we are unaware of?

Please call me at once so we can arrive at some workable agreement to settle your account.

If you cannot pay the full amount of your outstanding balance, please send us at least half of it at once.

We have enclosed a self-addressed and postage-paid return envelope for your convenience.

We have received your letter of June 18 relating to your company's past-due account of $3,700.00 and would like to propose the following solution to this problem.

SERIES 3—URGENT REMINDER COLLECTION LETTERS

Date

Name/Title
Business/Organization
Address
City, State Zip Code

Dear Name:

We are disappointed that we have not received any answer from you in response to our recent faxes as well as two registered letters regarding the payment of the bill for $10,321.76 that you owe our company. This amount is now more than four months overdue. Because you are a valued customer who has always been prompt in paying bills on time, we are wondering why we have not heard from you about this matter. However, we are also sure that you do not want to lose our company's credit standing. You know that our company policy prohibits extending credit to customers who have past-due charges outstanding. Is there a reason for the delay of this payment?

Please let us hear from you at once.

Sincerely yours,

Signature

Name

Date

Name/Title
Business/Organization
Address
City, State Zip Code

Dear Name:

Three months have passed since we mailed you our reminder letters about your outstanding balance of $1,139.07. However, we have not yet received payment of this amount.

Before this unpaid balance will affect your credit standing, please send us your payment right away or phone me at (000) 000-0000 to inform me of any reason why you should not do so.

Sincerely,

Signature

Name

Date

Name/Title
Business/Organization
Address
City, State Zip Code

Dear Name:

Our records indicate that your company still owes $6,331.00 from your last order. The account is significantly beyond the 30 days we agreed to when we opened your company's credit account last year. Please send payment by return mail since we cannot accept further delay. However, if for any valid reason you cannot pay at this time, call me as soon as possible so that we can discuss an alternative. We cannot believe that you would permit your account to become a forced collection matter.

Sincerely,

Signature

Name

Date

Name/Title
Business/Organization
Address
City, State Zip Code

Dear Name:

We are at a loss to understand why we have not heard from you regarding payment of $4,400.92, now more than four months overdue. Therefore, we must hear from you immediately, because on May 15, we will send our quarterly report to the Manufacturers' Credit Bureau. We are certain that you do not want your company's name on that list since it would seriously affect the national as well as regional credit rating of your organization.

Since we have not received your payment, we have no alternative but to withdraw your company's credit privileges, effective immediately.

This letter also serves as notice to you that unless you contact us by calling or writing within ten days from today, we will turn your account over for collection proceedings.

Sincerely,

Signature

Name

USEFUL SENTENCES FOR URGENT REMINDER LETTERS

Series 3

During the past four months we have had no response from you in answer to our reminder letters and faxes as well as telephone calls about our unpaid invoice for $17,551.00. We assume that this amount is correct, because you never questioned it.

We cannot understand why your company has failed to respond to all our inquiries, because your account is seriously in arrears.

If you are facing financial problems, please contact our credit department so that arrangements can be made regarding the overdue balance of your account.

If you need to work out an alternative plan for payment of your outstanding bill, call me at once at (000) 000-0000.

We are willing to offer you a flexible credit option to minimize the difficulty you face making monthly payments on the balance of your account. However, we must know your intentions immediately.

We do not want to see your good credit standing jeopardized. Therefore, we would like to cooperate with you to resolve this matter.

Because the $2,500.40 balance on your account is now three months past due, your credit rating is in jeopardy.

Please, save yourself the embarassment of a black mark on your permanent credit record and severe damage to your credit rating.

We are afraid you are placing your credit standing as well as the convenience of buying on credit in jeopardy.

If our credit department does not hear from you by September 15, we have no choice but to cancel your company's credit until payment in full, including applicable late charges, has been made.

We are unwilling to accept any further orders from your company except on a cash basis until you have settled your past-due account of $1,983.00.

Due to the unsatisfactory condition of your account, we hereby revoke the credit privileges that were granted to your company on January 25, 19__.

Since you have not answered our reminder letters and ignored our two telephone calls, we are now forced to take strong measures to collect the outstanding balance of your account in the amount of $8,990.34, which is 90 days overdue.

We regret the necessity of having to call your attention once again to your company's outstanding balance of $11,443.76, which is now more than three months overdue. Failure to remit the full amount within ten days from the date of this letter means that your bill will be turned over to our collection agency.

SERIES 4—FINAL ("ULTIMATUM") COLLECTION LETTERS

Date

Name/Title
Business/Organization
Address
City, State Zip Code

Dear Name:

Your bill of $2,459.10 is now overdue 120 days. Please remit this amount at once. If your payment is not received by March 1, your bill will be placed in the hands of our collection agency.

Sincerely,

Signature

Name

Date

Name/Title
Business/Organization
Address
City, State Zip Code

Dear Name:

This is to inform you that after three reminders and several telephone calls, you still have not made any effort to settle your past due account of $6,553.00. Therefore, we are now putting the matter into the hands of the Garland Collection Agency on May 14.

Sincerely,

Signature

Name

Date

Name/Title
Business/Organization
Address
City, State Zip Code

Dear Name:

Your disregard of our previous reminders and personal telephone calls concerning your account, which is long overdue and delinquent, leaves our company no choice but to serve this demand upon you for full payment. If your check for $4,480.55 is not in our hands by July 10, your account will automatically be referred to the Bernstein Collection Agency for forced collection. We do not like to take these drastic measures, but you leave us with no alternative.

Sincerely,

Signature

Name

Date

Name/Title
Business/Organization
Address
City, State Zip Code

Dear Name:

If payment of $346.89 is not received within ten (10) days of the date of this letter, we will have no choice but to refer your delinquent account to our credit and collection department for further processing.

- Don't let this happen

- Meet your obligations

- You owe $346.89

- Mail it today

Sincerely,

Signature

Name

Date

Name/Title
Business/Organization
Address
City, State Zip Code

Dear Name:

Our Credit Manager has decided that your delinquent account will be referred to our attorney for legal action in order to collect the outstanding balance of $9,881.72 due to us for more than four months.

Your continuing lack of response to our letters, faxes, and telephone calls and your unwillingness to cooperate leaves us no other choice.

Sincerely,

Signature

Name

Date

Name/Title
Business/Organization
Address
City, State Zip Code

Dear Name:

Our credit and collection department has just informed me of their intention to take legal action, because you have failed to answer any of our letters, faxes, telegrams, and telephone calls requesting immediate payment of $14,100.19, which is now five months overdue. Unless we hear from you within five business days—on or before February 12—we will turn your delinquent account over to our collection agency.

Sincerely,

Signature

Name

USEFUL SENTENCES FOR FINAL ("ULTIMATUM") COLLECTION LETTERS

Series 4

This is to inform you that unless your check for $3,109.23 is received by December 1, your delinquent account will be turned over to the John Doe Collection Agency.

We are turning over your delinquent account to the Marshall Collection Agency, which we have authorized to collect from you the past-due amount of $5,224.00, ten days from the date of this letter.

This letter is to notify you that we have no choice but to put your delinquent account into the hands of our attorney if your check for $991.00 is not received by August 10.

We are instructing our attorney to proceed with the collection of your overdue account, now five months in arrears, in whatever manner may be deemed necessary to protect our interests.

## CHAPTER 13

Job Application Letters, Résumés, and Employment Correspondence

There are two types of job application letters: (a) an unsolicited ("cold") letter of application, which is mailed to a company for which you would like to work even though the company has not advertised that there are any openings; and (b) an application letter in response to an advertisement in a newspaper or periodical for a particular position. In both cases, a job application letter (also known as a "cover letter" or "covering letter") must be sent with an accompanying résumé.

Cover Letters

The principal function of a cover letter is to inform a potential employer about the type of position you are seeking. It should also highlight the specific qualifications, accomplishments, and abilities or work experience (detailed in your accompanying résumé) that have a special relevance for the position for which you are applying.

If you are responding to an advertisement in a newspaper or magazine, always state that fact in the first paragraph of your cover letter.

Résumés

A résumé is a summary of a person's business or professional qualifications, educational background, and work experience for a particular position. The purpose of a résumé (also written as "resumé" or "resume" and also known as a "curriculum vitae" or "c.v.") is to interest potential employers in an applicant's capabilities, qualifications, and credentials for a given job. In this chapter you find a number of cover letters as well as sample résumés for various positions.

There are two basic types of résumés: chronological and functional. In a chronological résumé, which is the most common and the most readily accepted résumé format, you arrange your jobs in reverse chronological order beginning with your present or most recent position. The name and address of the company; the dates of employment; job titles or titles as promoted; and a description of your duties and responsibilities in order of importance must be provided.

In a functional résumé, you emphasize your responsibilities and duties, instead of your employers, exact employment dates, and job titles. Such a résumé should never be used if you have been steadily employed. A sample of a functional résumé is provided in this chapter.

Take a look at the résumés in this chapter before reading the information below.

A chronological résumé must include the following information:

—Your full name, mailing address and telephone number.

—*Employment Objective or Career Objective.* This can also be indicated with words such as "Position Desired," "Job Objective," "Professional Objective," "Position Sought," or "Career Goal/Professional Objective." If you are responding to an advertisement, you can omit the employment or career objective. However, employment or career objective should be mentioned in unsolicited cover letters to prospective employers.

—*Previous Employment and Work Experience.* This should include part-time experience if you are just starting your career. You can also use such words as "Employment," "Employers," "Employment History," "Professional Experience," "Occupational Experience," or "Business Experience." Brief descriptions of present and past jobs ("job descriptions") should be included. Your present or most recent job should be presented first.

—*Special Skills.* Qualifications, special skills, or experience. For example, proficiency in foreign languages; desktop publishing skills; familiarity with special business computer programs; or stenography ("shorthand") should be listed in this section.

—*Educational Background.* You can also use words such as "Education," "Formal Education," "Education and Training," "Technical Training," "Professional Skills," or "Education and Other Experience." Begin with your last educational program and work backward; include the name of the educational institute, its location, study program and the number of months or years attended. If you are a recent graduate, with little or no work experience, place your Educational Background section directly under the Employment Objective or Career Objective section.

—*Business and Personal References.* References are not necessary in a résumé. You can just write in your résumé: "References are available upon request." If employers want business or personal references or letters of recommendation, they will ask for them during an interview.

Employers are often asked to provide letters of reference or recommendation about former employees. The differences between these two letters are minimal. A letter of recommendation is a favorable statement by a former employer concerning an employee's qualifications, performance, character, and dependability, and endorsing or recommending that employee as being suitable for a particular job or position.

A letter of reference usually verifies facts about past employment (for example, dates of employment and job descriptions) of a person, although it often provides information about that person's capabilities, character, and performance. The person who provides such information or testimonial is known as a "reference."

It should be pointed out, however, that letters of reference and recommendation usually only say nice and positive things about a former employee without any reservation. Generally speaking, such letters do not contain negative or derogatory information or remarks, because such negative statements about a former employee could result in a lawsuit against his or her former employer. For that reason, letters of reference and recommendation, unless specifically requested by an employer, are frequently not as important as many job seekers believe they are. Instead, many employers prefer to talk with a candidate's superior or former boss by telephone in order to receive live answers to pertinent questions.

When writing letters of reference or recommendation, avoid the use of the once popular salutation "To Whom It May Concern." Instead, entitle such letters as "Letter of Reference for Ronald Bush," "Letter of Recommendation for Laura Webber," or "Recommendation for Peter Finch."

Unless specifically stated in the advertisement, do not mention anything about salary, your salary history, or your salary requirements in your cover letter or résumé. However, if a company wants to know your salary requirements, you can always write that your salary requirement is "negotiable." In this chapter, you find sample phrases dealing with salary matters.

Only when you think it is relevant to your application, do you mention anything about age, national origin, race, health, sex, religion, or marital status in your cover letter or résumé. Hobbies, community service, and other activities should only be listed on your résumé if they are directly related to the position that you are seeking.

Make sure that your complete job application, which comprises both your cover letter and résumé, is typed, grammatically correct, and neatly presented. Do not send handwritten letters and résumés, unless specifically required. Also, do not send a photograph or include copies of reference letters, recommendation letters, school transcripts, or diplomas. If employers want these items, they will specifically request them in a personal letter or during a personal interview.

Always try to write your unsolicited cover letter and résumé to a particular person by name, who is responsible for the job you desire. If necessary, call the company and ask for the full name (correctly spelled) and exact title of the person to whom you want to address your job application letter.

The sample cover letters, résumés, letters of reference and recommendation, job descriptions, and the numerous additional sentences dealing with applications and employment matters in this chapter provide abundant information and material to compose and write both your personal job-seeking cover letter and résumé.

This chapter consists of the following major sections:

- Unsolicited ("cold") cover letters to prospective employers.

- Cover letters or application letters responding to employment advertisements.

- Sample job descriptions for use in cover letters.

- Useful phrases to describe career or professional objectives.

- A series of sample résumés.

- Letters requesting a recommendation or information.

- Useful phrases for letters requesting a recommendation or information from an employment reference.

- Letters of reference and recommendation from employers.

- Useful phrases for letters of reference and recommendation.

- Employer's response to applications for employment.

- Useful phrases for responses by employers to job applicants.

- Letters of resignation.

- Useful phrases for letters of resignation.

- Miscellaneous company letters and announcements (e.g., promotions, increase in salary, dismissal due to redundancy and retirement).

UNSOLICITED ("COLD") COVER LETTERS TO PROSPECTIVE EMPLOYERS

Date

Name/Title
Business/Organization
Address
City, State Zip Code

Dear Name:

This is a letter of inquiry. I am writing to find out if your company has openings for a product manager in one of your pharmaceutical divisions.

The recent acquisition of Mencken Diagnostics, Inc. (for which I am currently working) by the Rextell Corporation has left the future of many employees uncertain. For this reason, I am seeking new challenges and options and have selected Barker Pharmaceuticals Corporation as one company whose reputation and leading position in the industry is unparalleled.

At present I am employed as a product manager for Mencken Diagnostics, Inc. in their New Jersey headquarters. My job involves the implementation of effective marketing plans in order that sales targets are met both on time and within budget. More specifically this involves the preparation of quarterly sales and analysis reports and forecasts, preparing product information packages for each new product launched, and producing promotional material for existing products.

After you have reviewed my résumé, I hope that we will have the opportunity to discuss my experience and qualifications further during a personal meeting. Thank you for your consideration.

Sincerely,

Signature

Name

Date

Name/Title
Business/Organization
Address
City, State Zip Code

Dear Name:

I am writing to inquire about the possibility of obtaining a position as a bilingual secretary (English-French) in your company's international marketing and promotions department. I am currently working as a private secretary for the senior vice president in charge of international sales of United Belgian Marketing Corporation in Milwaukee, Wisconsin.

Attached is my résumé outlining my qualifications and nine years of experience as a secretary for several mid-sized companies. I have excellent secretarial abilities, including shorthand (120 wpm) and audio (IBM AS 4010), and computer skills such as Word for Windows 6.0, business graphics, and desktop publishing (PageMaker 7.0). I can handle heavy responsibility and I have the ability to work on my own initiative and as part of a team. My experience with United Belgian Marketing Corporation is especially relevant to the qualifications you may seek. I would enjoy discussing this with you in a personal interview.

I look forward to your reply and hope to have the opportunity to meet with you during a planned visit to Chicago early next month.

Sincerely yours,

Signature

Name

_____

Date

Name/Title
Business/Organization
Address
City, State Zip Code

Dear Name:

I am presently a graduate student at Columbia University in New York City, working toward a Master of Science degree in geophysics. I will graduate in July 1999. Since my prior work experience during summer and part-time employment is in geophysics, the profile of your company was provided to me by Columbia's placement office. I am particularly interested in a position in your company related to geological exploration.

I have worked as a summer intern and later as a part-time employee for the Ferguson Oil & Gas Exploration Company in Madison, New Hampshire. I was involved in seismic interpretation and acreage evaluation in order to delineate existing and future fields and to define potential exploration targets. The attached résumé indicates my capabilities. I am available for an interview to discuss my qualifications and your requirements at your convenience.

Thank you for your consideration and I look forward to hearing from you.

Sincerely,

Signature

Name

Date

Name/Title
Business/Organization
Address
City, State Zip Code

Dear Name:

I received your name from Dr. Helmut Schwartz this week. I spoke to him regarding career opportunities with Silver Star Polymer Industries in Maryland. He suggested I contact you about the opening for a product development engineer in your company's engineering department in Hamilton.

I am currently employed as a product development engineer for Atlantic Polymer GmbH in Bonn, Germany. This company is well known in the field of polymer engineering. To ensure that their position in the German marketplace is consolidated and developed, the company employs me as a specialist engineer to build further relationships with their German customers. This position calls for a "hands-on" engineer who is capable of designing and developing new products from concept to manufacturing. This in turn requires the ability to build excellent relationships with customers.

I would welcome the opportunity to meet with you or a representative of your company to discuss the information on my enclosed résumé. May I call you next week to determine the most convenient time for such a meeting? Thank you for your consideration.

Sincerely,

Signature

Name

P.S. Please do not contact my present employer until mutual interest has been established.

Date

Name/Title
Business/Organization
Address
City, State Zip Code

Dear Name:

As you may know, my present company, Taylor Baker Inc., has recently merged with the Chatfield HiTec Corporation in Boston. As a result of this merger my position as a senior-level controller will be phased out in the very near future. For that reason, this letter and attached résumé is my application for a position in your company's financial department.

As a senior-level controller, I am an active participant in the development and implementation of Taylor Baker's financial strategies, combining creativity and experience to provide advice and guidance on both a divisional level and to corporate management. Focusing on overall profit-and-loss goals and objectives, my responsibilities include developing asset management programs, interfacing with engineering program management, and coordinating with the MIS group for ongoing systems development consistent with business needs.

I look forward to the opportunity to discuss the possibility of working for your company. Thank you for your consideration.

Sincerely yours,

Signature

Name

Date

Name/Title
Business/Organization
Address
City, State Zip Code

Dear Name:

My present employer—Harvest Insurance Company in Memphis, Tennessee—is a regional insurance company that offers limited opportunity for advancement. Therefore, I am seeking a new and challenging position with a major national insurance company, that will enable me to use my seven-year experience in the market research field. This confidential letter is to inquire into the possibility of an opening as research executive in your company's national marketing department.

I am currently working as a senior researcher in the marketing, planning, and research department, which plays a central part in the development and implementation of marketing strategy. This department commissions continuous and ad-hoc research designed to support new product development, market monitoring, customer analysis, and advertising and promotional development. My job involves all aspects of managing research projects, including liaison with internal marketing teams and research agencies. It also includes field and desk research and in-house presentations.

I would appreciate your time in reviewing my enclosed résumé and would welcome an opportunity to meet with you personally to discuss a position in your company.

Sincerely,

Signature

Name

Date

Name/Title
Business/Organization
Address
City, State Zip Code

Dear Name:

Within the next four months, I will be moving to Chicago where I would like the opportunity to put my ten years of accounting experience to work for your company.

I am currently working as a financial controller for the Morano Supermarket Group in Seattle, Washington, where I report directly to the group financial director. I am responsible for the group's financial direction and control, through tighter forecasting, budgeting, development of modern computerized controls, and more accurate reporting. As a result, I contributed significantly to the group's profitable growth during the past four years. In addition, I also ensure that all legal, taxation, and audit requirements are complied with and that appropriate statutory deadlines are met.

I have not yet informed my employer of my intention to leave the company. Therefore, I would appreciate your confidentiality in this regard. Should you wish to contact me, I can be reached on a confidential basis at (000) 000-0000 during the day, or else at my home phone during evening hours after 7:30 P.M.

Sincerely,

Signature

Name

Date

Name/Title
Business/Organization
Address
City, State Zip Code

Dear Name:

Having worked for the past four years as an international marketing assistant in the marketing unit of a prestigious and highly rated British bank in Chicago, I would like to apply for a challenging marketing position in your bank's international department in New York.

I currently work in a close-knit, professional team and I am responsible for a broad range of marketing activities: internal and investor communications, including regular newsletters, reports and brochures; production of materials for client presentations; and advertising and direct mail. My position demands marketing experience for the financial management and investment communities and in dealing with financial data and markets. It also requires excellent organizational skills and the ability to work to stringent deadlines.

I am enclosing a résumé of my qualifications for your review and I would welcome the opportunity to meet with you. I can be reached during evening hours at my home phone (000) 000-0000 or at my office (000) 000-0000 on a confidential basis during business hours.

Sincerely yours,

Signature

Name

Date

Name/Title
Business/Organization
Address
City, State Zip Code

Dear Name:

I am planning to return to the work force after an absence of eight years. During this period I raised two children, managed a busy household, and did volunteer work at the Essex City Hospital. I also retained my secretarial and administrative office skills and computer literacy with part-time work for my husband, who manages the Blackstone Insurance Agency in Essex City.

Since my family is well established, I am ready and eager to re-enter the job market once again in either a part-time or full-time position as a secretary or administrative assistant. For that reason, I enclose my résumé with additional information about my education, work experience, and other qualifications. Thank you very much for your consideration.

Sincerely,

Signature

Name

Louise Jensen
0000 Elm Street
New York, NY 00000
Tel. (000) 000-0000

May 5, 1999

Ms. Martha Peyton
Director of Personnel
ABC International, Inc.
000 Midwood Avenue
New York, NY 00000

Dear Ms. Peyton:

I am writing to you with the hope that you might have an opening now or in the near future for a personal assistant/secretary in the international sales division of your company. However, if you do not, I would very much appreciate if you could keep my enclosed résumé on file for future employment opportunities with Petersen International.

I am an experienced personal assistant/secretary with excellent administrative, organizational, and secretarial skills. I also would like to use my fluency in French and German, both written and spoken. I have a flexible approach to my work, together with the ability to cope with pressure and deadlines. The attached résumé details my working and educational experience. I would appreciate my application being treated as confidential, because I am currently employed as personal assistant to the senior vice president in charge of sales at an international specialist retail chain in New York City.

Looking forward to your answer to this letter and thanking you for your consideration, I am,

Sincerely,

Louise Jensen

Enclosure: résumé

(A chronological résumé)

Louise Jensen
0000 Elm Street
New York, NY 00000
Tel. (000) 000-0000

CAREER OBJECTIVE

Personal Assistant/Secretary position in a major international company with long-term career potential for advancement and growth.

WORK EXPERIENCE

Blackstone Shop Holdings Inc., Manhattan (N.Y.), 1990–Present

Personal Assistant to the senior vice president in charge of sales for 33 stores in the New York metropolitan area, 21 stores in France, 18 stores in Great Britain and 14 stores in Germany. This position at the company's headquarters in New York City demands excellent secretarial skills (105 wpm typing and 100 wpm shorthand), correspondence in three languages, travel arrangements; heavy client contact, organizational and well-developed communication skills, maturity, diplomacy, and fluency in French and German, both written and spoken. In addition, this position requires a good sense of humor and the initiative to anticipate the day-to-day of a busy senior executive.

Rosado Construction Company, Brooklyn (N.Y.), 1986–1990

Secretary to the General Manager of a construction company, which is well-known for its innovative office building projects in the New York Metropolitan Area.

Schaefer & Associates, Manhattan (N.Y.), 1984–1986

Receptionist/Telephone Switchboard Operator/Secretary with a busy law firm, specialized in business and commercial law. This was my first job after completion of my secretarial training and formal education.

EDUCATION

Volmer Language Training School in Manhattan: Advanced language instruction in French and German (evening courses; 1984–1988).

Richardson Business Institute in Manhattan: Two-year secretarial, administrative, and "computer literacy" training; 1983–1984.

High school education in France, Germany, and New York City.

REFERENCES

Available upon request

COVER LETTERS RESPONDING TO EMPLOYMENT ADVERTISEMENTS

Date

Name/Title
Business/Organization
Address
City, State Zip Code

Dear Name:

I am responding to your advertisement in the *Manchester Herald* of August 14 for an entry-level position as environmental analyst. As my résumé will indicate, I appear to fit the candidate description as specified in your advertisement. I have a strong interest in this position and I believe that my background, qualifications, and work experience appear to be well-suited to your company's specific requirements.

I received my Bachelor of Science degree in environmental chemistry from Manchester College last month. In addition, I have worked as a summer intern with several chemical companies in the Manchester area during the past three years.

Please accept my enclosed résumé in consideration for this position. Thank you for your time. I am looking forward to hearing from you.

Sincerely,

Signature

Name

Date

Name/Title
Business/Organization
Address
City, State Zip Code

Dear Name:

Your advertisement in this month's edition of *Management News* states that you are looking for several management trainees to add to your financial management staff in Boston. I would like to apply for one of these positions, because I believe my professional training and career objective are very much in line with your requirements.

I attended Columbia University in New York where I earned my bachelor of arts degree in Economics. I was awarded the master of business administration degree last year. I am currently working as a financial research assistant in the business planning and research department of the Mirabella Insurance Corporation in Washington, D.C.

I appreciate your time in reviewing my enclosed résumé and would welcome the opportunity to meet and discuss my qualifications and experience with you.

Sincerely yours,

Signature

Name

Date

Name/Title
Business/Organization
Address
City, State Zip Code

Dear Name:

The position of international Business Development Manager as advertised in the weekend edition of *The San Francisco Times* sounds like an interesting opportunity, especially since I am planning a move to the San Francisco metropolitan area. My international background, professional qualifications and fluency in Spanish and Portuguese appear to be an excellent match for this challenging position. Therefore, I am enclosing my résumé for your consideration.

I am currently employed as a business development manager for Jones & Bateman, a Chicago-based international organization providing a variety of management and marketing services to a wide range of clients in consumer and business-to-business markets in the United States, Canada, Mexico, and countries in Latin America. Business development managers have responsibility for maintaining and developing business among existing clients; identifying new clients for existing services; investigating and identifying new services and markets in which the organization should operate; providing appropriate proposals for participation in these markets; implementing agreed-upon plans for such new activities; and controlling revenue and profit budgets. I also manage a small team (five people) to carry out day-to-day contact with existing and new domestic and international clients.

Jones & Bateman has recently been sold to a Canadian conglomerate and the offices will relocate to Toronto, Canada. I am very interested in joining your organization in San Francisco.

Should you agree that my experience and qualifications, as outlined in the enclosed résumé, are a good match for your specific requirements, I would look forward to the opportunity of meeting with you personally in San Francisco early next month. Thank you for your consideration.

Sincerely,

Signature

Name

Date

Name/Title
Business/Organization
Address
City, State Zip Code

Dear Name:

I have read your advertisement for a planning manager in the Friday edition of the *Financial Times* with a great deal of interest. Comparison of my background and professional qualifications with your candidate description, as specified in this advertisement, suggests that I would be an excellent candidate for this interesting position. For that reason, I am forwarding my résumé for your review and consideration.

In my current position as planning manager for the Danzo Corporation—an international consumer-oriented marketing organization with corporate headquarters in Newark, New Jersey—I work on the development of two-year strategic and annual operating plans and in the critical area of allocating resources to meet the changing needs and objectives of the corporation. I report to the corporate planning manager. My job demands a strong backgound in corporate, strategic, and marketing planning in a large international consumer goods organization, where a sophisticated monitoring of international market and economic trends and the ability to respond rapidly to changing market conditions and directions is of vital importance. It also requires strong communicative and persuasive skills, together with the capacity to work effectively with senior management. I am willing to relocate for the right opportunity.

I would welcome the opportunity to discuss this challenging position with you personally.

Sincerely,

Signature

Name

Date

Name/Title
Business/Organization
Address
City, State Zip Code

Dear Name:

I am forwarding my résumé in response to your advertisement in the October edition of *International Oil* magazine for a director of client relations. This challenging position appears to be an exciting opportunity and has prompted me to submit my résumé for your consideration.

At present, I am employed as director of client relations for the USA-Euro Marine Spill Response Corporation in New York City. This corporation is an international, not-for-profit organization dedicated to providing a best-effort response to cleaning up catastrophic oil spills in the coastal and tidal waters of the countries bordering the Atlantic Ocean and the North Sea. I am responsible for client relations, including the negotiation and administration of a variety of contracts for oil spill response services with our clients, who are major producers, transporters and users of petroleum. In addition, I am responsible for the establishment and maintenance of an international network of specialized subcontractors in Europe, the United States, and Canada who assist the organization in meeting its oil spill response obligations. My position requires extensive knowledge of the oil industry (particularly transportation of petroleum products); excellent negotiating skills; and the ability to interact with all levels of management and government.

I am confident that I can make the transition from a small organization to a large international company smoothly. I look forward to your response and an opportunity to further discuss my international experience and qualifications and the possibility of working for your company.

Sincerely,

Signature

Name

Date

Name/Title
Business/Organization
Address
City, State Zip Code

Dear Name:

This week's *Financial Weekly* contained your advertisement for an experienced international financial transaction dealer. I appear to be an excellent match for your specific requirements.

As you can see in my enclosed résumé, I am currently working as an international financial transaction dealer at the corporate headquarters of Janssen International Finance BV in Curaçao, the Netherlands Antilles. I am a member of the capital markets and asset financing division, which is charged with bond issues of all types, including Euro equity issues, equity warrants and other international equity-linked products, swaps, and derivative instruments, infrastructure financing, and tax-based crossborder leasing. I am bilingual (English/Dutch) and I have a working knowledge of German and Spanish.

I would welcome the opportunity to meet and discuss my experience and qualifications with you. Since I will be in Miami at the end of this month, I will call you next week to set up a personal meeting.

Sincerely,

Signature

Name

Date

Name/Title
Business/Organization
Address
City, State Zip Code

Dear Name:

I read your advertisement for a bi-lingual personal secretary in the September 9th issue of *The Los Angeles Times* with considerable interest. This position sounds quite interesting and I have the qualifications that you are seeking. I am therefore submitting my résumé for your review and consideration. I am looking for a challenge and feel that I can meet the exacting standards you require.

Since 1991, I have been the personal secretary for the Director of the international department at the American-Scandinavian Investment Bank in Los Angeles. In addition to the usual secretarial duties, I am also responsible for the smooth running of the department's secretarial pool. My job includes the supervision of a small team of secretaries, extensive preparation of cost and expense reports, and constant liaison with New York headquarters. It also demands excellent shorthand, word processing skills, desk top publishing, a sound knowledge of Lotus 1-2-3, and strong personal qualities of initiative, maturity, loyalty, diplomacy, and confidentiality.

If my experience and qualifications are of interest, I would be delighted to meet with you to further explore career opportunities with your company.

Sincerely,

Signature

Name

Date

Name/Title
Business/Organization
Address
City, State Zip Code

Dear Name:

The position advertised in the October issue of *The Financial Post* for a risk management consultant is of special interest to me, because I appear to have the profile and qualifications that you are seeking.

I am currently working as a consultant in the risk management department of the Lanchart Consulting Group in Wilmington, Delaware. Reporting directly to the senior vice president in charge of the department, my position involves providing advice on alternative risk-financing solutions to medium-sized American and Canadian corporations. My duties include: high-level client contact and liaison with the Lanchart insurance network on all matters related to alternative risk financing; analysis of prospects and clients' insurance and risk management programs, including preparation and presentation of detailed feasibility studies.

The attached résumé details my business and academic background. I would be willing to relocate to New York City for the right opportunity.

I will be in the New York area from November 1 through November 6 and would be happy to meet with you regarding this position at that time. Would it be possible to arrange an interview with you during this period? I look forward to hearing from you soon. However, I would appreciate my application being treated as strictly confidential, as I am currently employed.

Sincerely yours,

Signature

Name

Date

Name/Title
Business/Organization
Address
City, State Zip Code

Dear Name:

Your advertisement for an experienced materials supervisor in this week's edition of *International Drilling* describes a position that I believe is well suited for my background, experience, and qualifications.

At present I am employed as materials supervisor for the Johanson's Drilling and Development Company in Houston, Texas. Johanson is an independent exploration and production company. As a key member of the company's production team, I am involved in all aspects of inventory control and procurement of goods and services relating to drilling and development operations in Texas and Louisiana. Sourcing suppliers and ensuring delivery of highest quality and reliability within rigidly applied cost parameters and timescales is a very important part of my job. This also applies to the ability to plan and schedule long-term procurement requirements. My position requires relevant experience in the oil industry and an extensive knowledge of domestic and international procurement, safety compliances, and computerized purchasing and materials management systems.

I would appreciate the opportunity of meeting with you personally to discuss my background and professional qualifications, as outlined in the attached résumé, in more detail.

Sincerely,

Signature

Name

Simon Kushner
0000 East 67th Street
New York, NY 00000
Phone: (000) 000-0000

September 16, 1999

CONFIDENTIAL

Mr. Lawrence Rendell
Director, Human Resources Department
XYZ Company, Inc.
0000 Michigan Avenue
New York, NY 00000

Dear Mr. Rendell:

I am responding to your company's advertisement for a marketing and promotions specialist in the September issue of *Marketing Promotions* magazine. This advertisement looks as if it has been written with my background, experience, and qualifications in mind.

As a marketing and promotions specialist for my present employer Durham Brown Company in New York (see attached résumé), I have considerable experience in all phases of marketing, promotions, advertising, and public relations. Although I enjoy the responsibilities and challenges of my current position, I am looking for the personal and professional growth that only a major company such as XYZ Company has to offer.

I would welcome the opportunity to meet with you to discuss my qualifications and the specifics of your company's requirements in greater detail. I prefer to leave the discussion of salary until my interview with you.

Sincerely yours,

Simon Kushner

(A chronological résumé)

Simon Kushner
0000 East 67th Street
New York, NY 00000
Phone: (000) 000-0000

JOB OBJECTIVE

A position in marketing and promotions offering increasing levels of responsibility and advancement and the opportunity to work for a quality organization.

WORK EXPERIENCE: 1988 TO PRESENT

Durham Brown Company, Marketing and Promotion Specialists
New York City: November 1993–Present

Supervisor of the consumer marketing and promotion department (seven persons). Responsible for all aspects of daily operation of the department, including planning, organizing, and implementing assignments of personnel and work flow; problem-solving and troubleshooting; preparation of news releases; public relations as well as marketing, advertising, and promotional materials; marketing and promotion plans; audiovisual presentations and press conferences. Also, participate in developing new marketing and promotional plans and objectives for clients.

Finch Palazzi Public Relations
New York City: July 1988–October 1993

Prepared public relations materials and news releases for small and medium-sized companies in the New York metropolitan area; audiovisual presentations; organized press conferences and press tours for trade journalists.

WORK EXPERIENCE (PART-TIME AND SUMMER JOBS DURING UNIVERSITY STUDY)

KEFG-Cable Television Channel 14 in Garden City, N.Y.
Part-time during 1987 and 1988.
Joined television crew on location and helped edit and present local cable television news reports.

Bergen Herald, Hackensack (New Jersey): 1984–1986
Full-time during summer; part-time (weekends) during remainder of the year.
Junior reporter (local and county news).

EDUCATION

Bachelor Degree in Marketing
Pace University (New York): 1984–1988

Completed six specialist courses in public relations and mass communications at the Mass Communications Institute of New York University: 1988–1990.

REFERENCES

Available upon request

Useful Sentences for Cover Letters Dealing with Job Applications

I am applying for the position of Marketing Assistant, which was advertised in last week's *New York Weekly Review*. I have completed my third year at New York University and intend to take a year off to supplement my education with relevant work.

Seven years as a personal assistant to the public relations manager of the Mancini PR Corporation in Pittsburgh have given me the background and professional experience to qualify for the position (Nr. 137) you advertised in last Sunday's *Pittsburgh Telegraph*. Therefore, I believe that my qualifications will meet your requirements for this challenging position with your company.

I have worked for the past four years as an international sales representative of a large industrial company, and I would like to apply for the position of Assistant Sales Manager that you advertised in the *New York Times* of July 22. This position calls for qualifications and experience that correspond to my professional background and job objective.

I am sending this letter and résumé to apply for the position of clinical technican with your institute. I believe that my background qualifications and work experience are very compatible with the requirements of this position you listed in your advertisement in this month's *Specialized Medicine Journal*.

I am forwarding my résumé in response to your advertisement in this week's edition of *Procurement News* for an Asian procurement specialist. This position seems tailor-made to my qualifications and long-time experience with several major companies in Southeast Asia.

As an experienced advertising sales representative, I believe that I am the qualified candidate you are looking for in this month's issue of *Advertising Sales Magazine*. I feel confident that I can make a significant contribution to your staff.

I am submitting my résumé in response to your advertisement for the position of program coordinator that appeared in the latest Sunday edition of *The Daily Sketch*. I believe that my qualifications and working experience are an ideal match for your requirements.

I am confident that my international experience qualifies me for the position of export sales representative in your marketing department. I am able to handle assignments individually or as a member of a team.

I feel confident that I can apply my qualifications, skills, and working knowledge of computer hardware development to your company.

I am interested in a part-time or freelance position in your advertising art production department.

I am currently seeking a position change and I believe that my management background in the construction industry might be of interest to your company.

I am considering a change in position with a law firm that offers increasingly greater responsibility and growth potential than is possible with my present employer.

Although my present position offers me decision-making responsibilities, I feel that it is time for a change as well as a new challenge.

I am seeking a new position because I believe that my educational background and long-time work experience in the software programming sector has prepared me for changes as well as a broader scope of management responsibility.

I am presently employed as a quality control engineer at Sendix Plus Industries in Rapid City, South Dakota. However, I feel that it is time for a change in position. Therefore, I am seeking a position with a large industrial company that is interested in my international quality control manufacturing experience both in the United States and Great Britain.

The reason for leaving my current position is the desire to work for a larger manufacturing company in the Southwest where my engineering qualifications, working experience, and commitment would positively contribute to that organization's manufacturing operations.

At the July convention of the SSBD in Los Angeles, I heard that Gresham Industries has several openings for technical sales representatives in the calculating and adding machines department. My desire to work for Gresham has prompted me to forward my enclosed résumé for your evaluation.

Marsha Hunt of Coastal Auto Leasing in Seattle suggested I contact you concerning my interest in locating a position in the field of automobile renting and leasing with your company in Chicago. I have enclosed a résumé to acquaint you with my background.

Robert Westwood recommended I submit my résumé for your review regarding the position of customer support representative. Please consider me a candidate for the job. A summary of my qualifications and working experience is enclosed.

At the suggestion of Roberta Johnson of the Perrett Corporation, I am submitting my résumé with regards to employment opportunities within your company's accounting department.

Lester Hines told me that the current catering manager of your hotel will retire in April and that his position will be open. It is upon his recommendation that I am sending you my résumé to acquaint you with my professional background in the hotel catering business.

Sandra Miller of Manganaro Company strongly encouraged me to contact you. Sandra and I are colleagues and we are working at Manganaro's quality control center.

I am writing to you at the suggestion of Ms. Mary Ann Januzzi, a close friend, about my decision to make a career move.

The management structure of Bryant Industries will be reorganized this year and for that reason I have elected to make this an opportunity for change and professional growth.

In June I will receive my Bachelor of Science degree in civil engineering from the University of Pennsylvania, and I am interested in obtaining an entry-level position with your company.

This letter and attached résumé is my application for an entry-level position as a secretary with your company. I have just graduated from the Piermont Business Studies Institute in Detroit and I am ambitious to start working.

This month I completed a two-year course of study in advertising and marketing at the International Advertising Institute in Zurich, Switzerland. My placement counselor, Ms. Anne Fisher, suggested I apply to you for an entry-level position as an assistant in your company's international advertising department.

I am looking to break into the airline catering business with a long-term goal of management. For that reason, I am sending you my resume with the hope you may have a management trainee opening on your staff in the near future.

Should you have an appropriate opening in your sales department, I would appreciate the opportunity to explore career opportunities with your company.

Should you have a need for a highly qualified and hard-working sales representative in the southwestern United States, I would welcome the opportunity to meet with you personally to explore the contributions that I could make to your company's sales division.

I believe my five-year experience with Vallejo Demarest Company is especially relevant to the qualifications you may require for a position with your company as a computer programmer. I would enjoy discussing my experience and qualifications with you in a personal interview.

The attached résumé details my five-year experience in marketing research. The past two years I have been with the marketing research department of the Walter Tappan Company, a small consumer product company, where I enjoy the challenges and responsibilities of my current position as supervisor.

However, I am interested in the opportunity to work for a major company such as Barton & Scheffer as a senior marketing research specialist.

I am open to relocating anywhere—in the United States or internationally—and can begin full-time employment with one month's notice.

If relocation is necessary, then I am ready to make that commitment.

I am presently planning to relocate permanently to the Atlanta area.

I am willing to relocate and future compensation packages are negotiable.

I am willing to consider relocation to Florida based upon salary and future opportunities for growth with your organization. I would be able to start work at the end of April.

My compensation requirement is negotiable. I am currently earning the market value for a mechanical engineer with seven years of experience with a major international company. I would be happy to discuss my salary requirement in a personal interview.

I will be glad to discuss the matter of salary with you during a personal interview, because I am sure we can arrive at a satisfactory arrangement.

If my qualifications are satisfactory, I would appreciate an interview at your convenience. Please let me know when we may meet.

May I call you for an interview early next week?

I will call you next week to discuss the possibility of a personal interview.

Personal and business references are available upon request.

References and letters of recommendation will be furnished after mutual interest has been established.

I will be glad to provide additional details if you wish.

I will be glad to furnish you with additional information about my qualifications and working experience.

I will be in Portland from May 10 to 15, during which time I would welcome the opportunity to meet with you. Thank you for your consideration. I look forward to speaking with you.

The enclosed résumé summarizes my experience and background. I would appreciate the opportunity to discuss my qualifications during a personal interview. I will follow up with a telephone call next week to arrange such a meeting.

The enclosed résumé is a brief summary of my experience. I would appreciate the opportunity to personally meet you. I would be glad to make myself available for an interview at your office to discuss my qualifications and skills.

I will call you within a few days to arrange a mutually convenient time to meet.

I would greatly appreciate the opportunity to present my skills and background in a personal interview.

I would be happy to talk to you in a personal interview and to provide you with details about my professional qualifications and international working experience in Europe and how they can best serve the Brandeis Corporation.

Since my present employer is not aware of my intent to search for a new and challenging position, I would appreciate that you keep my application with your company strictly confidential.

Since my present employer is unaware of my search, your strictest confidence is appreciated. Thank you for your consideration and response.

I am looking forward to your reply and thank you in advance for your consideration.

Thank you very much for considering my application.

Thank you for considering me for this position.

Thank you for reviewing my credentials. I look forward to hearing from you shortly.

Sample Job Descriptions for Use in Cover Letters

ACCOUNTING ANALYST—I am presently working as an accounting analyst for a subsidiary of the Philadelphia-based Collins Technology, a data technology company providing storage, management and access products for computer communications systems. I am responsible for the preparation of the financial statements of one of the company's subsidiaries, from journal entry to the trial-balance stage. I am also responsible for accurate measurement and reporting of the company's marketing and sales programs. This position requires extensive experience of general ledger and trial-balance preparation and reconciliation, intercompany accounting as well as sales, cost of sale, and general and administrative expenses reporting.

ART DIRECTOR—I am working as an art director with the Artox Design Studio in New York. This company has a strong blue-chip client base and works in industries as diverse as insurance, automobiles, travel, and business-to-business. Artox Design's work appears in North America and Europe. It also does a high proportion of press work and direct mail. My position demands the ability to develop strong ideas as well as skillful understanding of typography, design, and high-budget, low-volume work.

BACK OFFICE MANAGER—I am currently working as back office manager for a major bank in Tucson, Arizona. Reporting to the General Manager and working closely with the bank's management team, I am responsible for developing, establishing, and running all the relevant systems and procedures for the bank. Key elements of my job include settlements, information technology, accounting, planning, budgeting, and administration. My position requires a broad general understanding of international banking operations and wide experience and comprehensive knowledge of planning, implementing, and managing appropriate systems.

BUYER/FREIGHT FORWARDER—I am currently employed in New Orleans as a buyer/freight forwarder for FGS Sea Transportation Group, a major system integrator and sea-freight forwarder. I am responsible for promoting the import and export activities of the company in Great Britain. My specific responsibilities include product sourcing, negotiating with suppliers, organizing and tracking shipments, and collecting offers from suppliers and relaying them to the Group's partners. In addition, I provide general administrative support to the purchasing process.

CALL CENTER SUPPORT AGENT—I am currently employed as a call center support agent for the Wittax Company, a large producer and supplier of information and communication services, with headquarters in San Antonio, Texas. The company's customers are supported by a comprehensive range of technical services from a call center where support agents provide assistance to those customers who have difficulty in installing, configuring, or using Wittax equipment. My job requires a strong commitment to customer service, a background in computer technology and computerized systems and detailed knowledge of and experience in tape drives and CD-recordable technology.

CONTRACTS ADMINISTRATOR—I am presently working as a contracts administrator for the BEXO International Lease-Finance Company in Hartford, Connecticut, where I assist in the day-to-day management of an ever-increasing portfolio of commercial vehicles. I am a member of a small team acting as the catalyst for all contractual, financial, and technical management of the portfolio. My position demands a high level of computer literacy as well as an organized and methodical manner to support all elements of an international lease company.

CREDIT CONTROL MANAGER—I am currently working as a credit control manager for a medium-sized consumer goods subsidiary in Portland, Oregon, which is part of a multinational group with corporate headquarters in Omaha, Nebraska. My key responsibilities are: developing credit-control policy, identifying and resolving significant overdue accounts, recommending action on different debts, systems development, and considerable liaison with the company's sales teams. Reporting to the financial controller, I lead a department of six specialists.

DISTRICT SALES MANAGER—I am employed as a district sales manager for an American subsidiary of one of Germany's leading industrial companies. It manufactures a wide range of plastic consumer products. The main responsibilities of my present position are to identify and exploit business opportunities, to call on prospective customers, to arrange demonstrations, to manage regular promotional activities, and to close sales with senior decisionmakers. I report to the general sales manager and one of my specific roles is to develop and maintain close relationships with department stores, supermarkets, and major cash-and-carry sales organizations located within my sales district.

ENGINEER—I am working as an engineer for the customer technical support group (Fuels) of Stillmeyer Chemical Corporation in Tulsa, Oklahoma. Stillmeyer is a major marketer of industrial chemicals, polymer additives, pharmaceutical components, and fuel and lubricant additives. These products are sold in North America and the Asia-Pacific region. I specialize in fuels and demonstrate the suitability of the company's products to customers, by providing technical data and supporting the national and international sales function.

FINANCE AND INVESTMENT COORDINATOR—At present, I am employed as finance and investment coordinator for Kearns International, a subsidiary of Werner Oil Limited, in Dallas, Texas. Kearns International is primarily involved in the marketing and distribution of petroleum products in the European Union. I work within an international unit that provides an independent appraisal service to senior management. My areas of responsibility include investment and acquisition appraisal, competitor and market analysis, and production of relevant economic summaries and ad-hoc projects.

GEOPHYSICIST—I am employed as a geophysicist in the exploration department of the Columbus Oil Drilling Company in New Orleans, Louisiana, where I am involved in an exploration program aiming to increase the company's level of reserves. My specific duties include integrating well and depth conversion, advising on acquisition and processing of seismic data, and liaising with management and partners as well as government bodies on relevant matters. This position also requires a sound knowledge of all aspects of geophysical acquisition, processing, and interpretation, along with experience in the use of interactive seismic workstations.

INFORMATION TECHNOLOGY SPECIALIST—I am presently working as an information technology specialist with the Young & Webster Corporation, a multi-business group with headquarters in Tampa, Florida. I am responsible for the development and implementation of the corporate information technology strategy. The company's current systems environment consists of Protexx and Baana business systems, DEC Alpha, Novell and Microsoft Office technologies, and upgraded Lan/WAN infrastructure.

INVENTORY CONTROL MANAGER—As inventory control manager for the Bartlett & Morley Company, I am responsible for the stockholding and European distribution strategy of this company, which has its headquarters in St. Paul, Minnesota. With over 1,900 different electronic and electrical product lines being distributed internationally to each of the company's 184 specialized retail outlets in Great Britain, Italy, France, Germany, and Austria, one of my principal responsibilities is controlling computerized holding and stock replenishment procedures at the company's central warehousing facility in Milwaukee. Another key aspect of my job is the development and implementation of internal and external procedures, resulting in improved communications, service levels, and reduced stocks. This requires close working relations and information links with suppliers, critical thinking and problem-solving skills, computer literacy, and flexibility, especially when dealing with crisis situations.

LEGAL SECRETARY—I am currently working as a legal secretary for two corporate lawyers in a multinational company with headquarters in Akron, Ohio. I provide secretarial support, including shorthand, diaries, telephones, and travel arrangements. I also type and lay out agreements, correspondence, and contracts quickly and accurately. In addition, I keep track of spreadsheet figures relating to budget.

MARKETING COORDINATOR—I currently work as marketing coordinator for the Morton Company in Hartford, Connecticut, a leading manufacturer of hot-water appliances. This company is a wholly owned subsidiary of Morton International with corporate headquarters in London, England. My responsibilities include direct marketing; business-to-business and trade press advertising;

coordination of sales and promotional literature production; involvement in market analysis; provision of sales force support; and budget administration.

MEDICAL REPRESENTATIVE—At present, I am employed as a medical representative for the Sullivan Company, a medium-sized pharmaceutical company with corporate headquarters in Scottsdale, Arizona. I work in a recently established division to contact health-care professionals in hospitals. This position requires me to spend three to four months a year traveling throughout the Southwest in spells of one to two weeks duration.

PERSONAL ASSISTANT/SECRETARY—I am currently working as personal assistant/secretary to the senior vice president in charge of international information technology at Lippencott Management Consultants in San Francisco. This position demands excellent interpersonal skills and the ability to work in a role that requires not only the traditional blend of secretarial and organizational skills, but also the initiative and flexibility to thrive within a varied and often hectic environment. I am responsible for client liaison at international level, diary management, the organization of meetings and presentations, travel arrangements, as well as a variety of day-to-day functions. Other necessary qualifications are excellent shorthand and proficiency with a wide range of PC-based software packages.

PERSONAL ASSISTANT/SECRETARY—I am presently working as personal assistant/secretary for the head of the sales and marketing support department of the Van Nuys Corporation in Milwaukee, Wisconsin. In addition to the usual secretarial duties, I am also responsible for the running of the department's secretarial pool. This includes the supervision of eight secretaries and typists, extensive preparation of costs and expenses reports and frequent liaison with the company's regional offices in Chicago, Detroit, Indianapolis, Cleveland, Grand Rapids, and Cincinnati.

PRODUCTION GEOLOGIST—I am employed as a production geologist for the Hernandez Corporation in Baton Rouge, Louisiana, where I work as part of a closely knit professional team of geologists, geophysicists, and reservoir engineers. My specific responsibilities include constructing and maintaining detailed geologic models of operational fields and adjacent areas, proposing and justifying new development, appraisal of well locations, supervising well site activity, and management reporting and presentations. This position also requires a thorough knowledge of production geology, well site operations, exploration geology, plus a basic understanding of geophysics and reservoir engineering.

SAFETY MANAGER—I am currently working as safety manager for Mayfield Facilities, the manufacturing subsidiary of RDF Corporation, a leading healthcare company. With over 650 employees at its manufacturing plant near Birmingham, Alabama, health, safety, and environmental protection are of vital importance. This is reflected in the plant's safety and environmental department where I am responsible for providing and managing operational support in safety, fire, and environmental protection as well as strategic responsibility for training and systems development. My position requires a detailed understanding of the laws and regulations concerning safety, hygiene, and the work environment. It also demands a technical appreciation in accident prevention covering electrical and mechanical installations.

SALES COORDINATOR—I am currently employed as a sales coordinator in the document management systems department of the Finnesta Corporation in Eugene, Oregon. I coordinate support for new product introductions and sales and marketing activities, as well as business-oriented sales research. Moreover, I offer assistance to local sales companies in the areas of planning strategies, promotions, and distribution. My job requires extensive experience with new product introductions, a market and customer-oriented attitude, team spirit, flexibility, and excellent communication skills.

SALES REPRESENTATIVE—I am presently working as a sales representative for the Curtiss Brown Scientific Corporation, a manufacturer of sophisticated technical products for the medical community (physicians and nurses), with headquarters in Provo, Utah. In this position, I deal directly with decisionmakers in clinics and hospitals where I provide a consultative role analyzing and presenting solutions to their individual requirements. For that reason, my position not only requires considerable business experience in medical devices, but also negotiating skills and a thorough knowledge of the decisionmaking processes in hospitals and clinics.

SALES SUPPORT REPRESENTATIVE—I am currently working as a sales support representative for the XXZZ Database Corporation, a provider of specialized knowledge bases for safety and the environment, with corporate headquarters in Norfolk, Viriginia. Within the sales support department, I answer telephone calls, respond to customer and sales managers' requests and inquiries, and assist with proposals and quotes. Moreover, I provide general administrative support to the purchasing process and I have daily communication with our two other sales support offices in Houston and San Diego. My job requires excellent organizational skills, word processing experience (Microsoft), and the ability to work to stringent deadlines.

TECHNICAL SUPPORT OPERATOR—I am employed by the Manchester (Indiana)-based Elton Glenn Transaction Company, an information technology company providing software, hardware, and services to support high-volume transaction processing for sales outlets in retail industries. I am a member of the desktop support group where I am working as a technical support operator. This group is responsible for support and maintenance of the company's computer users, ranging from printing problems on the network to actually resolving problems users may incur with the operating systems. The troubleshooting includes use of remote support with sites all across Indiana, Michigan, and Ohio.

USEFUL SENTENCES AND PHRASES TO DESCRIBE CAREER OR PROFESSIONAL OBJECTIVES

Entry-level opportunity at an advertising agency.

An entry-level position in the field of personnel administration.

Entry-level position in financial services offering a chance to demonstrate initiative and abilities.

Seeking an entry-level position in the field of management with preference in sales promotion.

To secure an entry-level engineering technician position with the opportunity for advancement.

Trainee in a sales-oriented company offering the opportunity to advance to a position of increasing responsibility and career growth.

A management trainee position in a medium-sized direct marketing company with an opportunity to advance to management level.

To obtain a position as a sales management trainee that allows for career growth.

An assistant sales manager position with a large distributor.

A position as manager of a furniture department of a large department store.

A position as personal assistant/secretary with a major corporation.

Personal assistant/secretary position with a major international telecommunications company.

A position in the field of public relations where a background in journalism and consumer marketing may be utilized.

Management position in retail sales commensurate with 16 years of successful retail/supermarket sales experience.

Seeking a responsible position commensurate with nine years experience as a direct marketing specialist. I am looking for a chance to demonstrate a high level of motivation to succeed.

A sales management position in a communications company where I can use my promotion and sales experience.

A challenging supervisory position and active involvement in accounting with the opportunity for advancement and personal growth.

A line management position in a growth-oriented pharmaceutical company where I can apply my research, problem-solving expertise, and experience in medical chemistry.

A challenging and career-oriented position utilizing my experience and skills in office management and providing opportunities for advancement.

A position as a personnel manager where I can utilize my background and management experience in human resources and an opportunity to expand my areas of responsibility with further career potential.

A position in new product engineering providing an opportunity to apply my extensive technical experience.

Professionally and financially rewarding marketing management position offering challenge, responsibility, and an opportunity for advancement.

Seeking a full-time staff position offering career advancement and increasing responsibility in the field of international market research. I am willing to travel and relocate.

To seek a challenging position in the financial services field with the opportunity for professional growth based on performance.

To pursue an international sales position that offers advancement opportunities.

Seeking an opportunity to start a new career in audience and marketing research with a major television station.

To work in a managerial position with decision-making responsibilities in which I can utilize my long-time banking experience and professional skills.

To fully utilize my professional computer programmer experience in a position offering variety of challenging projects with growth potential in a major software company.

To find long-time employment in the accounting department of a major European organization that offers a career with advancement and expansion of responsibilities.

To obtain a position as an electronics engineer with a progressive Asian company engaged in advanced satellite research and development.

To obtain a challenging position in which I can utilize my diversified project engineering background and experience and an environment where individual achievements will be recognized.

Sample Résumés

(Chronological résumé: bookkeeper)

Christina Giachetti
0000 Bergen Avenue
Avondale, NJ 00000
Tel. (000) 000-0000

OBJECTIVE

> To work for a large company where I can utilize my experience and background in general accounting/bookkeeping and payroll administration.

EXPERIENCE

Jason International Trading, Inc., Teaneck, New Jersey
Bookkeeper: March 1995–present

Major responsibilities include accounts receivable, accounts payable, cost accounting, profit calculations, credit investigations on all new clients, and biweekly EDP payroll processing, including overtime, bonuses, sales commissions, and incentive awards for 157 employees. I supervise four people.

Simpson & Tague Company, Hackensack, New Jersey
Accounting Assistant: August 1988–February 1995

Duties included processing of invoices, checks, accounts receivable, and accounts payable.

EDUCATION

Fairlawn Junior College, Fairlawn, New Jersey
Associate Degree in Business Studies: June 1988

Fairlawn Junior College, Fairlawn, New Jersey
Diploma, Accounting I, II, and III: May 1990

Paramus Business Institute, Paramus, New Jersey
Certificate, EDP for Business Accounting: December 1991

SPECIAL SKILLS

Fluency in Italian (spoken and written)
Experience with computer hardware and software, including desktop publishing

REFERENCES

References will be forwarded upon request.

Please keep my application confidential at this time.

(Chronological résumé: certified public accountant)

Vincent Harrison
000 Chandler Avenue
Chicago, IL 00000
(000) 000-0000

CAREER OBJECTIVE

An accounting career with a large company that offers advancement opportunities and professional growth.

EMPLOYMENT

Bressler & Andersen, Certified Public Accountants, Chicago
Certified Public Accountant: August 1991–present

- Preparation of financial reports and statements and income tax returns (professional partnerships, corporations and institutions).

- Responsible for planning internal control evaluations and audit engagements of publicly and privately owned companies.

- Preparation of internal control comments for presentation to senior management.

Schwartz Company CPAs, Chicago
Financial Accounting Intern: June 1990–May 1991
Responsible for preparation of financial statements and monthly accounts analysis.

Hovert Trading Company, Chicago
Designed computerized accounts payable and receivable system: Summer 1988.

International Illinois Bank, Chicago
Assisted in developing revenue forecasts: Summer 1987.

EDUCATION

University of Chicago
Bachelor of Science Degree in Accounting: 1989
M.B.A. Degree: 1990

Certified Public Accountant (Chicago): 1991
Continuing professional education courses in federal taxes: 1994–present.

SPECIAL SKILLS

Fluency in German.

PROFESSIONAL AFFILIATION

American Institute of Certified Public Accountants

REFERENCES

Available upon request.

(Chronological résumé: a career in business management)

Marcia Turner
000 Bond Street
Boston, MA 00000
(000) 000-0000

OBJECTIVE:

A career in business management. Willing to travel and relocate.

EDUCATION

Columbia University, New York City
Bachelor of Business Administration: September 1994

WORK EXPERIENCE

MIRABELLA INSURANCE COMPANY, Hartford, Connecticut
Research Coordinator in Business Planning Division: October 1994–present
Conduct business, field, and desk research and make in-house presentations of results to senior management.
Coordinate and supervise system of current financial business news to department heads.

MARCUS BROWN, INC., Teaneck, New Jersey
Business Development Intern: Summer 1992
Worked in the areas of demographics and sales forecasts.

TIECO SALES CORPORATION, New York City
Business Intern: Summer 1991
Worked in the accounts payable and accounts receivable department.

DERBY INDUSTRIAL ADVERTISING, New York City
Business Intern: Summer 1990
Assisted Account Executive to develop promotion program for several industrial clients.

REFERENCES

Available upon request.

(Chronological résumé: hotel manager)

John Morrison
000 Saratoga Avenue
Miami, FL 00000
(000) 000-0000

PROFESSIONAL OBJECTIVE

A management position with a major international hotel chain.

WORK EXPERIENCE

The Colonade Hotel—Miami, Florida
Food and Beverage Manager: July 1989–present

Directly responsible for management of restaurant and kitchen operations (staff of 44) and purchasing in a 326-room hotel with a restaurant, coffee shop, and banquet facilities.

LaSalle Hotel—New York City
Assistant to Food Services Manager: September 1983–May 1989

Supervised dining room and bar staff of 38. Responsibility for meal planning and coordination of approximately 125 banquets and large private parties (50–400 guests) per year.

Orange Roof Restaurant—Passaic, New Jersey
Manager: October 1980–August 1983
Assistant Manager: July 1979–September 1980

Responsible for management of a 124-seat restaurant of a well-known popular restaurant chain with set menus at reasonable prices.

Continental Diner, New York City
Waiter: May 1978–June 1979

Waiter at a busy diner (open 24 hours) in midtown Manhattan.

EDUCATION

University of Miami
Bachelor's Degree in Business Administration: 1994

City College of New York
Successful completion of three Financial Management courses: 1982

Hotel-Restaurant Institute, New York
Completed six-month management training course (day/evening classes): 1979

Philadelphia Junior College
Associate Degree in Business Studies: 1978

REFERENCES

Available on request.

(Chronological résumé: personnel manager)

Martin B. Ritter
000 Baxter Avenue
Dallas, TX 00000
(000) 000-0000

JOB OBJECTIVE

A management position in the human resources department of a major manufacturing company.

WORK EXPERIENCE

DOLLINGER INDUSTRIES—Dallas, Texas
Personnel Manager: March 1990–present

Responsible for:

Recruiting, screening, interviewing, testing and hiring of personnel for secretarial, clerical, production, and research and development positions (approximately 175 positions per year). Dollinger Industries has 2,550 part-time and full-time employees.

Negotiate and commission contracts with employment agencies.

Participate in contract negotiations with labor unions.

Conduct compensation surveys and analyses; set salary and wage ranges.

Initiate, formulate, revise, and implement staff training programs, job evaluations, performance appraisals, and personnel policies.

Supervise the maintenance and retention of all employment records.

Update and revise personnel manual, covering employment, training, salaries, wages, and benefits.

Supervise a staff of eight.

COOPER PRODUCTS, INC.—Cambridge, Massachusetts
Assistant Director of Human Resources: July 1985–February 1990

Assisted the Director of Human Resources in areas of personnel screening, evaluation, and selection. Conducted performance appraisals and contributed to the company manual covering benefits, education, and training.

EDUCATION

Boston University.
Bachelor of Science degree in personnel administration: June 1985
Master of Science degree in personnel management: May 1987

The Institute of Personnel Administration of MIT, Cambridge, Massachusetts.
Certificate: six evening courses in personnel administration and EDP applications (including dBASE 6 and IBC II): 1988–1989.

References are available upon request.

(Functional résumé: systems programmer)

Brad Anaheim
00 Beech Avenue
San Jose, CA 00000
Tel. (000) 000-0000

PROFESSION

Systems Programmer

OBJECTIVE

A challenging position in the computer programming field where I can utilize my extensive experience and broad analytic design and problem-solving skills as a systems programmer.

EXPERIENCE

Member of a MVS/OS395 Parallel Systplexx Conversion Team.
Involvement in high exposure state-of-the-art environment, including OS395 Parallel Systplexx Conversions with full data sharing, Open Edition, and Internet Connection Secure Server.

Solid experience in the installation, maintenance, tuning, and debugging of MFFS/ESA (0S395), SMPE, JES3, TSO/ISPF, VTAN, TCP/IP and DB2 and CICS.

Ability to multitask and adaptability to multiple environments; implementing complex systems and network management applications.

EMPLOYMENT HISTORY

1993–present   Sonomax Conversion Systems, San Jose, California
1989–1991   ATRAXX Computer Associates, Palo Alto, California
1985–1988   Innova Computer Programs, San Francisco, California

EDUCATION

Bachelor of Science—Mathematics (1983)
University of California at Los Angeles

Master of Science—Computer Science (1985)
University of California at Berkeley

Letters Requesting a Recommendation, a Reference, or Information

(Letter requesting a recommendation)

Date

Name/Title
Business/Organization
Address
City, State Zip Code

Dear Name:

I am applying for a job as a bilingual secretary with the law firm of Martinez & Associates in Miami, Florida, because I am anxious to move to a position where I can use my Spanish. I have been asked for a recommendation from my Spanish-language teacher. As you may recall, I was in your advanced class from January to November last year. Your recommendation will undoubtedly enhance my chances of being hired. I hope you will allow me to use your name.

I look forward to hearing from you.

Sincerely,

Signature

Name

(Letter requesting a reference)

Date

Name/Title
Business/Organization
Address
City, State Zip Code

Dear Name:

Last year you offered to write a letter of reference for me if I would need one for future employment. Since I have been offered a position as a marketing management trainee with the well-known Lloyd Deltax Company in Boston, I would like to take you up on your generous offer.

Please address your letter to Ms. Arlene Slocum, Director of Marketing, Lloyd Deltax Company, 000 Colfax Avenue, Boston, MA 00000.

Thank you very much for your cooperation.

Sincerely,

Signature

Name

(Letter requesting information from an employment reference)

Date

Name/Title
Business/Organization
Address
City, State Zip Code

Dear Name:

Ms. Maria Ferrara has given us your name as a business reference. She has applied for a secretarial position with our company and we would be grateful for your opinion of Ms. Ferrara's proficiency in secretarial skills and her personality and ability to get along with other people.

We assure you that any information you supply about this applicant will be treated as strictly confidential. If we can reciprocate at any time, please let us know.

Sincerely yours,

Signature

Name

(Letter requesting information from an employment reference)

Date

Name/Title
Business/Organization
Address
City, State Zip Code

Dear Name:

Mr. Lawrence Roth is being considered for a position as international marketing manager and has given us your name as an employment reference. We would appreciate any comments you may wish to make about Mr. Roth's work, character, reliability, and his ability to work with other people.

We will, of course, keep any information you care to give strictly confidential and will reciprocate any time you ask. Thank you for your cooperation in answering this request.

Sincerely,

Signature

Name

(Letter requesting information from an employment reference)

Date

Name/Title
Business/Organization
Address
City, State Zip Code

Dear Name:

We are considering the application of Ms. Brenda Hertel for the position of personal assistant/secretary for one of our senior sales executives. We understand that Ms. Hertel was employed by your company as a personal assistant/secretary from May 1993 to January 1995 and we wish to verify that information. Can you also tell us why Ms. Hertel left your company, since she seems somewhat vague about her reasons for leaving? Your reply will, or course, be kept strictly confidential.

Sincerely,

Signature

Name

(Letter requesting information from an employment reference)

April 14, 1999

CONFIDENTIAL

WXYZ Company
Attention: Ms. Olga Madison
Director—Human Resources Dept.
000 Lakeview Avenue
Petersville, MS 00000

Subject: Personnel Record of Ms. Monica Singer

Dear Ms. Madison:

Ms. Monica Singer has applied to us for employment as assistant credit manager in our credit department. She has referred us to you for a testimonial of a recent similar position at your company. Would you be kind enough to provide us with the information requested below concerning Ms. Singer? Your answers and any other details that may be helpful in our decision to hire Ms. Singer will be sincerely appreciated.

- Date of employment with your company

- Title of position held

- Employee's reliability (good, average, poor)

- If discharged, reason

- Any other comments

Needless to say that all facts or remarks will be kept in the strictest confidence. If we can ever be of service to your company in return, please do not hesitate to contact us.

Thank you very much for your cooperation.

Sincerely,

Martha Trebine
Director of Human Resources

USEFUL SENTENCES FOR LETTERS REQUESTING A RECOMMENDATION OR INFORMATION FROM AN EMPLOYMENT REFERENCE

I am being considered for a position as marketing director with Hilberts Manufacturings Inc. in Philadelphia and I would be most grateful if I could give your name as a reference.

I am applying to various American and Canadian companies for a position as their sales representative in France. Would you be kind enough to let me use your name as a personal reference who can testify to my professional capacity in the international field and my ability to communicate in French?

We received an application from Ms. Carol Baker for the position of receptionist with our company. Ms. Baker indicated that she has worked for your organization and gave your name as an employment reference.

Mr. Brian Wilson has applied to us for the position of computer system manager, and your name was given as a reference. He informed us he held a similar position with your company and that he left of his own accord.

Mr. Peter Wertheim has applied for a position with our company as market researcher and has given your name as an employment reference. He stated that he worked for your company from October 1990 to March 1998. Could you supply us the exact dates of his employment?

Ms. Caroline Jones, one of your former employees, has applied for a position as legal secretary in our legal department and has given your name as a personal reference.

Ms. Michelle Norton has given us your name as a personal reference. She has applied to us for the position of assistant to the director of human resources and we are sufficiently interested in her experience and professional qualifications to seek further information.

We would be very grateful for any information you may wish to provide about Mr. Lipmann's character and professional skills that might aid us in making a decision to hire him.

Any information you care to supply will, of course, be held in strictest confidence. If there is ever an opportunity for us to reciprocate, we will be pleased to do so.

We know that your recommendation and remarks about Ms. Valentino's professional qualifications will be valuable, and request you to make them entirely frank. Please be assured that your comments will be held in strictest confidence.

We would appreciate receiving a straightforward appraisal of Mr. Oakley's ability to work well under pressure and without supervision as well as any other comments or professional opinions that you feel would aid us in making a decision about his application.

Answers to Letters of Reference and Recommendation

Date

Name/Title
Business/Organization
Address
City, State Zip Code

Dear Name:

I welcome this opportunity to respond to your request for a personal recommendation for Carol Woolley, who worked for our company as Assistant Sales Manager for the past five years.

We were very disappointed to lose Ms. Woolley. She left our company because her husband had been relocated to Detroit. Ms. Woolley's management skills and work have been exemplary and she was well liked by all her co-workers.

If your company requires a responsible, industrious, and dedicated Assistant Sales Manager, you should hire Ms. Woolley.

Sincerely yours,

Signature

Name

Confidential

Date

Name/Title
Business/Organization
Address
City, State Zip Code

Dear Name:

In response to your letter of July 7, I am pleased to write on behalf of Mr. Darryl Pfeiffer who has applied to your company for the position of inventory control supervisor. He worked for my company from February 1990 to September 1998 as assistant to the inventory control director. I found Mr. Pfeiffer's work to be entirely satisfactory and he has proven to be an intelligent, personable, hard-working, and reliable employee. I was genuinely sorry to see him go. Therefore, I am sure that Mr.

Pfeiffer will be an asset to your company and I highly recommend him for the position of inventory control supervisor.

If you have any further questions, please do not hesitate to contact me personally.

Sincerely,

Signature

Name

Date

Name/Title
Business/Organization
Address
City, State Zip Code

Dear Name:

In reference to your letter of February 19, I am pleased to confirm Margaret Atkinson's employment with Campbell Beltman Company from September 1994 through January 1999. Ms. Atkinson performed her responsibilities as the personal assistant of Mr. Beltman with competence, diligence, discretion, and complete loyalty. She will be an asset to any company and I can recommend her without reservation.

Sincerely,

Signature

Name

Date

Name/Title
Business/Organization
Address
City, State Zip Code

Dear Name:

I am happy to provide the information you requested in your letter of September 29 about the employment of Mr. Clint McCullen with our company. I found Mr. McCullen reliable, efficient, and entirely trustworthy. He was also liked by all his colleagues in the production department. I believe that any company would be fortunate to have him on its staff. Therefore, I feel very comfortable recommending Mr. McCullen to you and will be pleased to provide any additional information if necessary.

Sincerely,

Signature

Name

Date

Name/Title
Business/Organization
Address
City, State Zip Code

Dear Name:

Thank you for your letter of July 27 asking for a business reference for Ms. Gladys Conklin. I take genuine pleasure in recommending her as personal secretary to the chief executive officer of your organization.

Ms. Conklin worked for our company from May 1988 to June 1998. She started out as a secretary and became personal secretary to the vice president of our international marketing division after three years because she showed a marked talent for handling problems and meeting tight schedules and deadlines. She was absent only four days in the seven years she worked at our company. Ms. Conklin is also tactful, efficient, conscientious, and hard-working, and always pleasant to everyone. I strongly recommend her for the position as personal secretary to your company's chief executive officer. Our company was very sorry to lose Ms. Conklin and we would be very pleased to have her back on our staff.

Please feel free to call me for further information.

Sincerely,

Signature

Name

Date

Name/Title
Business/Organization
Address
City, State Zip Code

Dear Name:

In response to your inquiry of November 13, my wife and I are pleased to offer this personal recommendation on behalf of Mary Deegan.

Ms. Deegan worked for us for the past four years (five days a week) as a housekeeper and cook. She is intelligent, trustworthy, and a diligent worker who has always done an exceptional job. We could not have asked for better. Moreover, Mary has a very pleasant personality and our seven-year-old daughter was also very fond of her. We recommend Ms. Deegan to you without any reservation. We are sincerely sorry to see her go, but she wanted to live closer to her mother who recently was involved in a serious car accident.

Sincerely yours,

Signature

Name

Date

Name/Title
Business/Organization
Address
City, State Zip Code

Dear Name:

We find it rather awkward to answer your letter about Ms. Martina Willis, because her employment with our company—from February 15 to April 30, 1998—was brief. Perhaps Ms. Willis can provide you with other employment references with more relevant knowledge of her performance and secretarial skills. We suggest that you ask them for personal recommendations about her ability to perform the type of position as secretary she is applying for with your organization.

The above information is provided to you without legal responsibility.

Sincerely,

Signature

Name

Date

Name/Title
Business/Organization
Address
City, State Zip Code

Dear Name:

We received your letter of May 8 asking for the employment reference of Mr. Gerald Winter. We would prefer not to comment on his employment with our company although we found his work satisfactory and deadlines were always met. Mr. Winter worked for our company from July 1, 1996 through January 1999. He left our company on his own free will to pursue a more challenging position in Canada.

Sincerely,

Signature

Name

Date

Name/Title
Business/Organization
Address
City, State Zip Code

Dear Name:

I am sorry to inform you that we cannot provide any personal information about Mr. Howard Jackson since our company's privacy policy prohibits the release of personal data about our staff. However, I can verify that Mr. Jackson was employed by our company as a certified public accountant from March 1993 to February 1999 and that he left our organization of his own free will.

Sincerely,

Signature

Name

Date

Name/Title
Business/Organization
Address
City, State Zip Code

Dear Name:

Thank you for your letter of April 7 requesting information about Ms. Anne Klein's employment with our organization. We prefer not to comment on the employment of Ms. Klein with our company during the period (September 1997 until January 1998) she worked here as a typist in the secretarial pool.

Sincerely,

Signature

Name

January 3, 1999

LETTER OF RECOMMENDATION FOR LAURA WEBBER

Ms. Laura C. Webber was employed at our company during the period September 1992 to December 1998, most recently personal assistant to our national sales manager. She advanced to her current position in February 1996.

Ms. Webber is leaving our company on her own volition since she feels that she has advanced as far as possible under our current employment plan. For that reason, she has decided to look for a position in a larger organization.

We are sorry to see Ms. Webber go, because she has shown herself to be capable, resourceful, well-organized, intelligent, and pleasant. Therefore, we recommend her with enthusiasm since she should be a valuable asset to any company.

Joseph B. Baxter
Director of Human Resources

February 1, 1999

To Whom It May Concern:

The bearer of this letter, John A. Curran, has been employed by our company as a bookkeeper during the period April 1989 until January 1999. During this period, Mr. Curran proved reliable and trustworthy and performed his duties to our complete satisfaction. He is able to act on his own initiative and take on added responsibility where necessary. We can recommend him without reservation and if we can provide additional information, please do not hesitate to call.

Sincerely,

Jeanette McDonald
Personnel Director

Useful Sentences for Letters of Reference and Recommendation

We are happy to provide the information about Mr. Sidney Bialystock you requested in your letter of March 7 with the explicit understanding, however, that this information will be held in strict confidence.

It is with great pleasure that I recommend Dick Gross for the marketing position in your company.

I can recommend Ms. Jean Weinman, without any hesitation, for the position of assistant director of human resources in your organization. She is intelligent, accurate, personable, and discrete.

I recommend Mr. Leone without reservation, because I know you will find him an excellent sales representative. He is a serious and dedicated worker.

I am pleased to recommend Mr. Leonard Taylor, who worked in my department for the past five years as a truck driver. He is a dedicated and reliable worker and always has been generous with his time. In addition, he was willing to work late or during weekends when we asked him.

I am convinced that Mr. Derek Evans would bring credit to your organization. His integrity and reliability are above question.

I am pleased to vouch for Ms. Robinson's character and her professional qualifications.

During his employment with our organization, Mr. Osborne's proficiency in his job duties, attendance, and timekeeping record were excellent. He is also a very pleasant and thoughtful person.

I was very sorry to lose Ms. Clark and would readily rehire her if a suitable vacancy arose in our organization.

We were sincerely sorry to see Clark Brentwood, who has been employed as an administrative assistant in our bookkeeping department for three years, leave our company.

I was sorry to lose Ms. Quinn, because she was one of our best market researchers. Therefore, I do not hesitate to recommend her for any position she feels qualified to seek with your organization.

Mr. William Sherman has proven to be an efficient, hard-working, trustworthy, and very personable employee. I would not hesitate to offer Mr. Sherman employment again should he decide to return to the New York metropolitan area in the future.

Ann Johnson left our company because her husband had been relocated to Atlanta.

Mr. Asher left our organization of his own free will because he believed that freelance work would offer greater opportunities.

Ms. Jones left our company to take a position in Philadelphia that afforded her a better opportunity for advancement.

The only reason that we let Mr. Sheridan go last month was due to the fact that through the reorganization of our company, his position was eliminated.

When Ms. Kovacs left our company six months ago to get married, she was personal assistant to the vice president of our public relations department. We are very sorry that she left our organization.

Mr. Collins leaves our company at his own request because he feels that he should receive a higher salary than we can afford to pay.

Mr. Davis resigned to accept an international sales position with a competing company in London where he felt he would have greater opportunities for advancement and career growth.

Ms. Claiborne resigned in order to take up a position as director of public affairs of a major industrial company in her home town.

It was with deep regret that we accepted Ms. Dayton's resignation as national sales manager to seek new opportunities because we could not offer her the prospects of promotion that she deserved.

Mr. Bergen's position as a physical education teacher at Hiller High School was terminated because of a sharp reduction in federal funding for physical education.

Mr. Simon Danforth worked as a foreman in our computer manufacturing plant in Dearborn, Michigan. He left our company during a staff rationalization program in mid–1999.

Employer's Response to Applications for Employment

(A preliminary answer to a job applicant)

Date

Name
Address
City, State Zip Code

Dear Name:

Thank you for your application form and résumé for the position of media planner in our advertising department.

The response to our advertisement in *Media Weekly* has been overwhelming and therefore we will need approximately three weeks to evaluate all applicants. We will inform you as soon as possible if you will be scheduled to attend a personal interview at our head office in Fort Worth, Texas.

Thank you for your interest in Barnes Advertising Agency.

Sincerely yours,

Signature

Name

(A preliminary answer to a job applicant)

Date

Name
Address
City, State Zip Code

Dear Name:

Thank you for your application for the position of executive secretary with our company. Our human resources department is now reviewing your experience and professional qualifications. However, the response to this advertisement has been considerable. For that reason, it will take probably three or four weeks before all applicants have been evaluated and processed. You will be notified as soon as a final selection has been made.

Thank you very much for your interest in our organization as a potential employee.

Sincerely,

Signature

Name

(An invitation to an interview)

Date

Name
Address
City, State Zip Code

Dear Name:

Thank you for returning your completed application form for the position of production controller with our company. Your professional credentials and previous work record indicate that you may well have the qualifications that we are looking for. I would be grateful if you would come to this office for an interview on Tuesday, February 19, at 9:30 A.M. The interviewing procedure will take approximately two hours and will include a brief tour of our production facilities. You will be reimbursed for transportation, meals, and accommodation. Please call my secretary (Ms. Edwards; extension 315) to confirm this appointment.

I look forward to meeting you in person.

Sincerely yours,

Signature

Name

(A negative answer to a job applicant)

Date

Name
Address
City, State Zip Code

Dear Name:

This is to acknowledge your application for a position as sales representative with our organization. Our sales department has carefully reviewed your experience and qualifications. They are excellent, but I regret that we do not have an appropriate position open at the present time that fits your international background. Your credentials are impressive, however, and a person with your European background should have no trouble finding the right position with a major company in the United States or Canada. We wish you success in your career.

Sincerely,

Signature

Name

(A negative answer to a job applicant)

Date

Name
Address
City, State Zip Code

Dear Name:

I regret to inform you that, despite careful consideration of your experience and professional background, we are unable to offer you the position of systems analyst for which you applied. Although your credentials are excellent, we have offered this position to the candidate who had a great deal more practical experience in the computer programming and problem-solving field than yourself. We appreciate the interest you have shown in our company and wish you well in finding the position you desire.

Sincerely yours,

Signature

Name

(A preliminary response to a "cold-contact letter" for employment)

Date

Name
Address
City, State Zip Code

Dear Name:

Thank you for applying for employment with Unigrox Industries. Your background will be carefully reviewed to determine how your qualifications and interests match our present openings. This review process may take up to one month. If we identify a position suited to your qualifications, we will contact you and invite you to a personal interview.

If you do not hear from us within one month, you may assume that we have been unable to find a suitable position at this time. However, we always retain a file of the résumés of candidates and may contact you later regarding your interest in our company. We also advertise for current openings and invite you to respond in the future when applicable.

We appreciate your interest in Unigrox Industries and wish you success in your career goals.

Sincerely,

Signature

Name

(A negative response to a "cold-contact letter" for employment)

Date

Name
Address
City, State Zip Code

Dear Name:

We are sorry to inform you that we are not presently hiring financial planners in our investment division. However, we will keep your résumé on file in case there is a staff expansion or resignation. We are impressed with your business and financial qualifications and suggest you get in touch with us again in approximately four months if you are still interested in a position with our organization.

Sincerely,

Signature

Name

(A negative response to a "cold-contact letter" for employment)

Date

Name
Address
City, State Zip Code

Dear Name:

Thank you for sending us your résumé. We were quite impressed with your background and qualifications. At this time, however, we do not foresee any openings in our audiovisual department during the remainder of the year. Generally, these positions are filled internally.

We will keep your résumé on file and will be glad to contact you in the event that any openings do occur. Please, notify us of any changes in your address.

Sincerely,

Signature

Name

(A negative response to a "cold-contact letter" for employment)

Date

Name
Address
City, State Zip Code

Dear Name:

Thank you for your letter of September 17 expressing an interest in employment as a pharmaceutical sales representative within our organization.

I am sorry to inform you that at the moment there are no suitable vacancies in our national sales department. However, this situation may change within the next few months. For that reason, I would like to keep your résumé in our active file where it will be reviewed again in case an opening does occur in the department.

Thank you for your interest in Anderson Pharmaceutical Corporation.

Sincerely yours,

Signature

Name

(A negative response to a "cold-contact letter" for employment)

Date

Name
Address
City, State Zip Code

Dear Name:

Thank you for your letter and résumé inquiring about a marketing position in our company. At the moment there are no vacancies in our marketing department. Since you have excellent qualifications as well as marketing and sales experience, I will be pleased to hold your application and get in touch with you if there is a vacancy in our marketing department. However, I suggest that you continue your search for a position in other companies.

Thank you very much for your interest in the Tanno Services Corporation.

Sincerely,

Signature

Name

(Rejection of an applicant after an interview)

Date

Name
Address
City, State Zip Code

Dear Name:

It was a pleasure to meet with you at our Philadelphia office last month. Your long experience in telecommunications sales within Europe is impressive.

As we discussed during the interview, New USA Telecom Systems is looking for a mature person with a thorough understanding of the complicated European marketplace in both the public and private sectors of the telecom industry. This executive should have considerable management experience and should also be able to deal with strategic partners and officials at all levels and political environments. Because of your limited managerial experience, we are unable to offer you the position.

I wish you all the best for a successful continuation of your career in the telecommunications industry.

Sincerely,

Signature

Name

(Confirmation of a job offer to an applicant)

Date

Name
Address
City, State Zip Code

Dear Name:

I am pleased to offer you the position of personal secretary to Mr. Andrew Hanssen at our corporate headquarters in Dearborn, Michigan, commencing on July 1. I enclose two copies of your contract of employment for this position. Please sign both copies and return one to me before May 15. Your duties and responsibilities are detailed in the attached job description.

As discussed with you, the position is subject to a probationary period of two months. You will be offered a permanent position if the outcome of your probationary period is successful.

Sincerely,

Signature

Name

(Confirmation of a job offer to an applicant)

Date

Name
Address
City, State Zip Code

Dear Name:

It is with great pleasure that I am able to offer you the position of energy project engineer with our organization, starting on April 1, 1999. Congratulations on being selected and welcome to Lennox Projects Company.

The position pays $____ annually in equal increments every month and you will also receive the standard benefits package that we discussed in the interview.

I look forward to welcoming you to the company on April 1. Please plan to arrive at 8:45 A.M. If you have any questions, do not hesitate to call me.

Sincerely,

Signature

Name

(Confirmation of a job offer to an applicant)

Date

Name
Address
City, State Zip Code

Dear Name:

It is our distinct pleasure to inform you that, following your interview of last month, we can offer you the position of analytical chemist with our company. Congratulations on your selection.

You will be paid a starting salary of $____ per month and will receive three weeks paid vacation per year. In addition, you will receive standard health insurance and sick leave benefits and $ ____ of life insurance. If you have any questions about your conditions of employment, please get in touch with our personnel department.

We would like you to start on Monday, November 1, and look forward to welcoming you at our head office at 9:00 A.M.

Yours sincerely,

Signature

Name

(An applicant accepting a job offer)

Date

Name/Title
Business/Organization
Address
City, State Zip Code

Dear Name:

I have received your letter of September 12 offering me the position of software technician with your company. I am very pleased to accept your offer.

This afternoon I have submitted a formal notice to my current employer. I look forward to start working for your organization on October 1.

Sincerely,

Signature

Name

(An applicant declining an employer's job offer)

Date

Name/Title
Business/Organization
Address
City, State Zip Code

Dear Name:

Thank you for your letter of March 13 offering me the position of project geologist with your company. Unfortunately, I must decline your offer at this time. My company has offered me a promotion which I feel I cannot pass up. I am sure you will understand my decision.

Thank you so much for your confidence in offering me an opportunity to work for your organization. I am sorry if I have caused you any inconvenience.

Sincerely yours,

Signature

Name

(An applicant declining a job offer)

Date

Name/Title
Business/Organization
Address
City, State Zip Code

Dear Name:

I received your kind letter dated October 9, offering me the position of payroll supervisor with your organization.

However, after careful deliberation, I have decided to decline this position. The reason is that the relocation to San Diego would not be in the best interest of my immediate family as well as my grandparents who are also living with us.

I sincerely regret that I am unable to accept the opportunity to work for your company. Thank you for confidence in my professional skills and experience. I want to apologize for any inconvenience that my decision to decline your offer has caused.

Sincerely,

Signature

Name

Useful Sentences for Responses by Employers to Applications for Employment

This letter is to acknowledge receipt of your application for the position of electronics engineer in our Davenport Electro Division. We are now evaluating the applications and will be in touch with you soon.

I would like to discuss your application during a preliminary interview at 2:00 P.M., on Monday, September 9. If this time is inconvenient for you, please call me at (000) 000-0000. We will, of course, reimburse your travel expenses.

Thank you for sending us your résumé. Unfortunately, I must inform you that we have filled the position we advertised in *The Detroit Telegraph*. We wish you every success in your search for suitable employment.

We regret to inform you that we have filled the position of marketing trainee for which you applied last month.

I regret that there are no vacancies within our company at present, but would suggest that you try finding work with an international company to make full use of your language skills.

We have been favorably impressed with your work experience and portfolio and intend to consider you for a position in our advertising art department early next year. For that reason, we will keep your application on file until then.

We are sorry to inform you that the Penrose Company is no longer considering applications for its retail marketing positions.

We feel that your experience and qualifications do not match the needs of the management trainee position in our Philadelphia office.

Unfortunately, there is no opening for qualified mechanical engineers at the moment and we do not foresee any change in staff in the near future. However, we will keep your résumé in our active files.

We are sorry to inform you that we are unable to offer you the position of financial analyst, which we recently discussed. We hope that you are successful in your search for employment.

Congratulations on being selected as our exclusive sales representative in the state of New Mexico, effective March 15, 1999. We are sure that with your specialized knowledge and long-time experience in the toy market you will be able to make a substantial contribution toward introducing our "Anita Pretty Baby Doll" line in that state.

Confirmation of your appointment as office manager will be subject to your satisfactory completion of three months' probationary service.

Your specific working conditions relating to employment are detailed in our company's Employee Handbook.

It is with much regret that we have to advise you that you are being laid off in compliance with article 12 of our current labor agreement.

It is with regret that we have to inform you that we are unable to continue your temporary position in the maintenance department after May 15.

Letters of Resignation

Date

Name/Title
Business/Organization
Address
City, State Zip Code

Dear Name:

After considerable thought, it is with deep regret that I tender my resignation from the Warner Kingmere Company, effective May 1, 1999. I assure you that the decision to resign my position as credit manager was difficult to make, since my association with the company has been a pleasant one.

Sincerely,

Signature

Name

Date

Name/Title
Business/Organization
Address
City, State Zip Code

Dear Name:

I have been offered a position as assistant marketing manager with an Italian company in New York City. Therefore, I am submitting my resignation, effective May 1, 1999. I have enjoyed working at Brickstone Company and my decision to leave the company arises solely from my desire to make greater use of my European working experience and knowledge of foreign languages.

Sincerely,

Signature

Name

Date

Name/Title
Business/Organization
Address
City, State Zip Code

Dear Name:

After serious consideration, I have decided to resign from the organization, effective September 15, 1999. A growing family as well as increased financial obligations require me to move to a larger company where I can receive greater financial compensation and use my purchasing management skills to the fullest. I value the experience that I have gained at CCF Industries and thank you for your advice and support during the past seven years. It has been a pleasure to work with you and your staff.

Sincerely,

Signature

Name

Date

Name/Title
Business/Organization
Address
City, State Zip Code

Dear Name:

Please accept this as my formal letter of resignation, effective November 1, 1999. I have found my four years as assistant sales manager with ABCF Company thoroughly stimulating. I have enjoyed working at the company and have gained valuable experience.

I would like to thank you for your support and guidance during the past years. Without them I may not have had the confidence to attempt this new challenging position. However, I feel now is the right time to pursue my career further.

Sincerely,

Signature

Name

Date

Name/Title
Business/Organization
Address
City, State Zip Code

Dear Name:

This is to tender my resignation from Brennan & Cooper as international marketing representative, effective October 1, 1999. My decision to leave the company is based on personal considerations. I will return to Canada where I have accepted a challenging position with a major Canadian manufacturing company in Winnipeg.

I am sure you will understand my decision to leave Brennan & Cooper, because I have had several discussions with you about returning to my native country with my wife and children.

I want to thank you for the very valuable experience I have gained during my four years of employment with your company.

Sincerely,

Signature

Name

Date

Name/Title
Business/Organization
Address
City, State Zip Code

Dear Name:

This letter is to notify you that I will resign my position as junior account executive, effective March 31, 1999. I have enjoyed my two years at the Dillon Corporation where I have gained valuable experience which will be of great benefit to me during my career. I leave Dillon with many pleasant memories.

Thank you very much for all your help and your confidence in me. I will remember my colleagues and work here with pleasure.

Sincerely,

Signature

Name

Date

Name/Title
Business/Organization
Address
City, State Zip Code

Dear Name:

I am writing to inform you that I will leave Rinaldi Company on January 31, 1999. I have recently accepted a position as personal assistant to the vice president in charge of retail marketing with a major retail organization in Seattle, Washington. The reason for my leaving is that I want to widen my experience in the retail business.

The experience and knowledge I have gained at Rinaldi will certainly help me in the future. I will, of course, help in training the person you select to fill my position.

Sincerely,

Signature

Name

Date

Name/Title
Business/Organization
Address
City, State Zip Code

Dear Name:

Please accept this letter as official notification of my decision to resign my position as computer programmer with the Zextra Plus Software Company, effective August 31, 1999.

My reason for leaving Zextra is due to the fact that I would like to have more challenging work as well as additional responsibility. However, I very much appreciate the opportunity I have had at Zextra to gain valuable programming experience.

Sincerely,

Signature

Name

Useful Sentences for Letters of Resignation

This letter is to give formal notice of my intention to leave the company, effective immediately.

Kindly accept this letter as my formal resignation from my position as senior programmer on October 1, 1999.

Please be advised of my intention to resign from the company, effective April 15.

Please consider this letter as official notification of my intention to quit my employment with Alfred Johnson Limited, effective July 15, 1999.

Please consider this letter as my resignation, effective at once.

After considerable thought, I have decided to resign my position as supervisor at Riverdale Company, effective immediately.

According to the terms of my contract, I hereby give six weeks notice to terminate my employment as administrative assistant with Santa Fe Metals Company, effective September 1, 1999.

Circumstances have arisen, that make it necessary to be at home with my family in Woodbury. Therefore, I am submitting my resignation, effective November 15, 1998.

Miscellaneous Company Letters and Announcements

(Notification of an increase in salary)

Date

Name/Title
Business/Organization
Address
City, State Zip Code

Dear Name:

We have just completed our salary review for this year and are very pleased to inform you that your salary will be increased by $____ to $____ per year, effective January 1, 1999. This well-deserved salary increase reflects your hard work record, dedication, and added responsibilities. Your work record is excellent.

We genuinely appreciate your efforts and are delighted to have you on our staff. Keep up the good work!

Sincerely,

Signature

Name

(Notification of a promotion)

Date

Name/Title
Business/Organization
Address
City, State Zip Code

Dear Name:

I am very pleased to inform you that, after careful consideration by our Board of Directors, you have been promoted to executive vice president of our export division, effective November 1, 1999. Your promotion is well deserved and I offer you my congratulations and best wishes.

Sincerely yours,

Signature

Name

(Letter of dismissal of an employee due to redundancy)

Date

Name/Title
Business/Organization
Address
City, State Zip Code

Dear Name:

After long discussions with our plant manager, Alfred Drake, it is with deep regret that I must inform you that due to a drastic cutback in our manufacturing division, your services will have to be terminated. This letter, therefore, is a formal notice of the redundancy of your position as supervisor, effective March 15, 1999.

The specialized services of the outplacement agency engaged by our personnel department will be available to you to help you to find suitable employment with another company within our industry. We trust that with your background and experience as well as your strong supervisory qualifications, you will be able to secure a new position as supervisor with another organization. Of course, we will be pleased to provide any prospective employer with the best recommendation.

We want to thank you for your dedication and efforts during the past four years and wish you every success in the future.

Sincerely yours,

Signature

Name

(A personal letter introducing a new employee)

Date

Name/Title
Business/Organization
Address
City, State Zip Code

Dear Name:

I am pleased to announce that Dr. Martin Sanders has joined our company as personal assistant to the chief executive officer. Dr. Sanders will develop, monitor, and control the budget and prepare and present reports on cost projections. He will report directly to the chief executive officer.

Dr. Sanders, who holds a Ph.D. degree in economics from the University of Chicago, served as special assistant to the president of the Varick Consulting Group, a nationally recognized leader in providing innovative solutions to a variety of challenging management situations. Because of ongoing significant growth, we now have a need for a financial professional to join our organization.

Sincerely,

Malcolm Ericcson
Chief Executive Officer

(A personal letter introducing a new sales representative to customers)

Date

Name/Title
Business/Organization
Address
City, State Zip Code

Dear Name:

Next month you will be visited by Mr. George Sherman, our new sales representative in Connecticut and Massachusetts. Mr. Sherman will be in charge of servicing your company's account in these two states. He will replace Mr. Louis Nelson who, as you probably know, died suddenly last month in an automobile accident.

Mr. Sherman is a graduate of the Hartford Institute of Technology and holds a Bachelor of Science degree in mechanical engineering. For the last five years he has worked as a field representative for Seaton Engineering in Boston.

We are certain that George will be able to give you the kind of friendly service and professional advice you expect to receive from the Preston Sturges Company.

Sincerely,

Signature

Name

(A company memorandum introducing a new sales representative)

To: Sales Representatives
From: Ralph Torres, National Sales Manager
Date: September 18, 1999

Subject: Robert Frankenheimer Joins Field Sales Force

I am pleased to introduce our newest sales representative, Robert Frankenheimer. Robert is a broadly experienced sales representative and has an extensive background in pallet lift trucks and battery-powered skid trucks. Previously he worked for the Compton Corporation in Pittsburgh.

Robert and his wife Marina will be relocating to the New York area where he will join our Eastern Sales Office. Starting October 1, Robert will be handling accounts in New Jersey and Long Island.

(An interoffice memorandum announcing a promotion)

Date: November 16, 1999

TO: All Employees
FROM: Jeanne Crain, President

Re: Promotion to Director of Corporate Public Affairs

We are pleased to announce the promotion of Ms. Elizabeth Hartman to director of corporate public affairs. She recently won the prestigious Golden Pen Trophy Award of the Public Relations Association of America for her pioneer work in the corporate public relations field. Ms. Hartman will assume her new position on December 1.

(An interoffice memorandum announcing a promotion)

To: All Employees
From: Fred Z. Leonard, President and Chief Executive Officer
Date: June 9, 1999

Subject: David A. Miller Appointed Senior Vice President

We are pleased to announce the appointment of David A. Miller to senior vice president of the treasury underwriting department in our international reinsurance division, effective July 15. Mr. Miller will be responsible for marketing and underwriting both property and casualty treaties for our company's Canadian reinsurance operations.

Mr. Miller joined Mergenthall Insurance in Toronto in 1985, was promoted to manager in 1988 and was transferred to the treasury underwriting department at our New York headquarters in 1994. He earned a Bachelor of Business Administration degree from York University, Toronto, in 1980.

(Notice of employee leaving company)

February 23, 1999

Effective March 1, Mr. Rick Baker, regional sales manager of the Whiteman Consumer Division, will leave the company to pursue personal business interests. On that date, he will be replaced by Mr. Kurt Swift, sales manager of the Dickinson Group.

(Notice of employee leaving company)

Date: May 18, 1999

To: All Employees
From: Keith Branigan, Chairman of the Executive Board

It is with a great sense of personal loss that the executive board announces the resignation, effective immediately, of our valued director of human resources, Anthony Roget. He has worked for our company for more than seventeen years and we are sure that you all join us in wishing Anthony the very best in his new endeavors.

(Congratulatory letter on an employee's 25th anniversary)

Date

Name/Title
Business/Organization
Address
City, State Zip Code

Dear Name:

It is a great pleasure for all of us at Waltman Company to send our very best wishes and to extend our sincere congratulations on your 25th anniversary at our company. As director of customer services you have made numerous valuable contributions to Waltman.

On behalf of the company, I want to express my warmest appreciation for your ceaseless dedication and efforts during the past twenty-five years. We wish you every success for the years ahead.

Sincerely yours,

Martin Barton
President

(A memorandum announcing an employee's retirement)

Date: September 3, 1999
To: All Employees—Bertram Group   From: John Maxwell, President

Subject: Retirement of Jack Taurok

After more than 32 years of dedicated service with our organization, Jack Taurok, regional marketing manager of the Bertram Group, will retire on October 1.

I am sure you all know the numerous valuable contributions that Jack Taurok has made to the Group during all those years. Therefore, I know you will join me in extending our best wishes, deep appreciation and gratitude to Jack. We will certainly miss him and wish him the best of happiness and health in the years ahead.

On Thursday, September 30, at 4:30 P.M. in the blue meeting hall, we will hold a retirement party for Jack Taurok and everybody is invited to attend.

(An employee requesting a leave of absence)

Date

Name/Title
Business/Organization
Address
City, State Zip Code

Dear Name:

I am requesting a leave of absence for two weeks due to the death of my mother last week in an automobile accident.

My absence will start on Monday, April 5. I intend to return on April 19 to resume my present duties with Menillo Company.

I would appreciate a prompt consideration of this urgent request. Thank you very much for your cooperation.

Sincerely,

Signature

Name

(Nomination ballot for employee of the month program)

MARKS DEPARTMENT STORE

NOMINATION BALLOT   EMPLOYEE OF THE MONTH PROGRAM

Dear Customer:

Marks Department Store is committed to a company program that recognizes employees who truly excel in serving our customers. If one of our salespeople has done something truly outstanding for you, please take a moment to nominate that person in our employee of the month program.

Just complete this ballot and deposit it in the special ballot boxes at the main entrances.

Thank you very much for your assistance.

I would like to recognize:

Salesperson's Name _____

Department _____

Reason for Recommendation _____

_____

Customer's Name _____ Date _____

_____

(Nomination for employee recognition program)

SAN FRANCISCO BAY HOTEL

Employee Recognition Program

Dear Guest:

We award a monthly prize to the staff member who has tried the hardest to make your stay more enjoyable at the San Francisco Bay Hotel. If you have someone to recommend, please give us the details.

Employee's Name _____

Employee's Department _____

For (please be specific) _____

_____

_____

Other comments or suggestions related to any part of the hotel's operation are always appreciated.

_____

_____

_____

Guest Name _____ Room _____ Date _____

Please leave this form in the suggestion box at reception.

_____

## CHAPTER 14

NEWS RELEASES

News releases (also called press releases) convey news and information submitted by a company or any other organization to the media: consumer and special interest magazines, business and professional periodicals, newsletters, wire services, local, regional, and national newspapers, radio stations and television stations. A news release can cover any topic; for example, management changes, executive appointments, job promotions, retirements, operations, mergers and acquisitions, opening of a new plant, store or branch, introduction of new products and services, new technologies, special events, and dissemination of financial information.

News releases should be typewritten on plain standard typing paper on your regular business letterhead or on special company letterhead printed with the words "NEWS," "NEWS RELEASE," or "PRESS RELEASE." These words should also be used on the envelope if you mail the release.

The typewritten text of the release should be double-spaced and should, ideally, consist of one page. If a second page is used, type the word "more" at the end of the first page. The end of the release is usually indicated by symbols such as ### or ***. However, in order to avoid too much white space between lines in this chapter dealing with news releases, we do not double-space most of the sample releases. The releases in this chapter have been written in a format that is familiar to editors and news directors.

The important facts or events of a release—just as in a regular newspaper story—should be placed at the beginning and should provide the who, what, when, where, and, if possible, why or how as concisely and accurately as possible. Before you mail or fax a clean copy of your release to the media, compile a list of selected addresses of the local, regional, or national newspapers, periodicals and broadcast media whose audience you want to reach. An item of local interest should not be mailed to a regional let alone a national newpaper, periodical, or electronic medium. It is also obvious that you should not send a press release dealing with your company's financial statements or acquisition of a manufacturing plant to a monthly women's magazine. The editors of such magazines, however, would be interested to receive a timely and newsworthy press release about a new consumer product or service of interest to women. Your local public library can help you to find the names and addresses of the magazines, newspapers, and electronic media you want to send your release. A number of specialized directories with names and addresses are readily available in most public libraries. If you know or have found the editor's name (in the case with print media) or name of the news director (for electronic media such as radio and television) in directories, address your release by name to that person. If you do not know their names, then you should address your release to "The Editor" (for print media) or to "The News Editor" for electronic media.

(Executive appointment)

NEWS RELEASE

ABC CORPORATION
000 West 68th Street
New York, NY 00000

FOR IMMEDIATE RELEASE   September 3, 1999
Contact: Judy Taylor
      (000) 000-0000

The ABC Corporation is pleased to announce that Yvonne Gordon has been named national sales manager. Ms. Gordon has been east coast sales manager for seven years. Her new job responsibilities will include overseeing Lemont's national sales and promotion activities in the field of modern office furniture.

# # #

(Executive appointment)

PRESS RELEASE

XYZ MUSEUM OF ART
28th Street and Z Street N.W.
Woodville, NY 00000

FOR IMMEDIATE RELEASE   CONTACT: Carol White
April 2, 1999   (000) 000-0000

XYZ MUSEUM APPOINTS MARY LINDSAY AS NEW
VICE PRESIDENT OF DEVELOPMENT AND PUBLIC AFFAIRS

Woodville, NY—Terence C. Bradley, president of the XYZ Museum of Art, announces the appointment of Mary Lindsay as vice president of development and public affairs. Ms. Lindsay will head the reorganized department overseeing all fund-raising operations, public relations and special events. She assumes her post May 1.

Ms. Lindsay was formerly vice president of marketing and development for the Association for Basic Education Resources in Chicago. In addition to her experience in development and public relations, she has an extensive background in education and the arts. She is a frequent speaker on fund-raising and marketing and served as an art consultant to public and private agencies for more than seventeen years.

* * *

(Executive appointment)

IBT ENTERPRISES
New York, N.Y. 00000

NEWS RELEASE   Contact: Jack Nicholson
For Immediate Release   (000) 000-0000

IBT APPOINTS BOB WALSH
EXECUTIVE VICE PRESIDENT OF CORPORATE RELATIONS

New York, January 19, 1999—The executive board of IBT Enterprises today announced the appointment of Bob Walsh as executive vice president of its corporate relations department, effective March 1.

Mr. Walsh has extensive experience in domestic business issues. He is currently the director of corporate relations of Brewster TeleServices, Inc., a manufacturer of digital telecommunications equipment. Working with consumers, equipment suppliers and trade associations, he is responsible for conducting analyses on the impact of public policy decisions affecting trade and high technology on the telecommunications industry.

Prior to joining Brewster TeleServices, he served from 1983 to 1989 as administrative assistant to Congressman Dick Wagner. He helped Wagner take the lead on issues relating to international commerce and U.S. business competitiveness.

"Bob Walsh's experience in the public and private sector provides him with the collaborative spirit we want our Corporate Relations Department to possess," said George Firestone, chief executive officer of IBT, in announcing the appointment. "He has the kind of perspective and specific expertise that will help IBT Enterprises to keep its competitive edge in commerce."

Mr. Walsh has a master's degree in communications from Illinois State University and a bachelor's degree in political science from Chicago University.

# # #

(Executive appointment)

NEWS RELEASE

SOUTH PACIFIC AREA TRAVEL ORGANIZATION
Los Angeles, CA 00000

For Immediate Release   Contact: Margaret Welsh
January 18, 1999   (000) 000-0000

TPA'S JOHN NEWMAN ELECTED AS PRESIDENT OF SPATO

Los Angeles, California—TPA airline executive, John A. Newman, has been elected as president of the South Pacific Area Travel Organization (SPATO).

The industry veteran, who has been with Trans Pacific Airways (TPA) since 1979, was appointed to the Organization's top elected position at the SPATO Annual Conference held in San Francisco this week. He will hold office for the next three years.

SPATO, which was founded in Hawaii in 1966, now comprises a professional membership of over 1,200 tourism-related companies in North America involved in selling and promoting travel to the South Pacific region.

Mr. Newman is now the director of sales and services for TPA and also heads the Los Angeles–based regional sales and marketing operations for TPA in seven western states.

A bachelor of science graduate at the University of Dallas where he obtained his B.B.A. degree in 1959, John Newman earned his master's degree in business administration from the University of California at Los Angeles.

Formerly with the Zadokk Travel Organization, where he received the coveted "Salesman of the Year" Award, Newman was also recognized as the 1961 Student of the Year by the U.S. Marketing Organization.

* * *

(Executive appointment)

GODDARD CORPORATION
00 Hawthorne Avenue
Woodslawn, MO 00000

Pharmaceuticals	Consumer Products	Nutritional Products

N E W S

CONTACT: Rick Green   FOR IMMEDIATE RELEASE
(000) 000-0000

JACK TURNEY RETIRES AS PRESIDENT OF GODDARD CORPORATION

Woodslawn, Missouri (April 18, 1999)—At its annual meeting, Goddard Corporation announced that Jack A. Turney has retired as president of the company. Mr. Turney remains a member of the Goddard board of directors. The company said that there are no plans to name a new president.

Mr. Turney became president when Bergen Chemical Corporation merged with the Goddard Corporation on July 22, 1987. Prior to the merger, Mr. Turney had been chairman and chief executive officer of Bergen Chemical Corporation.

"Jack Turney can look with pride at a long career of distinguished service to this company and predecessor companies," said Mitchell Leiser, chairman and chief executive officer, Goddard Corporation. "He will be missed from our senior executive ranks, but we are delighted that we will retain the benefit of his counsel as a director."

Mr. Turney began his career as lawyer with the New York law firm of Wheeler & Mortimer. In 1968, he joined Denner Chemical Corporation as a member of the legal staff. He was named general counsel of Denner Chemical two years later. In 1972, Mr. Turney was appointed executive vice president at Bergen Chemcial Corporation with responsibility for the Denner Pharmaceutical Group. In 1984, he was elected chairman and chief executive officer of Bergen Chemical Corporation.

Jack Turney studied at the School of Public and International Affairs at Princeton University and was awarded an M.A. degree in 1956. He received an LL.B. degree from Harvard Law School in 1964.

# # #

(Announcing an international joint venture agreement)

ABC VIDEO TECHNOLOGY
00 Park Street
Burnham, MA 00000

NEWS RELEASE

Media Contact: Mark Finch
Tel. (000) 000-0000

Internet: http://www.abcvidtech.com
E-mail: Quinvdte@sun.qa.org.

ABC VIDEO AND EDUCATION JAPAN COMPANY SIGN JOINT VENTURE AGREEMENT FOR MULTIMACHINE EDUCATIONAL SOFTWARE

New York (April 15, 1999)—In a joint statement at the International Video Technology Show in New York, one of Japan's major developers of international educational media, Education Japan Company, and the American producer of video games, ABC Video Technology, announced a codevelopment agreement for an estimated 20 programs of "educationally oriented entertainment" for young personal computer users.

"The objective of this joint venture is to stimulate learning through entertainment," said Louis Hanin, president of ABC Video Technology. Hanin explained that the programs will include reading and mathematics. The first ten programs are due for delivery in November. The remaining programs will be released during the following two years.

"The consumer will benefit from the long educational experience of the Education Japan Company and also from the game development expertise of ABC Video Technology," Hanin said.

* * *

(A company acquiring another company in an exchange of stock)

NEWS RELEASE

XYZ Corporation   833 Grand Avenue   Chicago, IL 00000

Contact: Karen Lockhard   For Immediate Release
(000) 000-0000

XYZ TO ACQUIRE ABC COMPANY IN AN EXCHANGE OF STOCK

Chicago, Illinois, September 14, 1999—ABC Company and XYZ Corporation today announced a definitive merger agreement providing for the acquisition of ABC by Steiner.

Under the terms of the agreement, each outstanding share of ABC will be exchanged for ___ shares of the XYZ Corporation common stock. The terms in the agreement provide that the maximum effective price per ABC share will be no more than $____. The agreement is subject to approval by ABC shareholders at a special meeting to be held within six weeks.

Carlo Monti, president of ABC said, "The association with the XYZ Corporation is in the best interest of ABC and all of its shareholders. It will provide ABC with greater resources to facilitate its future growth plans. In addition, it will be particularly helpful in our research and development program in the field of musical instruments."

ABC, based in Lexington, Kentucky, is a developer, manufacturer, and marketer of guitars, violins, woodwind, and brass instruments. XYZ's principal businesses are also in musical instruments, especially in electronic keyboards, amplifiers, band and string instruments, and P.A. systems.

* * *

(Announcing a merger)

NEWS RELEASE   NEWS RELEASE

ABCD COMPANY
000 Richards Avenue
Globeton, MA 00000

FOR IMMEDIATE RELEASE
Contact: Alfred Lorentz
Tel. (000) 000-0000

MERGER OF ABCD AND EFGH COMPANIES

Globeton, Massachusetts, May 10, 1999—ABCD Company and EFGH Company have signed an agreement to combine companies in a merger of equals. This will create one of the largest suppliers of office equipment in the Globeton metropolitan area. The name of the new company will be ABEFGH with corporate headquarters in Globeton and significant operations in Brokeline, Oxford, Chelton, and Evanston.

Under a single name, the new company will build on its common strengths and provide its customers with great value, choices, quality, and innovative products and services.

In 1999, the combined companies had revenues of $____ million and earnings of $____ million.

* * *

(Announcing a merger)

NEWS

XYZ COMPANY   00 PALISADES AVENUE   BROCKTON, ID 00000

FOR IMMEDIATE RELEASE
Contact: Charlotte Donahue
Tel. (000) 000-0000

XYZ TO ACQUIRE 123 COMPANY

Brockton, Idaho, March 8, 1999—As part of XYZ's growth strategy in its core business of household service care products, XYZ Company has agreed to acquire the 123 Company of Ashland, Montana.

123 is the maker of 123 Oil Soap, one of America's best-known wood cleaners and a major factor in the markets for all-purpose cleaners. Terms of the transaction were not disclosed.

Greg Evans, XYZ chairman and chief executive officer, said: "This acquisition not only adds a growing brand to our company, but also represents the type of unique product that has significant international potential. Our plan is to develop appropriate new products and line extensions."

XYZ Company is a $____ million products company, focusing on the core of household surface and fabric care. The 123 Company also manufactures and sells a similar line of products. The 123 family will continue to own and operate certain aspects of the businesses.

* * *

(Announcing the completion of an acquisition)

NEWS

XYZ COMPANY	00 PALISADES AVENUE	BROCKTON, ID 00000

FOR IMMEDIATE RELEASE
Contact: Charlotte Donahue
Tel. (000) 000-0000

XYZ COMPLETES 123 ACQUISITION

Brockton, Idaho, April 2, 1999—XYZ Company today reported the completion of the purchase of the 123 Company, maker of 123 Oil Soap, one of America's best-known wood cleaners. The 123 acquisition is part of XYZ's strategy growth in household surface care products. XYZ Company intends to broaden product sales domestically and extend sales internationally. There will be no redundancies as a result of this acquisition although there will be some reorganization at the 123 company.

The purchase price, which included approximately 150,000 treasury shares of XYZ common stock, was not disclosed.

XYZ is a $____ million products company, focusing on the core business of household surface and fabric care.

* * *

(Financial news release)

NEWS RELEASE

ANYCO CONSUMER PRODUCTS, INC.
0000 Parker Avenue
Sand Pine, Ohio 00000

For Release   Media Contact: Paul Reiter
after 4 P.M., April 22   (000) 000-0000

ANYCO ACHIEVES INCREASES IN FIRST QUARTER EARNINGS

Sand Pine, Ohio—ANYCO Consumer Products achieved new sales and earnings records for the first quarter.

First Quarter ended March 31

Sales of $____ million were ahead ___ percent; volume increased ___ percent
Earnings before interest and taxes increased ___ percent to $___ million.
Net income increased ___ percent to $___ million.

John Ford, Anyco president and chief executive officer, said "Anyco achieved strong first quarter net income, despite recessionary conditions in key markets and the stronger U.S. dollar. Each of our geographic and business units participated; the largest operating profit increases were realized by Anyco-Pacific Division. It achieved outstanding profit growth as it continues to increase marketing and manufacturing efficiency."

# # #

(Financial news release)

NEWS

ABC Software Inc.   000 Sixth Avenue   Redington, IL 00000

Contact: Mitch Miller   For Immediate Release
(000) 000-0000

ABC SOFTWARE REPORTS SECOND QUARTER FIGURES

Redington, Illinois, July 25, 1999—ABC Software today reported a loss of $ ___ million, or __ cents per common share, on revenues of $ ___ million during the second quarter.

For the six month period, revenues were $ ___ million, up ___ percent from $ ___ million a year ago. Net income was $ ___ million, down __ percent from $ ___ million last year. First half earnings per common share were __ cents, down __ percent from __ cents a year ago.

Several factors affected second quarter results. One factor centers on the difficulty in developing BB/108, a generic software platform for the cellular telephone industry. Almost two thirds of the capitalized software cost ABC Software Systems (ABC) had incurred for BB/108 was written down. The balance of the investment in BB/108 appears to be sound and ABC is now working closely with its principal client to design a new system for them.

According to Barry Jones, President of ABC Software, the decrease also resulted from a general slowing of business. "All operating units were adversely affected by the recession during the second quarter. Our results are disappointing, but I have always said that we must set stretch objectives and take calculated risks in order to make our business grow. With that comes a risk of reaching too far. The important thing is that we realize problems and deal with them. We have done that. The long-term strength of our business remains intact. Our strategy is sound."

*   *   *

(Relocation of corporate headquarters)

NEWS   RELEASE

ABC COMPANY	0000 Alexander Avenue	New York, NY 00000

Contact: Claudia Weyer   For Immediate Release
(000) 000-0000   March 10, 1999

ABC COMPANY WILL RELOCATE ITS HEADQUARTERS TO HOUSTON

New York City—ABC Company will relocate its corporate headquarters from New York City to a new office location near Houston (Texas) next year, the company announced today. All of the approximately 150 management and nonmanagement employees at the company's current headquarters, at 0000 Alexander Avenue, will be affected by the move, which will take place next year.

Chief Executive Officer Ralph A. Murphy indicated that all employees at the company's headquarters in New York City will be offered a position in the new location. ABC management indicated in the employee meeting conducted this morning that the decision to relocate the headquarters was not taken lightly, that the potential disruption to both employees and their families was recognized, and that efforts would be taken to smooth the transition. Among the forms of assistance available for those who will be relocating are the company's relocation program and its spousal relocation assistance program. Those employees who choose not to relocate will be given outplacement assistance in finding other employment, an appropriate supplemental payment, and annuitant benefits for those who qualify.

"With the assistance of Graham Development Company," Mr. Murphy said, "we carefully considered a large number of locations over the past several years. We concluded that, on balance, the Houston area offered the best combination of factors from the standpoint of our employees' personal and professional lives and from an overall business standpoint. Both aspects were important in our final decision."

Move-in to the new permanent offices, located at the Century Office Complex in the city of Masterton, about 6 miles from downtown Houston, is not expected until the fall of next year.

# # #

(Regional microbrewery announcing the launch of a new draft beer)

NEWS RELEASE

XYZ Beer Company   0000 Grand Boulevard   Golden, WY 00000

For further information, contact   For Immediate Release
Bob Masters, tel. (000) 000-0000   April 8, 1999

BREWERY ANNOUNCES DEBUT OF XYZ DRAFT BEER

Golden, Wyoming—Reflecting the XYZ brand's proud heritage as one of the finest beers in Wyoming, and citing increasing consumer demand for packaged draft beer, XYZ Beer Company announced today the introduction of packaged XYZ Draft Beer. The product will be available at local retail stores in Wyoming and Montana on April 15.

"Consumers have made packaged draft beer one of the hottest segments in the brewery industry," said Lawrence Decker, XYZ brand director. "Our own market research tells us that consumers would react very favorably to a packaged draft beer that carries the well-known XYZ name," said Decker.

The introductory advertising campaign (regional television, radio, and print) from Barker Advertising Associates in Casper, Wyoming, will stress the cold-filtered nature of the XYZ Draft Beer, along with its all-natural ingredients and the brewery's long draught history.

A 12-ounce serving of XYZ Draft contains approximately 155 calories. Alcohol content is comparable to other domestic regular beers.

* * *

(Introduction of a new product)

N E W S from ABC'S OUTDOOR PRODUCTS

COMMAR COMPANY   0 Henderson Drive   Alton, GA 00000

FOR IMMEDIATE RELEASE   Contact: Carla Baker
                                                             Tel. (000) 000-0000

ABC COMPANY INTRODUCES THERMO-ELECTRIC COOLER

Alton, Georgia (February 7, 1999)—Ideal for vacations, road trips, and travel of all sorts, ABC's new Thermo-electric Cooler is a portable unit that not only cools but heats as well. Moreover, it can serve as a convenient auxiliary cooler or hot-dish warmer for special occasions at home.

On the road, the 32-quart unit plugs into the cigarette lighter of a vehicle and runs on 12-volt power. It cools without the hassle of ice. Simply reverse the power plug when a food warmer is needed.

With an AC adapter, which is sold separately as an accessory, the Thermo-electric Cooler functions as either a cooler or food warmer in motel rooms and at home. Its versatility makes it a serviceable appliance for parties or dinners, on the patio, in the garden, and around the pool.

The ABC Thermo-electric Cooler has been engineered for good looks without sacrificing superior function features. Thick insulation and a tight gasket seal provide top-notch temperature retention. Strong, comfortable handles are recessed to protect them from hard knocks while in transit, as well as enhancing the cooler's sleek lines. In addition to two-inch insulation in cooler walls, the tight-fitting lid is fully insulated for added thermal efficiency.

The unit, which measures 21 by 14 inches, weighs 14 pounds and 9 ounces, and draws 4 amps.

* * *

(Introduction of new consumer health-monitoring equipment)

NEWS

XYZ Electronics, Inc.   000 Broadway   Baton Rouge, LA 00000
Contact: Cynthia Kruger   IMMEDIATE RELEASE
(000) 000-0000

Baton Rouge, Louisiana, October 14, 1999—XYZ Electronics today announced at the annual Showcase Consumer Electronics Show in Phoenix, Arizona, that its own new line of health-monitoring equipment for the home will be available throughout the southwestern states in mid-November.

"Our theme for this consumer show—'Technology made pure and simple'—is embodied in every product we are showing this week," said Mark Roberts, president of XYZ Electronics. "Once again, XYZ proves that the most sophisticated technology can be built into consumer products that are innovative, affordable, and easy to use."

The American consumer has indicated a need for moderately priced, accurate health-monitoring equipment to supplement personal fitness and preventive programs. XYZ has responded by developing a line of health monitoring products that will enable consumers to chart basic health signs right in their own homes. The first products—a digital home blood-pressure monitor, a computerized scale, and an electronic thermometer—are being introduced in drugstores and pharmacies in the Southwest next month.

To date, the new health-monitoring products have been well received by the trade. "Close to 3200 drugstores and pharmacies will carry our new health monitors," said Jospeh Ryan, XYZ Director of Marketing Operations. "The trade's enthusiasm for these new consumer products has been very strong because marketing tests have demonstrated that health-conscious consumers are interested in such low-cost and easy-to-use electronic devices. The same precision, quality, and affordability built into all XYZ products now will help consumers maintain health and fitness, as well as monitor a condition diagnosed by a physician. We are also proud of the fact that these monitoring devices have met the rigorous standards of experts and health professionals."

* * *

(Announcing a local trade exhibition)

NEWS

ABC Franchise Organization   For Immediate Release
00 Chestnut Street   Contact: Judith Redwood
Seattle, WA 00000   (000) 000-0000

FRANCHISING EXPO TO BE HELD ON APRIL 21

Seattle, Washington, March 3, 1999—The ABC Franchise Organization will hold its annual franchise expo at the Mayfair Hotel Exhibition Center in Seattle on April 21. Many leading franchisers will display their franchise opportunities for consideration by prospective business owners in the Seattle metropolitan area. The expo will be open from 9:00 A.M. to 8:00 P.M. and admission is $___ per person.

"Franchise sales are outperforming the economy and many people are choosing the franchise method to go into business for themselves," says Robert Daniels, executive director of the ABC Franchise Organization. "The expo is like a shopping center that gives men and women of all ages a wide range of business ownership opportunities," he added.

During the expo, ABC provides free seminars about owning and investing in a franchise and about ways to expand business through the franchise method.

* * *

(Announcing a business information service)

NEWS RELEASE

NEWTON BUSINESSINFO SERVICES
0000 Harris Street
Marietta, CO 00000

Media Contact: Alice Simons   Release Date: March 23, 1999
Tel. (000) 000-0000

<u>INSTANT FINANCIAL AND CREDIT INFORMATION ON COLORADO COMPANIES
AVAILABLE ON NEWTON BUSINESSINFO SERVICES</u>

Marietta, Colorado—Detailed information about companies, partnerships, and sole traders in Colorado is now instantly available online through Newton BusinessInfo Services from April 1.

Newton BusinessInfo Services provides complete financial statements of more than 55,000 companies' annual reports and financial statements as well as business reports and credit details on 125,000 businesses.

Each Newton report provides a commercial and legal overview of a business. Standard information obtained from official and other reliable sources includes the legal status of a company or business, its registration details, principal executives, principal shareholders, legal history, and business activities. This is in addition to three years turnover and profit and key ratios for all registered companies.

Credit details are provided for each business including credit scores, credit limits, defaults, payments, commitments, and liquidity.

Newton BusinessInfo Services is a subsidiary of Newton Nationwide BusinessInfo Services, a major supplier of a wide range of high-quality business information services since 1971.

# # #

PRESS RELEASE

TEXAS REGIONAL AIR SHOW
Carlsbad Airport, Texas

FOR IMMEDIATE RELEASE
June 2, 1999

Media Relations:
Rick Taylor, Shirley Warner
(000) 000-0000

TEXAS REGIONAL AIR SHOW TO BE HELD IN CARLSBAD ON JULY 19 AND 20

Carlsbad Airport, Texas—The annual Texas Regional Air Show will be held at the Carlsbad Airport on July 19 and 20. Starting time: 1:00 P.M.

Dwight Prescott, the president of the Texas Regional Air Show Association, confirms that the show will have a topnotch line-up of performers this year. Confirmed participants include the Manning Aerobatic Team, the Flying Cowboy, the Hawker Hurricane Display Team, Jensen & Jensen Aerobatics as well as Ultralight and Vintage Aircraft. The well-known Texas Devils Aerobatic Team will also perform on both days.

The Texas Regional Air Show traces its roots back to the first Merlin Airshow organized by the late Russell Brian in 1968. After a 19-year hiatus, the Merlin Airshow returned in 1987 to become an annual event. Renamed the Texas Regional Air Show in 1990, it developed a reputation as a true enthusiasts' show. The Texas Regional Air Show Association is a nonprofit organization. Revenues from the air show are returned to the community for charitable purposes.

* * *

(A hotel announcing special weekly rates)

NEWS RELEASE

ABC HOTEL   000 East 30th Street   New York, NY 00000
Telephone: (000) 000-0000   Fax: (000) 000-0000

STUDIO ROOMS IN MANHATTAN FOR UNDER $125 A DAY

Manhattan, May 25, 1999—The ABC Hotel, located in central Manhattan, is offering what may be the best hotel value in New York City:

Studio Rooms for $124 a night and a special weekly rate of $595.
(all rates plus taxes)

Built with the concept of providing a "Home Away from Home" atmosphere for our guests, each studio features a bedroom, a full bath, a furnished living room and a kitchenette with a small refrigerator.

The 339-room ABC Hotel is an excellent choice for extended stay travelers and short-time travelers alike.

* * *

## CHAPTER 15

LETTERS TO SHAREHOLDERS

A LETTER TO SHAREHOLDERS

"A letter to shareholders"—also known as "chairman's letter to shareholders" or "chairman's statement to stockholders"—is frequently incorporated in a company's most important document, the annual report. It is written by the chairman of the board of directors and is often cosigned by the company's chief executive officer or president.

The chairman's letter provides an overview of the company's activities as well as its problems and difficulties during a given year. The annual report supplies more details and financial information and enables shareholders to evaluate their holdings in the company. The financial statements in an annual report consist of the statement of earnings and retained earnings (the so-called "profit and loss account"), the balance sheet, the changes in the company's financial position, and a financial review; together with notes to the financial statements and the report of the auditors.

The chairman often refers to the annual report in his letter to the shareholders. A typical chairman's letter to the shareholders covers or at least mentions many or all of the following subjects:

- Opening paragraph: for example, good year, bad year; turnover; optimistic or pessimistic view; profit, loss, and dividend.

- Company's performance in relation to the economic situation: for instance, inflation, recession, depression, a slowdown in the economy, booming economy, competition, national and international problems, and currency.

- Cost controls, cost reduction, and cost-containment programs; reorganizations.

- Acquisitions and divestitures.

- Research and development.

- Long-term goals, corporate strategies and objectives; and growth opportunities.

- Stock-repurchase programs.

- Directors and management, board of directors, management changes and appointments, organization and management.

- Personnel relations: for example, health insurance, medical and retirement plans, educational programs, and staff development programs.

- Corporate social responsibility, the company and the community.

- Thanking management and personnel for their work and efforts.

- Expression of confidence in the company's activities.

- Closing paragraph: "The Year Ahead," (also referred to as "Year Outlook," "Outlook," "Prospects," or "Future").

(Chairman's letter to shareholders)

Letter to Shareholders

For Randolph Industries, 1999 was a year of solid accomplishment. For the year ending December 31, 1999, your company reported the highest revenues and operating income and the second highest net income and earnings per share in its history.

Consolidated net revenues for the year ended December 31, 1999, were $___ million compared to $___ million for 1998; operating income was $___ million compared to $___ million for 1998. Net income was $___ million or $___ per share compared to $___ million or $___ per share for 1998. Most segments of the company produced fine results. Demand for nearly all our products held strong throughout the year. We made good progress with strategic plans and objectives for increasing total returns to our shareholders over time.

Record operating results came even though we sold off our hoist and crane division. We are investing the proceeds of this sale in growth projects that should begin to pay off in three or four years.

The year 1999 was ideal for our company. We already launched a strategic objective designed to enhance our national and international competitive strength and long-term growth. Economic conditions in the United States and overseas favored us in that process. So too, did the capital investments we have made in our facilities in recent years. Detailed information on your company's operating and financial results is contained in the chapters on operations, management's analysis, and the consolidated financial statements in this annual report.

You will see references to Randolph's strategic restructuring and its effects throughout this report. Our business strategies and objectives have been to:

- Undertake the acquisition and/or develop new products or businesses here and overseas in which we have significant technical and marketing strengths;

- Develop the corporate structure necessary for the acquisition and management of new and existing businesses;

- Intensify the search for new business opportunities outside our own industries to broaden the company's economic base and underlying asset value. For all our core businesses we will search out dynamic, sensibly priced acquisitions that extend our products and open new markets;

- Focus a larger part of our resources in businesses that are less susceptible to cyclical swings;

- Perform consistently in the top quarter of our industries, in terms of total capital; and

- Concentrate our energies on realizing the potential for domestic and overseas growth in our core businesses.

In January 1999, Bernard Drexel joined the company as vice chairman of the board with primary responsibilities in the areas of investment, acquisitions, and long-term corporate planning. Prior to joining Randolph Industries, Mr. Drexel served as executive vice president of the Sherman Realty Corporation.

John Wiseman, who had been president of Randolph Industries Development Company, retired from the company after 33 years of dedicated and highly appreciated service. Mr. Wiseman made many contributions to the growth and success of your company over the years. His presence will be missed by your management as well as by his many friends and colleagues throughout the country.

During 1999, John Pierce and Alicia Regan left our board of directors. We thank them for their numerous contributions and wish them well in their future endeavors. We are pleased to welcome to the board of directors of Randolph Industries Inc. Joyce Longstreet, Professor of Urban Affairs, New York University; and Alex Zimmerman, Director of the Alpha Beta Omega Foundation in Los Angeles.

We wish to express our gratitude to you, our shareholders, for your continued interest and support and to our fellow employees for their loyalty, professionalism, energy, personal commitments, and continuing outstanding contributions toward the success of our company.

Economic conditions here and abroad continued strong as the year got underway, although there are indications of a slowdown early next year. Whether that develops or not, we will be prepared. We are confident that the strengths we have gained will serve us well. Our optimism is based on the growing ability of Randolph Industries to recognize and fulfill the emerging requirements of the marketplaces it serves.

Daniel Gerstein
Chairman of the Board and
Chief Operating Officer

February 14, 2000

(Chairman's letter to shareholders)

TO OUR SHAREHOLDERS

Last year was an outstanding one for Asherton Company. Revenues grew and net income increased substantially. All our lines of business reported record operating profit. And recently completed capital projects not only increased productivity during the past year, but also demonstrated potential for additional profit gains in the years ahead.

The strong 1999 results enabled Asherton company to reach an important financial goal—___ percent return on equity. That target was set in 1996. At the time, it was an ambitious goal; Asherton's return on equity in 1991 was ___ percent.

Other key measures also demonstrate our company's growth during the past five years. Since 1991, revenues have increased more than ___ percent while operating profit and net income have almost tripled. The average annual return to shareholders, in terms of dividends plus stock appreciation, has been almost ___ percent.

A detailed description of the company's financial performance begins on page ___ of the annual report. In addition, the report this year includes a business profile section, which more fully describes the activities of our major subsidiaries.

STRATEGIES AND OBJECTIVES

Your company, as it exists today, is better positioned than ever to capitalize on opportunities that lie ahead. Through our planning efforts we have not only identified new businesses that appear to be promising; we have also reexamined and evaluated the long-range potentials for our existing operations. During the past year, for example, we have completed arrangements to sell two units that once fitted nicely into our organization, but today do not respond to our long-range growth plans. Thus, we have sold Technical Union Rochester and Astor Packaging. As part of our long-term growth strategy to strengthen our business, we also are acquiring companies that can add to the critical mass of our divisions.

In July 1999, we acquired Anacort Inc. at a price that was carefully balanced against the potential for future growth within our Spandexto Division.

COST-CONTAINMENT PROGRAMS

When we began our cost-containment program three years ago, we promised to improve profits by cutting costs and believed that this would become a way of life for every part of the company . . . and it has. In the coming years we will continue with the effort, seeking efficiencies and new savings, and imposing rigorous standards of performance and attention to the bottom line. We will also look for new ways to do more with less. The full impact of our stringent cost-reduction program will emerge as this year progresses.

STOCK REPURCHASE PROGRAM

Early last year, we announced that we would repurchase, from time to time, up to ___ shares of our outstanding stock. At the time this annual report went to press, ___ shares have been acquired in this manner at an average price of $___ per share. These shares, and other purchases within limit, will be available for contributions to employee benefit plans, stock option plans, and for future acquisitions.

DIRECTORS AND EXECUTIVE CHANGES

In March, Seymour A. Fincke, president of Witco Advertising, and Elisa F. Doyle, senior partner in the law firm of Kline, Wilton, & Divver were elected to the board of directors, expanding our board to nine members. Each is a valuable addition to the Board.

Effective January 1, 1999, Harry M. Ronner was appointed president of Asherton Company. Mr. Ronner brings to this position more than 25 years of successful leadership at several major Asherton subsidiaries.

Anne B. McCleary, formerly president of Asherton Brubaker Division, was appointed senior vice president—corporate planning and strategy of Asherton Company. During her 14 years with the company, Ms. McCleary has been instrumental in developing and executing a number of corporate strategies that resulted in our significant growth during recent years.

PERSONNEL, PROGRAMS AND BENEFITS

Effective June 1, 1999, significant improvements for our employees were made in the company's plans covering medical benefits. Maximum benefits under the company comprehensive medical plan were increased from $___ to $___ for each insured employee and covered dependent. Maternity benefits were substantially increased. Employees traveling on company business now also receive greater benefits in case of disability or accidental death.

Asherton's leadership in providing equal employment opportunities for minorities—already a voluntary commitment for decades—was underscored by substantial progress during the past year. Since 1974, when the company began keeping records, the percentage of management, sale, and general office positions held by minority employees more than tripled.

Our company's long-term affirmative action program is part of a larger effort to develop and train outstanding employees for management positions with Asherton. It includes regular review of each division's employment statistics, and the setting and monitoring of specific job-placement goals for minorities and women based on predicted openings.

OUTLOOK

Our principal subsidiaries hold strong positions in major markets that are growing at above-average rates. Our forecasts indicate that revenues will continue to grow at close to last year's pace despite certain industry-wide concerns about economic conditions. We share this national concern over the business outlook because some of our operations will inevitably be affected by it. However, our Asherton Fast Food Division is well-positioned to respond to softer market conditions expected as a result of increasing competition in the fast-food industry in North America.

The company will also continue to benefit from emphasis on customer service and cost-control measures. Our confidence is also bolstered by a strong balance sheet, with a debt-to-capital ratio of

___ percent. This permits additional borrowing, which together with increasing cash flow, can support our growth, whether by internal expansion or acquisition.

The greatest asset we possess is not machinery or brick or mortar. It is human—the extraordinary men and women who operate and produce Asherton's top-quality, high-value products and services. Their combined talents and commitments have fueled our company's significant progress over the years.

In summary, we believe that Asherton Company is in a good position to continue its record of profitable growth and earnings in the years immediately ahead.

Sincerely,

Donald H. Cahill
Chairman of the Board of Directors

March 16, 2000

USEFUL SENTENCES AND PARAGRAPHS FOR LETTERS TO SHAREHOLDERS

For your convenience, this section has been divided into the following categories:

- Opening Paragraphs

- Cost-Control and Cost-Containment Programs

- Acquisitions and Divestitures

- Corporate Strategies and Objectives

- Directors, Management, and Executive Changes

- Personnel, Programs, and Benefits

- Corporate Social Responsibilities

- Management's Tribute to Personnel

- Outlook: The Year Ahead

USEFUL SENTENCES: OPENING PARAGRAPHS

The Directors of Mercox Limited are pleased to present the seventh annual report of the company to the shareholders. The accompanying consolidated financial statements for the year ending December 31, 1999 include the accounts of Mercox and its subsidiaries, Centor Company and Derleth Company.

Revenues from retail activities reached a new low in 1999 of $___ compared with $___ in 1998. Pretax profits amounted to $___ in 1999 and were substantially lower compared with $___ in 1998.

The year 1999 was one of expansion and revenue growth for Quality Dental Supplies Company, with an improvement in net income arising principally from an excellent performance by our two subsidiaries in Mexico. Consolidated revenues for the year were $___ million compared with $___ million in 1998.

The year 1999 was a record one for Benn-Hill Company in both revenues and income before extraordinary items. Operating income reached $___ million, an increase of ___ percent over 1998's figure of $___ million.

Despite rising costs and depressed business conditions throughout 1999, Glaser Renaud Industries Incorporated managed to increase its revenues slightly and to maintain its income before extraordinary items at a level of only ___ percent below the 1998 level.

We are pleased to report satisfactory increases in both sales and earnings for 1999. In a highly competitive marketplace, these results reflect the dedication and fine performance of all Dougherty employees. Sales of $___ million increased ___ percent over 1998. Net income, exclusive of a one-time gain from the sale of Deakin, Inc., amounted to $___ million or $___ per share, an increase of ___ percent. The company's position was also strengthened during the past year by a significant reduction in long-term debt from over $___ million to approximately $___ million.

The opening figures in this year's annual report say clearly, without the need of extensive comment, that the year just ending was a good one for your company. The pages of the annual report provide ample evidence of why we are confident of the future, both for the year immediately ahead and long-term, as they discuss a number of new products and services that will contribute to our expansion here and abroad. Our confidence in the future was clearly expressed by the board of director's decision in February to raise our company's quarterly dividend. Effective with the March 15, 1999 payment, the dividend on the common stock was increased by ___ percent, to ___ cents per share.

Net income of Houseton Acoustics Company in 1999 was $___ million, on revenues of $___ million. The company continued to make progress despite the impact of the recession in North America. Our businesses strengthened their market positions and introduced an array of new products. We also developed new strategic priorities and began implementing them throughout the company. Higher operating earnings, however, were reduced by such special factors as a charge of $___ million against costs rising from staff reductions and a decline in interest income from lower cash balances. The elimination of those factors improve our outlook for this year. So, too, does a stringent cost-containment program inaugurated two years ago that is now beginning to take hold.

Business conditions during 1999 were among the most difficult in the company's history. Our problems in such inflationary conditions were no different from those of numerous other businesses. Our chief aim, in which we were successful, was to conserve our resources. However, we cannot remain permanently on the defensive, despite a general atmosphere of gloom and foreboding that is currently affecting every area of business and industry in our country. We cannot disguise the fact that we face serious short-term problems in all divisions of our company. Soaring costs, capricious raw material prices, political uncertainties, and a stagnant demand do not make for an easy life.

This time last year we said in our letter to shareholders in the annual report that we did not expect the business environment to improve significantly during the next twelve months since we could not see where any major upturn in economic activity was likely to come from. So it has proved. Economic activity has increased very little during the past year. However, the effects on Henderson Industries have been less profound than in the earlier phase of the recession. Although sales volumes do not appear to have increased, this is an improvement on the continuous reduction we witnessed during the previous year. In general, we have maintained our market shares, but in a number of cases at the cost of eroded margins.

A combination of recession and surplus capacity made this a difficult year for Fairbanks Corporation, particularly in Georgia. On the other hand, our manufacturing division has improved its market position in southern California and remains strong in Nevada.

Weak and changing markets together with intense competition have pushed back the time when Appexo Company might have been expected to make a profit. The business has therefore been refocused on a few of its more promising activities.

The economic problems that beset this country are well known and need not be recounted in this letter to shareholders. In some areas of great importance to our company, recovery of the economy was slower than expected.

Losses from retail activities, although within budget projections, were higher in 1999 as new sales outlets were constructed and existing outlets expanded.

Operating earnings for our company took a tumble as a number of dismal economic factors affected the sale of Finnish sauna equipment and supplies. Not only was the national economic climate weak, but one of our major markets, southern California and Arizona, was also in recession. As a result, earnings from continuing operations decreased to $___ million from $___ million in the prior year.

Recession took its toll on most of our company businesses during the past year. Sales volumes suffered from the weak market in Great Britain and Ireland and from customers running down stocks. Margins suffered from a fall in demand just as more capacity in the industry at large began to come on stream. Although its results are disappointing, the company showed a modest profit for the year.

USEFUL SENTENCES: COST-CONTROL AND COST-CONTAINMENT PROGRAMS

We will continue to manage costs vigorously. By keeping expenses in line year in and year out, we hope to maximize profits while avoiding the kind of disruptive downsizing that many companies have had to endure.

Some of our operations will inevitably be affected by the continuing and expanding slowdown in the economy. However, every manager in Costello-Hudak Enterprises has developed a deep cost-consciousness. New techniques, improved technology, and better cost-containment programs are being applied to the challenge of controlling expenses in the face of an inflationary economy.

In the face of difficult business conditions, F & M Enterprises as a whole has been cutting costs and raising productivity while concentrating on fewer businesses and seeking to expand them geographically.

We will continue to focus on cost-control and cost-containment programs and we recognize we can do more in this area, because a low-cost base gives us the leverage to realize substantial profit growth when economic conditions improve. We also worked hard to keep the number of employees low. Through attrition, voluntary retirement packages, buyout, and strict control of vacancies, the number of full-time employees declined __ percent last year.

Ultimately it is Maurello's employees who are responsible for this company's growth and strength. Their involvement and response to our company's new strategic priorities and cost-containment programs is impressive. We thank them for their enthusiastic cooperation, which is fundamental to our future success.

Somewhat better than might have been anticipated under the current difficult economic circumstances, Findlay Corporation's reasonable performance last year was in large measure attributable to the comprehensive cost-control programs instituted three years ago. Moreover, the efficiencies that have resulted from these stringent cost-containment programs plus the results of other actions taken during the past year should help the company make the most of any future improvement in general business.

Our company's sweeping cost-control efforts took many forms. Functions within each profit center were examined closely from the point of view of effectiveness, leading to decisions to continue, curtail, adjust, or discontinue. Some actions, particularly the institution of more efficient operating techniques in all subsidiaries, produced immediate results, achieving substantial savings and thus minimizing the effect of recent inflationary pressures. By year's end, the total staff had been reduced by five percent through attrition and early retirement as well as discharge.

USEFUL SENTENCES: ACQUISITIONS AND DIVESTITURES

Acquisitions play a continuing role in achieving our company's long-term goals. Since 1995, we have made seven significant acquisitions to support our business strategies and objectives. Consistent with our strategy of building on our strengths, all of these acquisitions have supported an existing subsidiary or market of opportunity. At the same time, we recognize the need to take action on businesses that no longer have the potential to contribute to the achievement of our corporate strategy. Over the past four years, we have divested or closed down three operations in order to maximize sustained future growth.

During the past year, we have carried out an extensive acquisition program. In July, we completed the acquisition of Steinbach Consumer Marketing Corporation, a regional supplier of lists, list enhancement, and other computerized consumer marketing services to the direct-mail industry. Steinbach's high-quality products and services are an excellent fit with our existing businesses. This acquisition enables us to further extend our company's full-service concept to our national and international customers. In October, we acquired Miller Electrical Contractors, Inc., an electrical company serving the Northeastern sector of the United States. In each of these two new companies we met with all the employees to introduce ourselves, to provide some background on our company's history and business philosophy, and to discuss our future together.

In line with our company's policy of continually reviewing long-term objectives, decisions were made during the past year to sell certain subsidiaries. Brooks Photocopy Services was sold, as was our majority interest in Hiller Retail, Inc. The advertising display company, CFB Outdoor Advertising, was sold to Hewig Gray Company in exchange for convertible preferred stock and cash.

Several strategic acquisitions and disposals were achieved this year as the board positions the company for further growth in the early part of the twenty-first century. The cost of acquisitions for cash considerably exceeded the proceeds from divestitures, so that during the course of last year the company moved from a net-cash position to a net indebtedness of $___ million. However, we have benefited in the past three years from a program of disposing of peripheral or low-yielding assets and redeploying the proceeds in building our core businesses in consumer appliances.

Our company is currently undergoing a radical reshaping, involving, among other things, the closing of unprofitable production facilities and the divestment of nonstrategic businesses. Among the year's divestments were two air conditioning equipment units and our shareholdings in precision-crafted automobile distributors, Tobin Ellis Inc. Employees of the divested businesses have, in the main, been kept on by the new owners and every effort has been made to redeploy others whose jobs have been affected.

USEFUL SENTENCES: CORPORATE STRATEGIES AND OBJECTIVES

For the immediate future, the main priority in our company's strategic planning is to obtain higher growth from existing businesses. We have set ourselves ambitious targets and objectives which will require the continuing improvement of our products and their marketing, and the active pursuit of every opportunity in all our marketplaces. Acquisitions, however, will continue to be important, as there are still many attractive projects and opportunities, but they are unlikely to be the prime engine for expansion.

Our corporate strategies and objectives can be simply stated: to be thoroughly competitive in everything we do; to be active in the markets in the United States and in selected countries of the European Union; to be innovative in all aspects of our business; and selecting those activities and markets where we see ourselves, both now and in the future, having distinctive technological strengths.

As a matter of corporate planning and strategy, we will continue for the foreseeable future to focus on our three corporate objectives—customer satisfaction, return on assets, and market share. However, our first priority will always remain customer satisfaction.

Our corporate strategy has been to withdraw from the weaker areas of our activities and to concentrate resources on the stronger ones—cutting costs at the same time. The benefits of this reshaping and cost-containment program will become apparent during the coming years.

Our company's future growth will come principally from our existing lines of business. Our corporate strategies and objectives—to invest funds in existing businesses to improve product quality, increase productivity, support long-term growth, and explore opportunities to augment growth of our existing businesses through acquisitions—remain in place.

As stated in our corporate strategy, we recognize that service and quality require a constant response to customer needs. To achieve this, it is important to manage for the long term: to reinvest the bulk of our earnings, to give unstinting support to research and development, and to remain sensitive to the needs and interests of our shareholders and employees.

With the sale of our fiber subsidiary, we are now focused on agrochemicals in California. These provide attractive and expanding marketplaces that will continue to provide us with opportunities for growth. We have long emphasized the wish in our corporate strategy to have a quality business, based on strong market positions, to provide consistent revenue and profit growth.

Our corporate strategy remains largely unchanged. As stated before, we intend to enhance our positions in consumer leisure travel services while, at the same time, maintaining strong luggage and fine leather goods interests in Italy. We place emphasis on quality, service, and market leadership and try to position ourselves in strong marketplaces in Europe. In building our company for the future, we aim to avoid speculation, but we are prepared to take calculated risks.

During the past twelve months we have continued our long-term corporate strategy to increase the emphasis on business electronics by disposing of our do-it-yourself businesses in July and by acquiring Stacy Business Electronics in October. We are now in the process of selling our remaining manufacturing facility in Centralia, Iowa. We expect by the end of this year to have achieved our objective of becoming a purely business electronics company. We are confident that as a result of this corporate strategy our company will emerge from this period of restructuring with a portfolio of small businesses that have a greater growth potential, less cyclical change and much stronger cash flow.

Our corporate strategy is to concentrate resources selectively on what we can do well and profitably. Therefore, we are pleased to announce that the company's program to dispose of consumer-related aspects of its business is expected to be completed toward the end of this year. We have signed agreements with Backer-Frederic Enterprises for the sale of our greeting card business and with Lilley Novak Company for the sale of the Bergen Art and Craft Company. In addition, we are having discussions with several prospective purchasers concerning the sale of Best Aqua Swimming Pools. The disposition of its consumer business will enable our company to devote its management and financial resources to its selected business markets.

The overall result of our company's activities is confirmation that the corporate strategies and objectives we have worked so hard to implement over the past few years are now bearing fruit. We will grow largely through our own efforts, but where we can acquire sound companies that fit our corporate planning and strategies, we will do so, provided the price is sensible. Our position in the Midwest—a vital market—has been strengthened by recent acquisitions and we will continue expanding there. Another area of great strategic importance to our company is the Pacific Northwest, which could account for around ___ percent of our growth by the year 2005.

A key to our company's corporate objectives and strategies is our constant enhancement of today's products and services along with the development of new ones through internal starts and acquisitions. We also focus considerable attention to the improvement of productivity, both through the application of new technology and the refinement of our current systems. For example, in the field of our Internet information systems, we repositioned our WEB MarketBiz Company for further growth through redefinition of the markets being covered and changes designed to serve those markets.

Fowler Inc. is a company in transition. Fundamental judgments are being made to determine the future direction of the company in the interest of increasing earnings, cash flow, and the rate of return on equity, thus enhancing our shareholders' value. In connection with our long-term business strategies and objectives, the company has created a new corporation (incorporated in the state of Delaware) as a wholly owned subsidiary. The present Fowler Industrial Supplies Company, under a new name, will serve as a holding company with the domestic industrial supplies business transferred to the new corporation.

The planned changes in our corporate structure as outlined in the annual report are the first steps to be taken to achieve the following corporate strategies and business objectives:

- Strengthen the company's position in the color copier market in the southwestern United States through new marketing, promotion, and advertising aimed principally at our ultimate business customers while supporting our traditional channels of distribution;

- Undertake the development and/or domestic or international acquisition of products that logically extend from our existing line of products and services based on high quality and value;

- Intensify the search for new business opportunities outside the color copier market to broaden the company's economic base.

USEFUL SENTENCES: DIRECTORS, MANAGEMENT, AND EXECUTIVE CHANGES

Two outside directors with distinguished careers in business joined the Hodon Company board of directors last year. Ward Kuhn, president of Industrial Utility Corporation, was elected to the board in May, and Helen O'Connor, president and director of Carrington Insurance Company, was elected in November.

Mr. Peter B. Guzzo, Philadelphia investor, was elected as a member to the board of directors on May 20, 1999. Ms. Dorothy Mintz, who had served on the Board of Directors since 1991, became director emeritus.

It is our pleasure to welcome as new directors of Hilbert-Duncan Corporation, Ralph T. Clark, Jr., president of Vernon Ellington Company, and Arlene C. Morley, chief executive officer of CDE Enterprises, Inc. In accordance with the company's retirement policy, Roy E. Schilling, former president of Evans Corporation, will not stand for re-election as a director at the annual meeting on April 4. Mr. Schilling has a special place in Hilbert-Duncan history. A director for 23 years, he actively supported the company during an unprecedented period of change and growth. He served as chairman of the board of directors from 1984–1996. His many contributions were invaluable, and he will be missed.

There were several important executive changes and elections to the board of directors during the year. Dr. Norman Oakland, who joined our company in 1973 and was president from 1979 to 1988, retired. Michael D. Cave, group vice president—international sales, was elected to the board of directors.

The vacancy on the board of directors by the retirement of David Stoebling was filled by Mark Hammer, executive director of Essex Science Institutes, who has been a large and supportive company shareholder for the past twenty years.

Mr. James Ronk, who was appointed a director by the board of directors at the 1998 Annual General Meeting of Shareholders, retires in accordance with the company bylaws and, being eligible, offers himself for re-appointment. The directors retiring by rotation are Ms. Anna Hall and Mr. Michael Jensen. Ms. Hall, who retired from her executive appointments in the company in 1991, intends to retire from the board and does not offer herself for re-appointment. Mr. Jensen, being eligible, offers himself for re-appointment.

Sir Dennis Heseltine ceased to be an executive director at the end of last year. He left to take on the full-time chairmanship of a major British manufacturing company, but has agreed to continue as a director in a nonexecutive capacity. This provides continuity in the contribution he has made to the company as a whole and particularly to the growth and restructuring of our business interests in Australia.

Ms. Margery Rooney, who has been with the company for 21 years, was forced through ill health to resign her directorship in July last year. The board of directors would like to place on record their deep appreciation and thanks for her loyal service to the company over the years, and wish her well in the future. At the end of September, Mr. Don Whiteman, senior vice president—financial affairs, who had been with the company for more than 35 years, retired. Again, the board would like to thank him for his long and devoted service and wish him many happy years of retirement.

At the end of the year, Marcia Westwood retired from the board of directors. Marcia joined Shea Corporation in 1970 and was vice president—human resources from 1972 to 1994. She saw the corporation through many changes, approaching every transition with skill and common sense. We are very grateful for her sound advice over the years.

Leonard P. Taylor, whose association with Ward-Sullivan Inc., spanned more than 29 years and included service as vice chairman and president of our company, retired as director last year. He takes with him the respect and affection of all of us who worked with him. Nancy A. Decker and Albert H. Graham also retired as members of the Board of Directors. They, too, contributed to the company's affairs and will be missed.

We would like to recognize the contribution of an outstanding member of our board of directors. Walter D. Wilcox, chairman and chief executive officer of Sellman Reid Inc. and a director since 1987, died on January 19, 1999. He was a valued advisor and he will be sorely missed.

With deep sorrow this annual report notes that Ms. Amelia T. Petersen, retired executive vice president—international marketing services and a member of the board of directors, died last March after a long illness. A distinguished businessperson, she began a 30-year career in marketing in 1968 when she joined the Quigg Corporation. She became vice president of MDD International in 1979 and during subsequent years played a decisive role in the expansion of our company's international business and marketing activities.

In February, death came to Lloyd A. Kester, president of the company from 1970 to 1988, and chairman of the board of directors from 1985 to 1994. His legacy can be measured in numerous ways. Under his strong and inspired leadership BPL International entered a period of dynamic development and rapid growth. However, development and growth alone would be an inadequate measure of his contributions. Those men and women who worked with him will remember Lloyd Kester best for his willingness to let those around him grow. In so doing, he developed scores of dedicated managers who carry on today. The successful attainment of our future corporate objectives will be a direct result of his confidence in the people who worked for him.

In October, we welcomed to the Astoria board of directors Dr. John T. Baines, president of the Indiana Institute of Advanced Computer Technology. As detailed on page 16 of the annual report, a number of outstanding new executives also joined the company last year, while many other men and women, not all of whom are mentioned, were promoted to new responsibilities, received awards of excellence, and made other important contributions.

A number of important executive changes, which were made during the past year, are described on page __ of this annual report. Last year's favorable operating results are tangible evidence that this management transition worked well and quickly. We are confident that we now have in place a management team geared to take full advantage of the opportunities and challenges that face our company.

In January, Shirley Hersch was appointed vice president of Crevani Company. She previously had served as vice president—advertising sales. Ms. Hersch joined our company in 1990. In recognition of the growing importance and complexity of human resources, three new responsibility areas have been developed: Paul Schneider was appointed vice president—management development; Mildred Hawthorne was appointed vice president—employee benefits; and Mario Bussagli was appointed vice president—management training programs.

A new corporate operating company—GGE Services—has been formed comprising the five subsidiaries active in the catering industry. In July, Marianne Damad was appointed president of this new operating company. Before joining our company, Ms. Damad had broad experience in the hotel management field and had been with the Deegan Hotel Organization in Pennsylvania. In another executive change, Hubert Oostenbrink was named executive vice president of the Harrison Rexon Company. He succeeded Martin Schikker who resigned to engage in private investment activities.

No chief executive has worked harder than Edmond O'Brien, who retired last July after 37 years with the company. He carried with him the affection and good wishes of his colleagues and the special thanks of the board of directors.

Early this year, we suffered a great shock at the untimely death of Nicholas Devine. Nicholas joined Werner Brothers in 1980 as chief financial officer. He played a particularly important role during the major restructure of our company in the early 1990s. He was distinguished in his profession and, had he survived, would this summer have been nominated to become chief executive officer of Werner Brothers. He will be sorely missed.

USEFUL SENTENCES: PERSONNEL, PROGRAMS, AND BENEFITS

Improvements that will benefit employees were made in our company's life insurance and medical insurance plans. Medical benefits were broadened to cover additional illnesses. Effective January 1, 2000, the amount of group life insurance coverage provided free to all active employees was increased from $____ to $____.

An important event at Carrier Contractors, Inc. was the introduction of the company's employee stock ownership plan (ESOP). This action can influence the profitability of the company for years to come. The ESOP acquired stock—amounting to 14 percent of Carrier Contractors' ownership—will be allocated to employees over the next five years.

Since January, all full-time employees are now eligible to participate in our company's Retirement Income Plan at age __ (compared with age __ before) with __ months of employment. Vesting is now quicker: employees earn a guaranteed pension benefit after __ years of qualified service with the company.

Several significant changes were made in the company's employee retirement plans during the past year. The benefit formula of the retirement program was altered to provide more pension payments upon retirement. The plan was also amended to provide additional payments to current members who had been unable to join the plan at an earlier date because of previous restrictions on age and length of service.

Our company's career opportunities program, introduced in 1990, gives any employee the chance to be considered for a job opening anywhere in KKL Industries. More than __ employees have been transferred or promoted within the company as a result. As part of KKL's continuing concern for clear employee communication, last year we formalized an "employee right to know" policy that spells out the right of KKL men and women to review their personnel files and to request corrections or changes.

Holden company's personnel policies and benefit programs are designed to create the best possible climate for employees' satisfaction on the job, to help them attain their career goals and to aid in their personal growth—in the highest sense to make the company a "good place to work." Several improvements in our personnel programs were made during the past year. In a major liberalization of the tuition refund plan, employees can now receive ___ percent reimbursement of all approved courses that provide opportunity for continued development. In addition, a new career opportunities program was introduced to increase employees' opportunities for advancement within the company whose qualifications meet the job requirements.

USEFUL SENTENCES: CORPORATE SOCIAL RESPONSIBILITIES

There are many ways beyond normal contributions that a corporation can reach out to help its community. Last year, for instance, our company provided conference and exhibition space in our buildings for many worthwhile nonprofit events and donated equipment and material to hard-pressed schools and hospitals. In addition, Morton Marketing Services people perform a variety of volunteer services for their communities. Last year, we tested a program for backing up their personal efforts with corporate funding. It was initially tested in Dayton (Ohio) and is being further implemented in other Morton locations in five different states. Our summer camp fund, supported through voluntary contributions of our employees, has granted more than ___ camperships during the past five years.

A commitment to the community—the localities as well as the broader society of which the company is a part—has long been a philosophy at Perkins Corporation and represents a major and important activity. During the past year, the company as an organization, and its employees as individuals, contributed to their communities in many ways. For example, in Detroit, the company pioneered with a training program in clerical skills for women on work-release from prison. Since 1989, the company has sponsored high school and college scholarships for promising students from underprivileged areas. For the past ten years, high school students in Detroit enrolled in Perkins' work study program in the company's Detroit office, have completed their high school education by attending classes at Perkins and gaining valuable work experience through jobs at the company.

Useful Sentences: Management's Tribute to Personnel

The effort and commitment of our employees have once again been of critical importance to our success last year and we are most grateful to them.

The credit for past year's achievement and progress lies largely with our management and staff at all levels. We are very grateful for their support and continuing positive contributions.

Last year's success was due largely to the efforts of our employees at all levels throughout the company. The directors express their thanks to all of them for their continuing support and dedication.

The past year was a better one for Peterson Corporation and we are optimistic this improvement will continue. None of this would be possible, however, without the dedication and talents of the men and women who work for our organization as well as the confidence and support of our shareholders.

We are grateful for the dedication and hard work of all our management and staff—at times under very trying circumstances—throughout the year. We want to thank all those men and women for their continuing support, which we believe will be well rewarded. Our strategy provides exceptional opportunities and we are confident that Bedford Enterprises will become strong and more profitable.

This year as in the previous three years, the company's employees have faced up to numerous problems affecting the environment of their business lives. It is to their great credit that the financial year ended with a significantly better position than could have been envisaged in the early months of the year under review. My colleagues on the board and I wish to thank everyone for their contribution and hard work.

The optimism about prospects for Kubelik-Mirowitz, Inc. rests in very large part on our confidence in all the men and women of our company. We would like to express here our pride in, and gratitude for, their hard work during the past year.

We would like to thank all management and staff for their contribution to Halberstone's good results. These could not have been achieved without their full support and commitment.

To those men and women who work in Lamberty Corporation, we would like to pay tribute to their dedicated performance in these difficult times, and to look with them to better years ahead.

The driving force behind our company's profitable growth will continue to be our people whose skills, professionalism, and dedication are essential to our continuing success. Once again, we express our thanks to them all.

As a company, Marlow Equity Corporation is responding to changes. However, in the final analysis, it is the people of our company who are identifying and meeting those challenges. Their talents are our most important asset. By providing an environment in which those talents may be fully utilized, Marlowe Equity is providing an important contribution to our shareholders and to society in general.

Our determination to maintain leadership underlies our continuing emphasis on human resources development. We have no more important task than to attract, retain, and motivate the best and most innovative men and women. We are indeed fortunate to have an exceptionally talented staff, because this is the principal resource for successful financial performance.

We appreciate the enthusiastic support and diligently applied capabilities of our employees, who individually and in total comprise the great asset of CTT Company. They make the difference that gives assurance of the company's continuing success.

We extend our sincere appreciation to the shareholders and to all employees of Meyer & Grant Company for their continuing support and encouragement. Their contributions and commitments are a vital part of our company's progress and success.

Achievement of our company's goals will depend, as always, on the loyalty and skill of the men and women who work for Fourman Company. Their combined efforts are responsible for the progress our company has made last year and are the best guarantee to our stockholders that the company can achieve the corporate objectives we have set for the years ahead.

To our shareholders, who continue to support and encourage our efforts, and to our loyal employees who work diligently to improve the company's results, particularly during this especially difficult period for the computer software business, we express our sincere appreciation. To those men and women—the people of Sturges Software—we dedicate this letter to our shareholders and our annual report. Their varied talents are responsible for the past successes of this company. Because of them, we look to the future with optimism.

Like all business enterprises, FCX Corporation operates in a rapidly changing financial, economic, and technological environment. The board of directors as well as management, however, recognize that all of these changes in our operating environment signify challenges and opportunities. The answer to meeting and capitalizing on them is the maintenance and enhancement of our organization led by a corps of able men and women who will make the most of the company's inherent strengths by doing an even better job anticipating and responding to change.

I want to express my sincere appreciation to my senior executive colleagues and to all employees of the company for their achievements during the past year. We have been fortunate in their commitment to Logan Internet Services and are determined to build upon it in future years. Dedicated people are the key to our success.

USEFUL SENTENCES: THE YEAR AHEAD

We believe that the year ahead will be another strong syear, one in which we will continue to build on past achievements and continue to generate growth in earnings and revenues.

We expect a continuation of the present high level of capacity utilization of our manufacturing plants during 1999. Therefore, we anticipate that 1999 revenues and operating income will approximate last year's levels.

In spite of a number of uncertain factors, which may have repercussions in both circulation and advertising, the Brandon Magazine Group expects net earnings for 1999 to equal 1998 levels.

The year ahead poses uncertainties for our company. While it is unrealistic to expect significant gains, we are confident that, in 1999, we will again surpass our long-term annual growth objective by at least four percent.

Looking ahead, we are well aware of difficulties and challenges. Nevertheless, we look forward to a continuation this year of profitable growth, expanded opportunities and improved earnings.

Effects of the previously announced reorganization of our consumer electronics unit will become visible during this year. Even though we do not aniticipate growth in revenues, we expect that operating income will closely resemble last year's levels.

At this writing, there is a great deal of uncertainty regarding the economic outlook for 1999. However, unless the economy is more adversely affected than many economists are currently forecasting, we believe the company's earnings could be among those of our better years.

The two companies acquired in 1999 will all contribute to DCB's operating income in 2000 and along with internal growth from existing companies, we anticipate a significant increase in revenues and earnings.

The company, having improved the efficiency of its ongoing operations, having rid itself of some economically unattractive business activities and having prepared itself to participate in several promising new ventures in the northeastern United States is now in a good position to capitalize on improvement in the general economy in the year ahead and to renew the pattern of growth in revenues and earnings that has sustained Hills-Hays, Inc.

We do not expect a market recovery for our personal computer activities during 1999. However, as a positive result of the effects of our recent reorganizations, we anticipate an improvement in operating income.

Although Boland Industries is not recession proof, our company's performance during prior turndowns in the business cycle has shown us to be relatively recession resistant when compared with most other domestic and international companies in our industry. All this considered, we anticipate good performance and growth this year.

Our company has not been immune to the sagging economy that adversely affected our country. However, this will not deter us from continuing the pursuit of quality in all our endeavors for the year ahead. The executive board expects that revenues, net profit as well as the profit per share for 1999, will at least equal the figures for 1998.

While there is uncertainty about the state of the overall economy in North America, we are fundamentally optimistic regarding the strength of our business. If economic conditions do deteriorate, we believe that Professional Internet Services Company should fare better in the year ahead than most businesses since our products and services enable our customers here and overseas to make better decisions in many business areas.

Riverson Enterprises is confident about the immediate future despite the many challenges we will face. We believe that our continued determination to improve profitability and expand our core businesses here and overseas position our company to achieve a new era of growth.

It seems clear that the economic recession is behind us and that a measured business recovery is under way. The threat of renewed inflation remains, however, and certain other continuing pressures are of particular concern. However, we look to the coming year with considerable optimism. We confidently expect, therefore, that our company will participate fully in the resurgence of the economy.

We believe we now have the people and the organizational structure to react efficiently and aggressively in what we believe will be a more competitive business environment in the near future. We also firmly expect an increasing proportion of our future potential to be realized through our own organic growth programs and stringent cost-containment efforts. Therefore, we anticipate that 1999 will be a strong year in which we will continue to build on past achievements.

Much still remains to be done to sustain and improve our company's competitive position, both at home and abroad. However, when the economy in Mexico moves out of recession, this company is well poised to benefit and we are confident that it will grasp the opportunities presented. The current year has started better than the early months of last year and we expect that the year ahead should produce some further improvements.

Although the decline in storm door and storm window unit sales during the past two years is not encouraging, we are committed to an aggressive program of strengthening our company's position in the market, gaining market share, and searching for new markets and new products to expand our national sales. In addition, we continue to review the structure and processes of the business and have intensified the search for new and better ways to operate our business. Looking ahead, we anticipate another difficult year in 1999. Unless there is a significant improvement in the nation's economy, sales will remain sluggish. Nevertheless, our company's long-term prospects are good.

For the past few years, our company has been primarily concerned with the reorganization and consolidation of its activities. This stage is now behind us, and in 1999 we began to reap the benefits of our development policies of the previous years. There is, in our view, good growth potential in most of our divisions although we must anticipate that our activities will continue to be affected by cyclical movements in the national economy. Nevertheless, we look to the year ahead with optimism though operating income is expected to decrease slightly in 2000.

While it is still too early in a very uncertain year to forecast results with any reasonable degree of precision, it appears at this time that some of the extraordinary factors that contributed to record performances in 1998 will not be repeated this year. Inflation and a slowing economy are affecting the operations results. As a consequence, 1999 is not likely to equal our company's outstanding performance and results of 1998. Moreover, as a result of the negative effects of 1998 currency fluctuations, we expect 1999 earnings to decline.

We do not expect a recovery in our audiovisual division during 1999. Furthermore, we anticipate greater competition throughout the organization; accordingly, revenues and earnings will decline further this year. However, we remain confident about our company's future.

During the first three months of 1999, we have not seen improvements in the economies in the southwestern states in which we operate. Compared to the corresponding period of 1998, operating income remained approximately the same. In light of uncertainties in our markets, we abstain at the present time from forecasting 1999 earnings for QWF Corporation as a whole.

FORMAL NOTICES OF AN ANNUAL MEETING OF SHAREHOLDERS

ABC, INC.
00 William Avenue
Boston, MA 00000

NOTICE OF AN ANNUAL MEETING OF SHAREHOLDERS
March 18, 1999

NOTICE IS HEREBY GIVEN that an annual meeting of shareholders of ABC, Inc. will be held in Commerce Hall, 000 King Street, Boston, Massachusetts on March 18, 1999 at 2:30 P.M., for the following purposes:

(a) to receive the consolidated financial statements of ABC and its subsidiary companies for the financial year ended December 31, 1998 together with the report of the auditors thereon;

(b) to elect directors;

(c) to appoint auditors and to authorize the directors to fix their remuneration; and

(d) to transact such further and other business as may be properly come before the meeting or any adjournments thereof.

Dated at Boston the 10th day of February, 1999.

BY ORDER OF THE BOARD OF DIRECTORS

James A. Wilson
Vice President and Secretary

If you are unable to attend the meeting in person, you are requested to date, sign, and return the enclosed form of proxy in the envelope provided for that purpose.

Consolidated XYZ Company   00 Macmillan Place   Chicago, Illinois 00000

NOTICE OF ANNUAL MEETING OF STOCKHOLDERS

The annual meeting of stockholders of Consolidated XYZ Company will be held at the Langford Hotel, Grand Ballroom Entrance, One Swinden Plaza, Chicago, on February 27, 1999 at 11.00 A.M., for the transaction of the following business:

1. To receive and consider the audited financial statements for the financial year ended December 31, 1999, and to declare a final dividend.

2. To re-appoint Ms. R. S. Thompson and Mr. J. C. Williams as members of the board of directors.

3. To re-appoint Bryan & Simsom as auditors of the company.

4. To consider and pass the following resolution that will be proposed as an ordinary resolution:

   That the authorized share capital of the company be increased from $___ million to $___ million by the creation of new ordinary shares of $___ each.

5. To transmit any other ordinary business of an annual meeting.

By order of the board of directors

Gerald H. Murray
Vice President and Secretary

## CHAPTER 16

LETTERS OF CONDOLENCE AND SYMPATHY

Condolence letters are probably the most difficult letters to write. For that reason, we have included a large selection of sample letters as well as a large number of helpful sentences expressing sympathy and understanding. A personal letter or note of condolence should be handwritten, particularly if you know the deceased person's family very well. Such letters or notes should be brief and tactful, because a few well-chosen and sincere words of sympathy can often give great comfort.

In addition, a series of (paid) death notices, which are often published in a newspaper announcing a person's death, are included in this chapter. Death notices (also known as "funeral notices") are alphabetical listings that include such information about a death as funeral arrangements, memorial contributions, and survivors.

Several model letters as well as a number of helpful sentences expressing sympathy to an injured or ill person are also given. Tact and sincerity are also of great importance when writing letters of sympathy. The length of this type of letter is usually based on the degree of mutual friendship that exists.

LETTERS OF CONDOLENCE

Date

Name
Address
City, State Zip Code

Dear Name,

I learned with deep regret of the recent passing of your father and wish to extend my sincere sympathy in your bereavement.

With deepest respects,

Signature

Name

Date

Name
Address
City, State Zip Code

Dear Name,

This is to convey to you our deepest sympathy in your recent bereavement.

With sincere condolences,

Signature

Name

Date

Name
Address
City, State Zip Code

Dear Name,

Upon my return to the office this afternoon, I was grieved to learn of the sudden passing of your husband. You have my deepest sympathy. I only wish there were some way in which I could lighten your burden of sorrow.

With sincere condolences,

Signature

Name

Date

Name
Address
City, State Zip Code

Dear Name,

It was a great shock to us all to hear of your sudden loss of your wife. We would like to convey with deep sincerity the sorrow with which all of us here received the news. Please accept our heartfelt condolences.

Sincerely yours,

Signature

Name

Date

Name
Address
City, State Zip Code

Dear Name,

We cannot tell you how sorry we are to hear of the death of your wife. Our deepest sympathy to you in your great loss.

Yours sincerely,

Signature

Name

Date

Name
Address
City, State Zip Code

Dear Name,

I was stunned to learn of the accidental death of your father today. Albert was a colleague and I knew him as a man of integrity, ability, and kindness. I will certainly miss him. Please accept my deepest sympathy.

Sincerely yours,

Signature

Name

Date

Name
Address
City, State Zip Code

Dear Name,

The news of Peter's accidental death came as a great shock to us at McNamara Corporation. All of us here at the office extend our deepest sympathy to you. We also want you to know that our thoughts are with you at this time of grief.

With kindest regards,

Signature

Name

Date

Name
Address
City, State Zip Code

Dear Name,

This morning Mr. Archer told me the sad news of your mother's sudden death. Although I had known for a long time that she was dangerously ill, the news of her passing still came as a shock. Please accept my sympathy and heartfelt condolences. If there is anything I can do for you, now or in the future, please let me know as soon as possible.

With deepest respects,

Signature

Name

Date

Name
Address
City, State Zip Code

Dear Name,

We are deeply grieved by Fred's unexpected death. Sandra and I want to express to you and the children our most heartfelt sympathy. May the love of your family and many friends comfort and strengthen you in the difficult days ahead.

Affectionately yours,

Signature

Name

Date

Name
Address
City, State Zip Code

Dear Name,

We were deeply saddened to hear the news of your husband's sudden death of heart failure. On behalf of the management and staff, I tender our deepest sympathy to you and your family.

His death is a great loss to our company. We, who had the privilege of knowing and working with your husband for many years, will remember Andrew as a very kind and humorous person who enjoyed everyone's respect. We have lost a valued colleague and his friendly presence will be greatly missed.

Please accept our sincere condolences. If there is any way that we can help, please let me know.

With kindest regards,

John Barnes
President

Date

Name
Address
City, State Zip Code

Dear Name,

We at the Chilton Company were shocked and saddened to hear that your husband died last night and wish to extend our deepest sympathy. We will remember your husband not only as a knowledge-able and talented businessman, but also as a kind and cheerful person. Jack was a wonderful person to work with, always witty and full of enthusiasm and energy. We will all miss him terribly and grieve with you at his passing.

Cordially,

Lester Taylor
Chairman of the Executive Board

Date

Name
Address
City, State Zip Code

Dear Name,

The sad news of your wife's death, while not unexpected, was nevertheless a severe blow to us. Laura and I remember that you often spoke of how difficult Annette's long-time battle with cancer was. Al-though we are deeply saddened by the death of your beloved wife, we share your understanding and relief that Annette, who has suffered so long, has finally found release and is now at peace. She was a very courageous and brave woman. You can also take great comfort from the fact that you did every-thing possible to make Annette's last days as easy as possible for her.

The time of grief is always difficult, but we know it will be greatly eased by the loving support of your son and daughter. If we can help you and your family in any way, please do not hesitate to call.

With deepest sympathy,

Signature

Name

USEFUL SENTENCES FOR LETTERS OF CONDOLENCE

Opening Sentences

All of us here at Martin's Department Store are deeply saddened by the untimely death of your wife.

My colleagues and I were shocked and saddened to hear about your husband's tragic automobile accident.

We are saddened by the news of your daughter's passing. Please accept our sincere sympathies.

We have just learned with profound sorrow of the death of your son and send you our heartfelt sympathy.

The sad news of Norma's sudden death is something that we can still hardly believe.

The news of Arlene's death came as a deep shock.

We were deeply shocked to hear of the death of your daughter, Linda.

We have just heard with profound sorrow the sad news of your wife's death.

We were saddened to hear that your mother died yesterday and wish to extend our deepest sympathy.

We were very sorry to hear the news about George's untimely death in an airplane accident.

We were deeply saddened by the news of Joan's passing.

We would like to offer our sympathy to you and your family on the passing of your sister.

This is to tell you of my deep sympathy in your recent bereavement.

Our family was deeply saddened today when we heard from William that you have lost your father.

There are no words to adequately express my deep shock and grief when I heard this morning of the sudden death of your little baby, Mickey.

It was with sincere regret that Tony and I heard this evening of the untimely death of your father to whom we know you were deeply devoted.

I was deeply shocked and saddened to learn of the unexpected passing of Brenda on Sunday.

I am so very sorry to hear of the death of your mother.

I was terribly sorry to hear of the death of your son.

Please accept my heartfelt condolences on the untimely passing of your wife.

Marion's sudden death has saddened us beyond words.

Other Sentences

There are no words that can express our deep sorrow about the death of your daughter.

There is not much one can say to ease your deep sense of loss, but Margery and I want you to know our thoughts are with you in this time of grief.

There is little anyone can say or do at a time like this to ease the burden of your grief, but all of us at Sanderson's Warehouse express our deepest sympathy to you on the great loss of your husband.

We would like you to know you have our deep sympathy in your bereavement.

May we extend our heartfelt sympathy to you and the whole family on your great loss.

Susan was always well liked and she will be greatly missed. Her death is a great loss to all of us.

Your sorrow is shared by everyone who knew and loved Eve.

Everyone who knew Angela loved her.

Your wife's death is a great loss.

My heartfelt condolences and deepest sympathies and understanding in your time of sorrow.

We think of you at this time and extend our understanding and deepest sympathy.

We grieve with you at your husband's passing and feel grateful for having known him.

We hope it will be of some comfort to you and your wife to know that your many friends share your deep sorrow.

It is difficult to convey my deep sadness, but my thoughts and love are with you.

We hope the love you and Edward shared will help comfort you in the days ahead.

I wish it was in my power to soften your deep sorrow.

My colleagues and I send you our warmest regards.

My colleagues and I, who knew your father well, had a genuine respect for him.

We can well appreciate what a great loss this must be to you and your family.

I hope that time will soon heal your sorrow.

Our thoughts are with you now, and we send you our deepest sympathy.

Our thoughts and sympathy are with you.

We are all thinking of you and send our deepest sympathy.

Be assured of our loving concern and availability to help in any way John and I can. Call on us, please.

Carla was a wonderful person. We are sure that you and your daughters will be sustained during the difficult days and weeks ahead by many happy memories.

Let me first extend my heartfelt sympathy to you and your family.

We send you our warmest regards and our most sincere sympathy.

If I can help you in any way, please do not hesitate to call me.

Please, accept my sincere condolences and call on me if there is anything I can do.

If there is any way Warren and I may be of help to you during the difficult days and weeks ahead, please always feel free to call on us.

We hope that we may help you in some way at this very difficult time.

If there is some way that I can help you and your family, let me know.

You know that if there is anything I can do, you have only to tell me.

If Martin and I can help in any way, please do not hesitate to get in touch.

If there is anything that I can do to be of assistance, I would regard it as a favor if you would let me know.

We will drop by in the next few days to see if there is anything we can do to help you.

Please call on us if there is anything we can do to help.

In the meantime, let us know if there is anything we can do for you and your family.

We would be grateful if you would turn to us for any help we might give. Janet will call next week to see if there is anything we can do.

I will phone you in the next couple of days to see when I might visit.

Anne and I are only a phone call away if there is anything we can do for you.

Please call me if you just want to talk.

Please remember that we are always here if you want to talk with someone.

Closing Sentences

Please accept our sympathy.

Please accept our sincere sympathies.

Please convey my condolence to your family.

Please accept our love and sympathy.

Please accept our sincere condolences.

Please accept my sympathy and best wishes.

With deepest sympathy to you and your family.

Our heartfelt sympathy to you.

May our sympathy help to comfort you.

My sincere condolences to you and your family.

I wish to express my deepest sympathy to you.

I send you my heartfelt sympathy.

We want to share our sympathy with you.

With love and sympathy to you both in this great loss.

Please accept our heartfelt sympathy in your time of great sorrow.

May I extend my deep sympathy to you and your family.

God bless you and your family.

Our thoughts and prayers are with you.

You are in my thoughts and prayers.

My heart and tears are with you.

We share a deep feeling of loss.

I share in your grief and send you my love.

My thoughts are with you at this sad time.

Our thoughts and prayers are with you.

I want you to know I am thinking of you.

Closing Phrases

With affection and heartfelt condolences,

With sincerest sympathy,

With deepest sympathy,

With deepest sympathy to you in your great loss,

With best wishes,

With respect and affection,

REPLIES TO LETTERS OF CONDOLENCE

Replies to condolence letters can be made either by a formal printed card or by a brief personal letter or note.

(Formal printed card)

> Mrs. Dionne Guinan and Family
> gratefully acknowledge
> and wish to thank you for
> your message of sympathy

(Formal printed card)

Mr. Brian Cahill
wishes to thank you most sincerely
for your note of sympathy

(Formal printed card)

The family of Angela Warren
wishes to acknowledge with gratitude
your kind expression of sympathy

(Personal thank-you note)

I want to thank you most sincerely for your expression of sympathy during my time of grief. Your kind words were very comforting and I appreciate your thoughtful offer of assistance if the need should arise.

USEFUL SENTENCES THANKING FOR EXPRESSIONS OF SYMPATHY

Thank you very much for your kind words.

Thank you for your kind letter.

Thank you sincerely for your kind expression of sympathy.

I deeply appreciate your kindness in writing to me.

Your visit during our time of grief brought us great comfort and encouragement.

My husband and I wish to thank you for your kind and encouraging words during our bereavement.

My wife and I wish to thank you for your kindness and sympathy in our bereavement.

Your help and expression of love and concern have given me hope and encouragement during my period of grief.

Your kindness and understanding sympathy have been a great comfort. They have helped us to accept our daughter's death more courageously.

During my time of grief, your family's expression of love brought me great comfort and encouragement.

It was heartwarming to receive your kind expression of sympathy upon the death of Marie Louise.

Sally and I want to thank all of you for comforting us in our time of need.

Formal Acknowledgments in a Local Newspaper

The family of the late Mary Williams, extends sincere thanks to relatives, friends, and neighbors for the sympathy letters and cards of condolence received during their bereavement. Thanks also to those who gave donations to the Ridgewood Nursing Home and to everyone who attended the funeral.

The family of the late Major Carl Holmes wishes to thank all relatives and friends for their kind messages of sympathy, support, and donations received during their recent sad bereavement. Sincere thanks to the Reverend Peter Mulder for his kind ministrations and to all who attended the funeral service.

The family of the late Father Donald O'Hara wishes to express its sincere gratitude to Mr. Anthony Dixon, the staff and boys of St. Bernhard School, to Captain R. E. Ashley and all naval and civilian personnel of *U.S.S. Thomas Jefferson*, and to all who helped to transform a sad departure into the commemoration of a full, happy, and rewarding life.

We are grateful to all our relatives, friends, and associates for your expressions of kindness and sympathy during our recent loss. Mrs. Mary Conley and Family.

Mr. and Mrs. David Walker wish to thank their many friends for their expressions of condolences and the many moving tributes paid to the memory of their daughter Janet. Thank you for your contributions to the National Cancer Foundation.

Mrs. Margaret Dixon and family express their sincere thanks to all relatives, friends, neighbors, and colleagues for their kind messages of sympathy, cards, and floral tributes received in their sad loss. Please accept this as the only intimation.

Andrew Grisewood and the family of the late Anne Taylor wish to thank everyone for the warm letters of sympathy and support, kindness, and help received at this very sad time. They are grateful for the very large number who attended the funeral service on Tuesday, May 7, and for the beautiful flowers sent and the donations given to the Red Cross in her memory. We also wish to thank the doctors, nurses, and staff of St. Anthony Hospital for all the attention and kindness shown to her. It is hoped that this acknowledgment can be accepted as an expression of their most grateful thanks.

DEATH NOTICES IN LOCAL NEWSPAPERS

Valerie Anne Rossitter (née Dougherty), much-beloved wife, sister, mother, and grandmother and friend to so many, died peacefully on August 23 after a long illness which she faced with spirit and great courage. The funeral will take place on August 28 at 12 noon at St. Paul's Church, Wall Street, Perrysburg. Family flowers only. Donations if desired, to a charity for the relief of suffering. Funeral arrangements by Richard Brinkhurst, 000 Kimberly Avenue, Perrysburg.

On February 12, peacefully at home with her family, after a long illness, Kathleen Reeves, aged 83 years passed away. Much-loved mother of Christopher and Mary. Cremation on Tuesday, February 15, at 2:30 P.M. Family flowers only. Donations, if desired, please send to Asthma Research Fund, Worthing Road, Woodlawn.

On April 17, passed away peacefully in St. Anthony Hospital, Fairlawn, John G. Fowles, aged 74 years. Will be sadly missed by his loving wife and family. Funeral services wil be held at Hope Park Church, Ridgewood, on Friday April 22 at 12 noon, followed by committal at Ridgewood Crematorium.

On January 4, Andrew Livingston, much-loved husband of Alexis and father of Lucy and Rachel and stepfather of Angela and Henry. Private family funeral on January 8. Memorial service to be announced. Family flowers only, but donations if desired, for the Arlington Charity Foundation may be sent together with any inquiries to Albert Dawson Funeral Services, 00 Guildford Street, Guildford. Tel. (000) 000-0000.

On Sunday, January 13, at Hinton Hospital, John Patterson passed away after a brave fight against cancer. He is now at peace. A strong, caring, peace-loving man, John will be much missed by all who knew him. The funeral will take place on Thursday, January 17 at 11:30 A.M. at Cedarhurst Crematorium.

Maurice Hunter—on August 12, peacefully after a short illness at home in Monterey, aged 70 years. Beloved husband and companion of Susan for 48 years. Dearly beloved father of Mary, Jennifer, and Arthur. He will be sadly missed by all his family and friends. Service at All Saints' Church, Tiverton, on Thursday August 17 at 1:30 P.M., followed by interment at Tiverton Cemetery at 2:30 P.M. Family flowers only, please. If desired, donations in his memory to the American Heart Foundation. All inquiries to Joyce and Arthur Hunter; tel. (000) 000-0000.

Andrew B. Christie—On March 24, of complications from AIDS, aged 28. Died at home, with courage and dignity. Beloved son of Peter and Betty. Brother of Jane, Tom, and Elizabeth. Long-time companion of Jack. Funeral services will be held at the Vale Crematorium, Overton Street, Centerport, on Tuesday, March 28 at 3:00 P.M. No flowers by request. Donations, if desired, for the AIDS Research Foundation, c/o William Harrison, Funeral Directors, 7 Charlotte Square, Centerport.

On October 8, tragically in the course of duty, Captain Dick Anderson, aged 29. Dearly loved son of Ethel and James, brother of Michael and Susan. Devoted fiancé of Laura. Regarded with great affection and respected by all his friends. Dick will be sadly missed. Funeral service will be held at Holy Trinity Church, Claresholm, on Monday, October 13 at 2 P.M. prior to cremation at Claresholm Crematorium.

The staff of Glendale General Hospital at Glendale, New Jersey, record with great sorrow the sudden passing of their dear friend and colleague Dr. Daniel A. Sokolosky. He was an inspiration to staff and patients. He leaves a great legacy of courage and will be remembered with respect and affection. We extend our sincere sympathy to his family. The staff of Glendale General Hospital.

The board of governors, members, and staff of the Regional Hospital Association note with extreme sadness the untimely death of Daniel A. Sokolosky, M.D., who served as president and chief executive officer of the Midtown Medical Center of Rockville from 1972 to 1994. A former chairman of the Regional Hospital Association and a long-time member of its board of governors, Dr. Sokolosky served as a member of distinguished boards, including the board of the League of Voluntary Hospitals where he made an important mark upon the health-care community. The Regional Hospital Association recognized him upon his retirement in 1994 for his vision, leadership, determination, and dedication to the improvement of the delivery of health-care services. We extend our deepest sympathies to his son Anthony Sokolosky, his grandchildren Dinah and Suzanne, and all the members of his family. Andrew C. Butwin, M.D., chairman, Regional Hospital Association.

USEFUL SENTENCES FOR DEATH NOTICES

On June 26, peacefully in her sleep, following a stroke, Mary Anne Burgess, aged 59.

Peacefully on February 3, having accepted his cancer with courage and dignity, Thomas Cotterell, aged 44.

On Saturday, July 8, passed suddenly and peacefully away in the hospital, Alan Simpson, aged 76. Dearly beloved husband and companion of Ann and friend of many others.

On September 28, suddenly in the garden of his home at Aberdeen, Richard Arkwright, aged 54.

On Sunday, May 4, peacefully at Haven Manor Rest Home, Turpin Hills, at peace with God and man and thinking of others to the very end, Maria Fleming. Beloved wife of Nick, dearly loved mother of Nora and Jane, and wonderful grandmother to ten.

On November 7, after a long illness bravely borne, Dorothy Slack (née Watson), dearly loved wife of David, and much-loved mother of Margaret and James and grandmother of Alexandra. Her warm friendship and cheerful disposition will be sadly missed by all who knew her.

Tragically on Thursday, November 17, while on holiday in France, Richard Edwards, dearly loved son of David and Rose, loving brother of Jeanette, cherished grandson, and devoted uncle.

Nora Hodges, very dear wife of Richard Hodges. Died instantly in a car crash Sunday, August 6.

Requiem Mass at St. Paul's Church, Lexington, at 12 noon, Friday, August 4, followed by interment in the churchyard.

Service will take place at St. Mary's Church, Boston, on Tuesday, May 19 at 3:00 P.M., followed by private cremation.

Relatives and friends are kindly invited to attend the funeral services at New Hope Baptist Church, 200 Christie Street, Elizabeth, on Wednesday, June 19, at 10:30 A.M.

Friends may call on Thursday, May 7, at the Lee Funeral Home, 000 Fairfax Drive, Arlington, from 10:30 A.M. until the time of service at 12 noon. Interment at Arlington National Cemetery.

The officers and members of Fort Colmaro Post 000 of the American Legion of War Veterans are hereby notified of the death of comrade Joseph A. Gaines on December 4. Visitation at Gilmore Funeral Home, Wednesday, December 7 from 10 to 11 A.M. Legion services at 10:30 A.M.

Family flowers to Herbert Copeland & Sons, Funeral Directors, 000 Forton Avenue, Grossport.

Floral tributes to Grimley Funeral Serices, 00 Tunbridge Street, Davenport. Requiem Mass at 10.00 A.M. on Wednesday, April 22, at St. Francis Church in Stockbridge.

All flowers and any inquiries to Jonas Weller & Son, Funeral Directors, 00 West Street, Belleville; tel. (000) 000-0000.

Immediate family flowers only. Donations, if desired to a charity of one's own choice.

No flowers please, but donations to the United Heart Research Institute would be appreciated.

Expressions of sympathy may be made in the form of flowers or memorial contributions to the charity of your choice.

Donations instead of flowers to Institute for the Deaf, Hartsdale. Enquiries to Hartsdale Funeral Directors, 00 Fulham Road, Hartsdale.

In lieu of flowers, contributions may be made to a favorite charity.

In lieu of flowers, the family suggests that expressions of sympathy may be made in the form of contributions to the National Diabetes Foundation.

In lieu of flowers, remembrances may be made to Hospice Care, 00 Nashua Road, Nickerson.

Expressions of sympathy in her memory may be donated to the National Cancer Society or the Jewish Rehabilitation Center.

Expressions of sympathy in Mr. Franklin's memory to the charity of your choice would be appreciated.

The family prefers donations in Joanne's memory to the Scholarship Fund, c/o East Greenwich College, East Greenwich, CT 00000.

The family requests that expressions of sympathy be in the form of contributions to the First Baptist Church of Ashland Park.

Donations in Suzanne's name would be appreciated to the Visiting Nurse Association in Eastham.

LETTERS OF SYMPATHY

(Letter of sympathy to an injured person)

Date

Name
Address
City, State Zip Code

Dear Name,

Barbara and I were very sorry to hear that you were injured in a car accident and we want to let you know how concerned we are. We are hoping that you will make a speedy recovery and will soon be out of the hospital.

So hurry and get well!

Warmest regards,

Signature

Name

(Letter of sympathy to an injured person)

Date

Name
Address
City, State Zip Code

Dear Name,

Marina and I were shocked and distressed to learn the news of your wife's automobile accident. We hope Jenny will recover quickly. We will come to see her at the hospital as soon as she is able to receive visitors.

Sincerely,

Signature

Name

(Letter of sympathy to an ill person)

Date

Name
Address
City, State Zip Code

Dear Name,

We have just heard of your illness and of your admission to Claremont General Hospital last week. We understand that you will be hospitalized for three or four weeks. Therefore, we hope that by the time you receive this letter, you will soon be all right again. William and I intend to visit you on Sunday, April 4th.

With best wishes,

Signature

Name

USEFUL SENTENCES FOR LETTERS OF SYMPATHY TO INJURED OR ILL PERSONS

I was very sorry to learn that you have been hospitalized.

We were greatly shocked to hear about William's heart attack.

We understand that you will be hospitalized for a few weeks.

We hope to see you back soon.

My wife and I are hoping for your rapid recovery.

We hope you will soon again be up and about.

We are certainly relieved to know that you will be out of the hospital in about two weeks.

With the best wishes of the entire staff for a speedy and complete return to health.

We are sending you our best wishes for your quick recovery.

We would like to visit you at the hospital when you are feeling better.

We do hope that you will soon be on the way to complete recovery.

All of us at the head office are sending you our best wishes and hope you will have a quick recovery. We look forward to your return.

We are sure it will not be long before you are back again at the office. We all feel your absence and sincerely hope you will recover quickly.

Please accept our best wishes for a fast recovery.

Your colleagues at the Somerset Hotel were very sorry to hear of your little son's serious accident.

We hope that soon your wife will be well on the road to complete recovery.

We all miss you.

Best wishes for a speedy recovery.

You have all our best wishes for a fast recovery.

We are all hoping for you to get better very quickly from your emergency surgery.

We are hoping that you are feeling better every day and that you will soon be back on your feet. The office is not the same without you.

USE OF PUNCTUATION MARKS IN WRITING

Punctuation marks are marks or signs such as the period (.), comma (,), colon (:), semicolon (;), question mark (?), exclamation point (!), hyphen (-), dash (—), parentheses (); ellipsis points (. . .), slash (/) and quotation marks (" "). These marks are used to punctuate business and academic writing. The purpose of punctuation is to make the structure and meaning of the written word clear to the reader.

PERIOD

A period (.) or full stop is used to mark the end of all sentences, except for exclamations and questions.

Examples:

The Federal Reserve System issues new currency.

Ecology is the science that studies the interaction between living organisms and their environment.

The period is also used after most abbreviations and decimals.

Examples:

Co.	Mr.	Ms.	R.S.V.P.	U.S.A.
A.M.	P.M.	5:15 A.M.	3:34 P.M.	etc.
0.2	5.87	7.339	23.4 percent	9.42 yards

However, abbreviations of organizational names (for example, IRS, FBI, NASA, CIA, GM, UN, EU, UNESCO, and IBM) do not require a period.

COMMA

A comma (,) indicates a slight break in thought and is used to separate words, phrases, or clauses in a list.

Examples:

The development of the business system in Great Britain depends on transportation, communications, and banking services.

My only brother, Harold, has been hired as a sales representative.

Mr. Dodd, our European marketing director, will visit you next week.

I believe, however, that business functions in a complete environment are influenced by independent legal, social, cultural, economic, and technological forces.

Commas are also used in addresses; in dates; in numbers with more than three digits; with degrees, titles, and abbreviations that follow a name; in correspondence (salutation and closing in a letter); and in phrases identifying direct quotations.

In dates

September 12, 1999   Saturday, December 7, 1995

In addresses

55 West 42nd Street, New York, NY 10036
Grand Plaza Building, Suite 2109
P. O. Box 377, Washington D. C. 20202-4456

In numbers with more than three digits

1,754   35,689   157,600   8,971,562   43,124,755

With academic degrees, titles, and abbreviations that follow a name

Anthony Valentez, C.P.A.   Susan Morris, M.D.
Carl Lewis, Ph.D.   Lincoln Brothers, Inc.
Mackenzie & Douglas, Ltd.   Michael Lindsay, President

In correspondence (salutation and closing)

Dear Mrs. Jones,   Dear Walter,
Sincerely,   Sincerely yours,

In phrases identifying direct quotations

Ronald Markham is now manager of Fortax Plastics. "My scientific training," he says, "gave me discipline. It showed me how to tackle a problem."

Wilma B. Taylor said, "Almost all computers require the person to compensate for the technical capability."

COLON

A colon (:) is most often used after a word or sentence that introduces a list or series of texts and extracts, a long speech or a long quotation. A colon is also used after the salutation in a business letter, to indicate time in hours and minutes, and in biblical references (chapter and verse).

Colons used to indicate a series or summation

The preparation of a report involves the following four steps:

The largest and best known industrial unions in the United States are the following: the Transport Workers Union, the United Mine Workers, and the United Steelworkers of America.

An analysis of this letter points up two conclusions: (1) a new proposal to merchandise the invention; and (2) management specifically contemplated that before the parties were to be bound, there was to be the signing of a formal agreement.

Salutation in a business letter

Dear Sir/Madam: Dear Ms. Grant:

Indication of time in hours and minutes

5:45 A.M.   11:08 P.M.

In biblical references (chapter and verse)

Isa. 53:4   Luke 7:3   Phil. 3:1–4:1   Acts 7:54–60

SEMICOLON

The semicolon (;) is a mark of punctuation that is much stronger than a comma but less pronounced than a period.

The problem is not necessarily inexperience in management; many such plans were offered only after a company was on the verge of bankruptcy.

In summary, mergers lead to bigness; bigness does not necessarily lead to better service, better products, or better pricing.

QUESTION MARK

A question mark (?) is used to end a sentence expressing a direct question.

What are you doing?

Who invited Mrs. Jones to the reception?

How often have you felt victimized by an accounting error attributed to a malfunctioning computer?

A question mark within parentheses is used to indicate the writer's uncertainty or doubt about the correctness of the preceding word, date, figure, or statement.

You ordered a dozen (?) copies of this reference book.

Geoffrey Chaucer was born in 1340 (?) and died in 1400.

Do not use a period or a comma after a question mark.

"Are you really married?" she suddenly asked.

EXCLAMATION POINT

An exclamation point (!), also known as an exclamation mark, follows an abrupt, forceful, or excited cry, utterance, outburst, or comment. It can also be used at the end of a single word.

Hurry!   No!   Go away!   Help!

What a splendid view!

HYPHEN

The hyphen (-) has a number of uses, although the use of hyphens varies considerably. In many cases, you will need to consult a dictionary to ascertain whether you have to use hyphens or not. Therefore, newspapers and publishing companies often consult their own style manuals regarding the consistent use of hyphens. Hyphens are frequently used to form a compound word from two or more other words (e.g. secretary-treasurer, self-made man, daughter-in-law). A hyphen is often used to join two or more words serving as a single adjective before a noun (e.g. blue-green eyes, computer-generated marketing maps, time-consuming processes).

PREFIXES

A hyphen is frequently used when attaching prefixes.

Examples:

all-	all-Canadian
anti-	anti-Communist
ex-	ex-President Reagan
mid-	mid-October
non-	non-Christian
pan-	pan-European
post-	post-Vietnam War
pre-	pre-Renaissance
pro-	pro-British
self-	self-help
un-	un-American
well-	well-preserved

Hyphens are always used in compound numbers from twenty-one to ninety-nine (or twenty-first to ninety-ninth).

Examples:

twenty-two   forty-seven   fifty-six   ninety-eight

nineteen hundred and ninety-six

twenty-fifth anniversary   ninety-eighth birthday

The hyphen is also used to split a word between syllables at the end of a line. Major American dictionaries provide detailed word division information because they divide all entry words into syllables.

Examples:

in-struc-tion	in-stru-ment	in-sur-mount-a-ble
non-ex-is-tence	gen-tle-man	qual-i-fi-ca-tion

Advice: if in doubt about a word division, check a good dictionary.

DASH

A dash is a mark of interruption or separation in a sentence to mark a sudden break or abrupt change in thought. On a word processor or typewriter, the dash is made with two hyphens (--).

Examples:

A job specification generally lists measurable information -- years of schooling, length and type of experience, and characteristics -- that would most likely describe a suitable employee.

Dust, dirt, unsanitary washrooms, chemical fumes -- and even noise -- endanger health.

PARENTHESES

Use parentheses ( ) to insert explanations, phrases, comments, examples, figures, details, and quoted material when a separation stronger than a comma is desired within a sentence. Parentheses are also frequently used around figures or letters to enumerate or designate each item in a series.

Direct mail is the solicitation of customers by mail (telephone, television, or magazine advertisements may also be used) and fulfillment of these orders by postal or commercial delivery.

The ability of personal computers to precisely duplicate software has led many software companies to include devices that make unauthorized copying difficult (copy protection).

Form I-9 (employment eligibility verification form) must be filed with the Immigration and Naturalization Service (INS) within three days after every new employee has been hired.

Enclosed is my personal check for seventy-eight dollars ($78.00).

Sole proprietorships are so prevalent because they have four important advantages: (a) ease of setting up, operating, and closing a business, (b) complete ownership of all profits, (c) tax advantages, and (d) high credit standing.

After studying this booklet you should be able to: (1) relate the purpose of the marketing distribution system, and (2) recognize and explain the various distribution channels.

ELLIPSIS

An ellipsis (. . .) is a punctuation mark of three space periods to indicate that one or more words or sentences have been left out within a quoted passage. An ellipsis is also used to mark a hesitation, an interruption or a pause.

Example:

The policy underlying these principles is that: ". . . damages . . . have never been considered to be a cause of legal action . . . because the function of such an action is not merely to compensate the plaintiff for wrongs committed by the defendant but, . . . to present them, by removing all inducement to attempt dealing for their own benefit . . ."

SLASH

A slash (also known as a virgule) is a diagonal mark (/) used especially to separate alternatives.

Examples:

B/L (bill of lading)   c/o (in care of, care of)

and/or   4/5 (fraction)   1995/1996   miles/hours

The bottle exploded because of carbonation pressure and/or the weakness of the bottle.

QUOTATION MARKS

Double quotation marks (" ") are used when directly quoting sentences or paragraphs from a book or magazine or a speaker's words. Quotation marks are always used in pairs, before and after the quoted material.

Examples:

Soon the day will come for management to decide: "Do we strike out on our own?"

Remembering the axiom, "A fool and his money are soon parted," he decided to be nobody's fool.

Shirley Jackson calls herself "the first black woman to make a million dollars in chemical manufacturing."

"The business of America is business," said president Calvin Coolidge, and he had good reason for saying so.

One of the most successful trade union tactics was the implementation of a "corporate campaign" to "isolate the RBB Corporation from the mainstream of the business community."

"People may doubt your ability," Mary Hill advises, "so you must know your specialty area better than anyone else." Hill added that life in upper management can also be "a very lonely experience."

After a four-week training program to learn about new company procedures, each "graduate" is awarded a diploma.

According to John Smith, employees in "the old days" were glad just to have a job. "Nowadays people are no longer motivated to perform well," complains Smith.

Grand's Department Store in Toronto is described by its owner (Richard Benson) as "one of the most expensive men's stores in Canada." "Our customers want the best," explains Benson.

CAPITALIZATION

The rules to capitalize words are often unpredictable and complex, although there certain basic rules and standard conventions. The following words are always are written or printed with a capital letter.

FIRST WORDS

The first word of a sentence or exclamation:

The experiment started last week.

He served in the army during the Second World War.

Hello!   Help!   Fire!

The first word of a direct quotation that is a complete sentence:

A feared business tycoon once said, "Most people seem to think I am the kind of guy who shaves with a blowtorch. Actually, I am bookish and worrisome."

"I never started out meaning to have my own business," Margery Dixon said. "It just accidentally happened."

The first words of a quoted fragment is not written with a capital letter:

The Italian historian Giacomo Vittori denies that there can be such a thing as a "philosophy of business history" or that "business history has any real meaning."

The novels of Hans Lessing are written in a style that is "deliberately prosaic and purged to chemical purity of all poetry."

"We are not," the board of directors stressed, "particularly happy about this new development."

My professor always considered accounting as "the major source of internal information about a company itself."

The first word of a complete sentence that follows a colon (:) is capitalized.

Her first question was: Why are people so stupid to pay these extravagant charges?

The first word of a line of poetry is always capitalized:

> I have seen better faces in my time
> Than stands on any shoulder that I see
> Before me at this instant
> —William Shakespeare King Lear 2.2.94-96

TITLES OF WRITTEN MATERIAL

Capitalize the first word and the last word and all other important words (pronouns, nouns, verbs, adjectives, and adverbs; with the exception of such words as "a," "an," "about," "and," "for," "in," "the," and "to") in the titles of books, newspapers and magazine articles, themes, plays, films, television programs, or headings.

Examples:

Business in Action: An Introduction to Business Practices

Dynamics of World Business

Mr. Johnston and the Knight's Companion

"A Break in the Action," *Time and News*, April 27, 1995, pp. 52–53.

Much Ado About Nothing

Good for Nothing: A New Play for Young People

SALUTATION AND COMPLIMENTARY CLOSING

The first word of a complimentary closing of a letter as well as the major words of the salutation are written with capital letters.

Examples:

Dear Mrs. Brown: Dear Madam: Gentlemen:

Dear Sir: Dear Senator Maxwell:

Sincerely,   Sincerely yours,   Cordially,   Yours truly,

PROPER NOUNS

Always capitalize the names of the Supreme Being, people, groups, languages, religions, government bodies, countries, states, organizations, institutions, schools, hospitals, universities, trademarks, commercial products, heavenly bodies, holy books, months, days, holidays, holy days, historical events, and documents.

Examples:

God   Allah   the Lord   Jesus   Zeus   the Holy Spirit

Archimedes   Socrates   Emperor Nero   Napoleon

President Clinton   Queen Elizabeth   King Albert

the French people   the British   Americans

Japan   Latin America   Venice   Amsterdam   Los Angeles

Islam   Buddhism   Methodism   Hinduism   Protestantism

Christianity   a Christian   the Jesuits   a Baptist

the Bible   the Koran   the Old Testament   the Epistles

the United Nations   the United States Senate

British Medical Association   Madison Avenue   the White House

Main Street   Atlantic Ocean   North Sea   Northern Ireland

South Korea   Panama Canal   Hong Kong Island   the Far East

Civil War   Rotary Club   Summer Olympics   Red Cross

Oxford University   World Trade Center   Sears Building

Democratic Party   D-Day   World War II   Second World War

New York Public Library   London Hospital   Louvre Museum

Battle of the Bulge   Treaty of Versailles   Magna Carta

Western Hemisphere   Antarctica   Arctic Circle

Nobel Prize   Academy Award   Coca-Cola   the First Amendment

U.S. Constitution   Independence Day   Christmas   Easter

the Crusades   House of Lords   Wars of the Roses

WORDS LIKELY TO BE CONFUSED

There are a number of words that often sound nearly alike, but have different spellings and also different meanings. As a result of their similarity in spelling or sound these words are likely to be confused or misspelled.

Word	Meaning
absorb	to take in, to assimilate
adsorb	to take up by absorption
accede	to yield, to consent, to comply with
exceed	to surpass, to go beyond

accept	to take, to receive
except	to exclude, to omit; not including
access	admittance, entrance
excess	surplus, superfluous, too much
adapt	to adjust, to conform, to fit, to suit
adept	skillful, skilled, proficient
adopt	to take as one's own, to accept
adverse	unfavorable, negative, opposed
averse	unwilling, hesitant, reluctant
advice	suggestion, counsel, guidance, information
advise	to consult, to recommend, to suggest, to inform
affect	to influence, to act upon, to inspire
effect (noun)	result, consequence, outcome
effect (verb)	to produce results, to cause, to come into use
affective	emotional, moving
effective	producing a desired or intended result
aisle	passageway
isle	island
already	previously, by this time
all ready	entirely prepared
altar	place of worship, communion table
alter	to change
altogether	completely, entirely, thoroughly
all together	all in one place, everyone in one group
always	forever, continuously, invariably
all ways	in every way
allusion	indirect or casual reference
illusion	fantasy, dream; magician's trick
apprehend	to arrest; to foresee, to anticipate, to know
comprehend	to understand, to grasp
apprise	to inform, to notify, to tell
apprize	to cherish, to treasure, to rate

appraise	to estimate, to make an official valuation
apprise	to inform, to tell, to warn, to notify
ascent	advancement, rise; soaring, climbing
assent	consent, agreement, concurrence
astrology	foretelling the future by the stars
astronomy	science of the planets, stars, and galaxies
awhile	for a short time
a while	a period of time
bail	security for an appearance in court
bale	bundle
beside	at the side of
besides	in addition to
biannual	twice a year, semiannual
biennial	every two years
bimonthly	happening every two months
semimonthly	happing twice a month
biweekly	happening every two weeks
semiweekly	happening twice a week
biyearly	happening every two years
semiyearly	happening twice a year
born	to give birth to, to deliver, to bring forth
borne	carried, endured
calendar	a system of reckoning time
calender	a machine for processing paper or cloth
canvas	coarse woven fabric; painting
canvass	to scrutinize, to examine, to study, to solicit
casual	accidental, fortuitous, incidental
causal	implying or constituting a cause or result
cease	to stop
seize	to grasp, to grab, to take
climactic	relating to a climax
climatic	relating to climate

clothes	garments, wearing apparel
cloths	fabrics
coarse	vulgar, common
course	route, way, passage, direction, curriculum
complacent	satisfied, smug, self-contented
complaisant	amiable, good-natured, obliging
complement	something that completes; full number
compliment	to acclaim, to praise; congratulation, praise
comprehensible	understandable, intelligible
comprehensive	all-round, general, inclusive
condole	to sympathize
condone	to forgive, to excuse, to pardon
confidant	trusted friend
confident	secure, certain, self-assured
confidentially	in strict confidence
confidently	with assurance
contemptible	despicable, deserving or held in contempt, vile
contemptuous	scornful, expressing or showing contempt
conscious	alive, awake, aware, alert, watchful
conscience	qualm, moral and ethical principles
continual	of frequent recurrence, successive, intermittent
continuous	uninterrupted, permanent, ceaseless
corps	a body of people, a part of an army, party
corpse	a dead body, carcass, cadaver
council	legislative body, a group of appointed or elected people, assembly in consultation
counsel	to advise, to recommend; advice, guidance; lawyer
councilor	member of a council
counselor	adviser, attorney, lawyer, trial lawyer
credible	believable, reliable, plausible
creditable	respectable; creditworthy

decease (noun)	death
decease (verb)	to die, to expire
disease	illness, sickness
deceased	dead
diseased	ill, unhealthy, affected with disease
decent	respectable, morally upright, proper
descent	slope, a downward incline; lineage
dissent	to disagree; disagreement
depravation	corruption, moral perversion
deprivation	loss, dispossession
deprecate	to disapprove
depreciate	to cheapen or disparage; to go down in value
die	to cease living, to expire, to pass away
dye	to color; color, dyestuff
discreet	cautious, careful, considerate, prudent, modest
discrete	distinct, diverse, separate, several
disburse	to pay out money
disperse	to spread, to scatter
economic	of a country's or company's finances
economical	thrifty, frugal, sparing
elicit	to extract, to evoke, to draw out
illicit	unlawful, illegal, not legal, unauthorized
eligible	suitable, qualified, fit to be chosen
illegible	unreadable, undecipherable
emigrant	a person who leaves his country
immigrant	a person who comes to and settles in a country
eminent	famous, prominent, distinguished, illustrious
imminent	about to happen, impending, near at hand
ensure	to make sure
insure	to take an insurance policy

exceptionable	debatable, objectionable
exceptional	extraordinary, unusual, well above average
expose	to reveal, to disclose, to exhibit
exposé	public revelation or exposure, explanation
farther	more distant
further	additional
formerly	once, previously, some time ago
formally	in form, in a formal manner, with regard to form
fortuitous	happening by chance, accidental
fortunate	lucky, bringing or having good luck
genteel	cultured, cultivated, refined, urbane
gentle	not rough, mild, lenient, soft
human	relating to humankind
humane	charitable, good, kind, benevolent
immigrate	to enter and settle in a country
emigrate	to leave one country and settle in another
immoral	unprincipled, bad, corrupt, unscrupulous
immortal	not subject to death, undying
imperial	of or relating to an empire or emperor
imperious	proud, overbearing, dictatorial
industrial	of or relating to industry
industrious	hardworking, diligent
ingenious	inventive, clever, skillful, shrewd
ingenuous	frank, natural, simple, innocent, unsophisticated
intelligent	clever, rational, logical
intelligible	understandable, clear, comprehensible
interment	burial
internment	detention, confinement
judicial	relating to courts of law or judges
judicious	wise, prudent, having sound judgment

lay	to place
lie	to rest; to tell a lie
loath	reluctant, unwilling, hesitant
loathe	to detest, to hate
lose	to fail to win, to forfeit, to mislay
loose	not fixed, free, lax, slack, idle, not tight
material	substance, yard goods or cloth
materiel	equipment, outfit, apparatus, gear
masterful	domineering, overbearing
masterly	expert, skillful, skilled, proficient
momentary	short-lived, fleeting, transient
momentous	important, significant, meaningful
maybe	perhaps
may be	might be
moral	virtuous, righteous
morale	esprit, mental state of confidence and discipline
negligent	careless, disregardful, lax, casual
negligible	small, unimportant, slight
none	not any, not one
no one	nobody
notable	remarkable, worthy of note or notice; celebrity
noticeable	attracting attention, outstanding, conspicuous
official	authoritative, formal, one who holds an office
officious	informal, unofficial, meddlesome
ordinance	law, rule, regulation
ordnance	weapons, military materiel
overdo	to do in excess, to do something too much
overdue	past due, late, past the proper time
participation	division
petition	formal request

persecute	to oppress, to harass, to torment
prosecute	to take legal action against somebody
personal	individual, private
personnel	employees, staff of workers
perspective	view, vista, outlook
prospective	likely to happen, possible
practicable	feasible
practical	useful, usable
prescribe	to order, to enjoin, to set down as a rule
proscribe	to denounce, to condemn, to prohibit
principal	chief; most important; capital, head
principle	code of conduct, tenet, fundamental truth
procede	to occur before in time
proceed	to go forward, to continue, to go on, to advance
proceeds	earnings, profit, gain
reality	actuality
realty	real estate
residence	house, dwelling
residents	people who reside in a particular place
seasonable	timely, opportune, suitable to the season
seasonal	occurring or depending on a particular season
sewage	liquid and solid waste
sewerage	drain or sewage system, a system of sewers
spacious	roomy, having plenty of space
specious	deceptive, erroneous, false, inaccurate
stationary	not moving, fixed, immovable, static
stationery	writing supplies, writing materials
statue	sculpture
statute	law, decree, rule, regulation
than	as compared to, in comparison with
then	at that time, in that case

| therefor | for that, for this |
| therefore | hence, consequently |

| undo | to annul, to erase, to reverse |
| undue | excessive, exceeding what is appropriate |

| urban | relating to or characteristic of a city |
| urbane | cosmopolitan, civilized, cultural, well-bred |

| vendee | purchaser, buyer |
| vendor | seller |

| veracious | truthful, honest, precise, accurate |
| voracious | greedy, exceedingly greedy in eating |

| waiver | release |
| waver | to be undecided, to hesitate |

Forms of Address for Use in Correspondence in the United States

The words "full name" in the second column below indicates that the full name of the recipient of the letter must be used; for example, the Honorable John G. Barnes.

The word "surname" (or last name) in the third colum below indicates that only the last name of the recipient of the letter must be used; for example, Dear Mr. Levitt; Dear Ms. Purcell. Note that the name of the recipient in the salutation is followed by a colon.

FEDERAL GOVERNMENT

President of the United States

| *Letter Address:* | The President |
| | The White House |

| *Salutation:* | Dear Mr. President; Mr. President |

Former President of the United States

| *Letter Address:* | President (full name) |
| | Address |

| *Salutation:* | Dear Mr. (surname) |

Wife of the President of the United States

Letter Address: Mrs. (full name)
                    The White House

Salutation: Dear Mrs. (surname)

The Vice President of the United States

Letter Address: The Vice President
                    United States Senate

Salutation: Dear Mr. Vice President; Sir

Cabinet Members

Letter Address: The Honorable (full name)
                    Secretary of (name of the department)

Salutation: Dear Mr./Madam Secretary; Sir/Madam

Attorney General

Letter Address: The Honorable (full name)
                    Attorney General of the United States

Salutation: Dear Mr./Madam Attorney; Sir/Madam

Postmaster General

Letter Address: The Honorable (full name)
                    Postmaster General

Salutation: Dear Mr./Madam Postmaster General; Dear Sir/Madam

Senator

Letter Address: The Honorable (full name)
                    United States Senate

Salutation: Dear Senator (surname); Sir/Madam

Representative

Letter Address: The Honorable (full name)
                   United States House of Representatives

Salutation: Dear Representative (surname); Dear Mr./Ms./Miss (surname)

Director of a Federal Agency

Letter Address: The Honorable (full name)
                   (Title, Name of Federal Agency)

Salutation: Dear Mr./Ms./Miss (surname)

Chief Justice

Letter Address: The Chief Justice
                   The Supreme Court of the United States

Salutation: Dear Mr./Madam Chief Justice; Sir/Madam

Associate Justice

Letter Address: The Honorable Justice (surname)
                   The Supreme Court of the United States

Salutation: Dear Justice (surname); Sir/Madam

Judge of a Federal Court

Letter Address: The Honorable (full name)
                   Judge of the (name of the court)

Salutation: Dear Judge (surname); Sir/Madam

DIPLOMATIC OFFICIALS

Ambassador, United States

Letter Address:	The Honorable (full name) Ambassador of the United States
Salutation:	Dear Mr./Madam Ambassador; Sir/Madam

Chargé d'Affaires, United States

Letter Address:	(full name), Esq. American Chargé d'Affaires
Salutation:	Dear Mr./Ms./Miss (surname)

Consul, United States

Letter Address:	The Honorable (full name) American Consul
Salutation:	Dear Mr./Ms./Miss (surname); Sir/Madam

Vice Consul, United States

Letter Address:	The Honorable (full name) American Vice Consul
Salutation:	Dear Mr./Ms./Miss (surname); Sir/Madam

Foreign Ambassador in the United States

Letter Address:	His/Her Excellency (full name) Ambassador (name of country)
Salutation:	Dear Mr./Madam Ambassador; Excellency

Foreign Minister in the United States

Letter Address: The Honorable (full name)
Minister of (name of country)

Salutation: Dear Mr./Madam Minister; Sir/Madam

Foreign Chargé d'Affaires in the United States

Letter Address: Mr./Ms./Miss (full name)
Chargé d'Affaires of (name of country)

Salutation: Dear Mr./Madam Chargé d'Affaires

Foreign Consul in the United States

Letter Address: The Honorable (full name)
Consul of (name of country)

Salutation: Dear Mr./Ms./Miss (surname); Sir/Madam

Secretary General of the United Nations

Letter Address: His/Her Excellency (full name)
Secretary General of the United Nations

Salutation: Dear Mr./Madam Secretary General; Sir/Madam

American Representative ("Ambassador") to the United Nations

Letter Address: The Honorable (full name)
United States Representative to the United Nations

Salutation: Dear Mr./Ms./Miss (surname); Sir/Madam

United Nations Representative ("Ambassador"), Foreign

> *Letter Address:*   His/Her Excellency (full name)
> Representative of (name of country) to the United Nations
>
> *Salutation:*   Dear Mr./Madam (surname); Sir/Madam

STATE AND LOCAL OFFICIALS

Governor of a State

> *Letter Address:*   The Honorable (full name)
> Governor of (name of state)
>
> *Salutation:*   Dear Governor (surname); Sir/Madam

Lieutenant Governor of a State

> *Letter Address:*   The Honorable (full name)
> Lieutenant Governor (name of state)
>
> *Salutation:*   Dear Mr./Ms./Miss (surname); Sir/Madam

Secretary of State

> *Letter Address:*   The Honorable (full name)
> Secretary of State (name of state)
>
> *Salutation:*   Dear Mr./Madam Secretary; Sir/Madam

State Senator

> *Letter Address:*   The Honorable (full name)
> The Senate of (name of state)
>
> *Salutation:*   Dear Senator (surname); Dear Mr./Ms./Miss (surname)

State Representative, Assemblyperson or Delegate

Letter Address: The Honorable (full name)
House of Representatives

Salutation: Dear Mr./Ms./Miss (surname); Sir/Madam

Judge

Letter Address: The Honorable (full name)
Judge of the —— Court

Salutation: Dear Judge (surname); Sir/Madam

Mayor

Letter Address: The Honorable (full name)
Mayor of (name of town)

Salutation: Dear Mayor (surname); Sir/Madam

Alderman or Alderwoman

Letter Address: The Honorable (full name)
Alderman/Alderwoman

Salutation: Dear Mr./Ms./Miss (surname); Sir/Madam

THE ACADEMIC WORLD

President of a College or University (with a Doctorate)

Letter Address: Dr. (full name)
President (name of institution)

Salutation: Dear Dr. (surname); Dear Sir/Madam

President of a College or University (without a Doctorate)

Letter Address: Mr./Ms./Miss (full name)
President (name of institution)

Salutation: Dear Mr./Ms./Miss (surname)

Professor

Letter Address: Professor (full name)
Department and Name of Institution

Salutation: Dear Professor (surname)

Holder of a Doctorate

Letter Address: Dr. (full name)
Address

Salutation: Dear Dr. (surname); Dear Sir/Madam

CLERGY

Pope

Letter Address: His Holiness the Pope
Vatican City

Salutation: Your Holiness; Most Holy Father

Roman Catholic Cardinal

Letter Address: His Eminence Cardinal (surname)
Archbishop of (place name)

Salutation: Dear Cardinal (surname); Your Eminence

Roman Catholic Archbishop

Letter Address: The Most Reverend (full name)
Archbishop of (place name)

Salutation: Dear Archbishop (surname); Your Excellency

Roman Catholic Bishop

Letter Address: The Most Reverend (full name)
Bishop of (place name)

Salutation: Dear Bishop (surname); Your Excellency

Roman Catholic Monsignor

Letter Address: The Right Reverend Monsignor (full name)
Name of Diocese or Church

Salutation: Dear Monsignor (surname)

Roman Catholic Priest

Letter Address: The Reverend (full name)
Name of Church

Salutation: Dear Father (surname)

Roman Catholic Mother Superior

Letter Address: The Reverend Mother Superior (full name)
Name of Convent

Salutation: Dear Reverend Mother; Reverend Mother

Roman Catholic Nun

Letter Address: Sister (full name or given name)
                      Name of Religious Order

Salutation: Dear Sister (surname or given name)

Roman Catholic Brother

Letter Address: Brother (given name)
                      Name of Religious Order

Salutation: Dear Brother (given name)

Anglican Archbishop

Letter Address: The Most Reverend (full name)
                      Archbishop of (place name)

Salutation: Dear Archbishop (surname)

Protestant Episcopal Bishop

Letter Address: The Right Reverend (full name)
                      Bishop of (place name)

Salutation: Dear Bishop (surname)

Pastor, Minister, Clergyman and Clergywoman (with Doctorate)

Letter Address: The Reverend Dr. (full name)
                      Name of Church

Salutation: Dear Dr. (surname)

Pastor, Minister, Clergyman and Clergywoman (without Doctorate)

Letter Address: The Reverend (full name)
                      Name of Church

Salutation: Dear Mr./Ms./Miss (surname)

Rabbi (with Doctorate)

Letter Address: Rabbi (full name)
                      Name of Temple

Salutation: Dear Dr. (surname); Dear Rabbi (surname)

Rabbi (without Doctorate)

Letter Address: Rabbi (full name)
                      Name of Temple

Salutation: Dear Rabbi (surname)

PROFESSIONS

Dentist

Letter Address: (full name), D.D.S.
                      Address

Salutation: Dear Dr. (surname)

Physician

Letter Address: (full name), M.D.
                      Address

Salutation: Dear Dr. (surname)

Veterinarian

Letter Address: (full name), D.V.M.
                      Address

Salutation: Dear Dr. (surname)

ARMED SERVICES

When addressing letters to commissioned officers of the United States Armed Services, the full rank (plus branch of the military) is written. For officers of the U.S. Army, the U.S. Air Force and the U.S.

Marine Corps, the military ranks (in descending order) are: General, Lieutenant General, Major General, Brigadier General, Colonel, Lieutenant Colonel, Major, Captain, First Lieutenant, and Second Lieutenant.

For officers of the U.S. Navy and U.S. Coast Guard, the ranks (in descending order) are: Admiral, Vice Admiral, Rear Admiral, Commodore, Captain, Commander, Lieutenant Commander, Lieutenant, and Ensign.

In salutation, the full rank is often shortened. Thus, the mode of salutation for General, Lieutenant General, Major General and Brigadier General is "Dear General" (with surname): *Dear General Taylor.*

The salutation for a Colonel or Lieutenant Colonel is "Dear Colonel" (with surname) while the salutation for a First Lieutenant or Second Lieutenant is "Dear Lieutenant" (with surname): *Dear Lieutenant Jones.*

The salutation for an Admiral, Vice Admiral, and Rear Admiral is "Dear Admiral" (with surname): *Dear Admiral Hughes.* The salutation for both a Commander or Lieutenant Commander is "Dear Commander" (with surname): *Dear Commander Williams.*

In all cases, the mode of salutation "Dear Sir" or "Dear Madam" may also be used for all ranks. Thus, you may either use the salutation "Dear General Taylor" or simply "Dear Sir" or "Dear Madam."

COUNTRIES OF THE WORLD

The name of the country is shown in bold type, while the adjective of the country and the name in general use for an inhabitant or native of this country is shown in roman type.

Country	Adjective	Inhabitant
Afghanistan	Afghan	Afghan
Albania	Albanian	Albanian
Algeria	Algerian	Algerian
Andorra	Andorran	Andorran
Angola	Angolan	Angolan
Antigua	Antiguan	Antiguan
Argentina (also the Argentine)	Argentinian Argentine	Argentinian Argentine
Australia	Australian	Australian
Austria	Austrian	Austrian
the Bahamas	Bahamian	Bahamian
Bahrain	Bahraini	Bahraini
Bangladesh	Bangladeshi	Bangladeshi

Barbados	Barbadian	Barbadian
Belgium	Belgian	Belgian
Belize	Belizian, Belizean	Belizian, Belizean
Benin	Beninese	Beninese
Bermuda	Bermudian	Bermudian
Bhutan	Bhutanese	Bhutanese
Bolivia	Bolivian	Bolivian
Botswana	Botswanan	Botswanan
Brazil	Brazilian	Brazilian
Britain	British	British
Brunei	Bruneian	Bruneian
Bulgaria	Bulgarian	Bulgarian
Burundi	Burundian	Burundian
Cameroon	Cameroonian	Cameroonian
Canada	Canadian	Canadian
Cape Verde Islands	Cape Verdean	Cape Verdean
Chad	Chadian	Chadian
China	Chinese	Chinese
Colombia	Colombian	Colombian
Comoros	Comoran	Comoran
Costa Rica	Costa Rican	Costa Rican
Cuba	Cuban	Cuban
Cyprus	Cypriot	Cypriot
Czech Republic	Czech	Czech
Dahomey	Dahoman, Dahomean	Dahoman, Dahomean
Denmark	Danish	Dane
Djibouti (also	Djiboutian	Djiboutian
Jibouti, Jibuti)	Jiboutian, Jibutian	Jiboutian, Jibutian
Dominica	Dominican	Dominican
Dominican Republic	Dominican	Dominican
Ecuador	Ecuadoran, Ecuradorean	Ecuadoran, Ecuadorean
Egypt	Egyptian	Egyptian
El Salvador (also	Salvadorian	Salvadorian
Salvador)	Salvadoran	Salvadoran
England	English	the English
Eritrea	Eritrean	Eritrean
Ethiopia	Ethiopian	Ethiopian
Fiji	Fijian	Fijian
Finland	Finnish	Finlander, Finn, the Finns
France	French	the French
Gabon	Gabonese	Gabonese, the Gabonese
Gambia	Gambian	Gambian
Germany	German	German
Ghana	Ghanaian, Ghanian	Ghanaian, Ghanian
Gibraltar	Gibraltarian	Gilbraltarian

Great Britain	British	the British
Greece	Greek	Greek
Grenada	Grenadian	Grenadian
Guatemala	Guatemalan	Guatemalan
Guinea	Guinean	Guinean
Guyana	Guyanese	Guyanese, the Guyanese
Haiti	Haitian	Haitian
Holland (see **Netherlands**)		
Honduras	Honduran, Hondurean, Hondurian	Honduran, Hondurean, Hondurian
Hong Kong (also Hongkong)	Hong Kong Hongkong	Hong Konger Hongkongite
Hungary	Hungarian	Hungarian
Iceland	Icelandic	Icelander
India	Indian	Indian
Indonesia	Indonesian	Indonesian
Iran	Iranian	Iranian
Irak (also Iraq)	Iraki Iraqi	Iraki Iraqi
Ireland, Republic of	Irish	the Irish
Israel	Israeli	Israeli
Italy	Italian	Italian
Jamaica	Jamaican	Jamaican
Japan	Japanese	Japanese
Jibouti, Jibuti (see **Djibouti**)		
Kenya	Kenyan	Kenyan
Kuwait	Kuwaiti	Kuwaiti
Laos	Laotian	Laotian
Lebanon	Lebanese	Lebanese, the Lebanese
Liberia	Liberian	Liberian
Libya	Libyan	Libyan
Liechtenstein	Liechtenstein	Liechtensteiner
Luxembourg (also Luxemburg)	Luxembourg Luxemburg	Luxembourger Luxemburger
Malta	Maltese	Maltese, the Maltese
Mauritania	Mauritanian	Mauritanian
Mauritius	Mauritian	Mauritian
Mexico	Mexican	Mexican
Monaco	Monacan, Monegasque	Monacan, Monegasque
Mongolia	Mongolian	Mongolian
Morocco	Moroccan	Moroccan
Namibia	Namibian	Namibian
Nepal	Nepalese	Nepalese, the Nepalese
Netherlands, the	Dutch	the Dutch
New Zealand	New Zealand	New Zealander
Nicaragua	Nicaraguan	Nicaraguan

Niger	Nigerian	Nigerian
North Korea	North Korean	North Korean
Norway	Norwegian	Norwegian
Pakistan	Pakistani	Pakistani
Panama	Panamanian	Panamanian
Paraguay	Paraguayan	Paraguayan
Peru	Peruvian	Peruvian
Philippines	Philippine, Filipino	Filipino, the Filipinos
Poland	Polish	Pole, the Poles
Portugal	Portuguese	Portuguese
Puerto Rico	Puerto Rican	Puerto Rican
Qatar	Qatari	Qatari
Rumania (also	Rumanian	Rumanian
Romania, Roumania)	Romanian, Roumanian	Romanian, Roumanian
Russia	Russian	Russian
Rwanda	Rwandan	Rwandan
Salvador (see El Salvador)		
San Marino	San Marinese	San Marinese
Saudi Arabia	Saudi	Saudi
Senegal	Senegalese	Senegalese
Seychelles	Seychellois	Seychellois, the Seychellois
Sierra Leone	Sierra Leonean	Sierra Leonean
Singapore	Singaporean	Singaporean
Slovakia	Slovakian	Slovakian
Somalia	Somali	Somali
South Africa	South African	South African
South Korea	South Korean	South Korean
Sri Lanka	Sri Lankan	Sri Lankan
Sudan	Sudanese	Sudanese, the Sudanese
Surinam (also Suriname)	Surinamese	Surinamese, the Surinamese
Swaziland	Swazi	Swazi, the Swazi
Sweden	Swedish	Swede, the Swedish
Switzerland	Swiss	Swiss, the Swiss
Syria	Syrian	Syrian
Taiwan	Taiwanese	Taiwanese, the Taiwanese
Tanzania	Tanzanian	Tanzanian
Thailand	Thai	Thai, the Thai
Togo	Togolese	Togolese, the Togolese
Tonga	Tongan	Tongan
Trinidad and Tobago	Trinidadian and Tobagonian	Trinidadian and Tobagonian
Tunisia	Tunisian	Tunisian
Turkey	Turkish	Turk
Uganda	Ugandan	Ugandan

Ukraine	Ukrainian	Ukrainian
United Kingdom	British	the British
United States of America	American	American
Uruguay	Uruguayan	Uruguayan
Vatican City	Vatican	Vatican
Venezuela	Venezuelan	Venezuelan
Vietnam	Vietnamese	Vietnamese
Zaire	Zairian	Zairian
Zambia	Zambian	Zambian
Zimbabwe	Zimbabwean	Zimbabwean

ABBREVIATIONS OF AMERICAN STATES

The following two-letter abbreviations of American states are used in conjunction with the so-called ZIP Code *(Zone Improvement Program)*, a postal code system to expedite the sorting and delivery of mail by assigning a five-digit or nine-digit number to each postal delivery area in the United States of America. The five-digit or nine-digit numbers are placed after the state abbreviation.

Examples:

Eatontown, NJ 07724; Washington, DC 20013-7127.

American State	*ZIP Code*
Alabama	AL
Alaska	AK
Arizona	AZ
California	CA
Colorado	CO
Connecticut	CT
Delaware	DE
District of Columbia	DC
Florida	FL
Georgia	GA
Hawaii	HI
Idaho	ID
Illinois	IL
Indiana	IN
Iowa	IA
Kansas	KS
Kentucky	KY

Louisiana	LA
Maine	ME
Maryland	MD
Massachusetts	MA
Michigan	MI
Minnesota	MN
Mississippi	MS
Missouri	MO
Montana	MT
Nebraska	NE
Nevada	NV
New Hampshire	NH
New Jersey	NJ
New Mexico	NM
New York	NY
North Carolina	NC
North Dakota	ND
Ohio	OH
Oklahoma	OK
Oregon	OR
Pennsylvania	PA
Rhode Island	RI
South Carolina	SC
South Dakota	SD
Tennessee	TN
Texas	TX
Utah	UT
Vermont	VT
Virginia	VA
Washington	WA
West Virginia	WV
Wisconsin	WI
Wyoming	WY

ABBREVIATIONS OF CANADIAN PROVINCES AND TERRITORIES

Canadian Province or Territory	*Abbreviation*
Alberta	AB
British Columbia	BC
Manitoba	MB
New Brunswick	NB

Newfoundland	NF
Northwest Territories	NT
Nova Scotia	NS
Ontario	ON
Prince Edward Island	PE
Quebec	PQ
Saskatchewan	SK
Yukon Territory	YT

NUMERICAL EXPRESSIONS

NUMBERS

The usage of numbers in a written text varies. Generally speaking, the numbers from one to ten are written as words. Numbers above ten are usually written as figures, although in many books and periodicals figures under one hundred are also written as words. In addition, many writers also prefer to write numbers that can easily be expressed in one or two words (e.g. two thousand dollars; four million years).

When a sentence begins with a number, the number must be written as words (*wrong*: 5000 employees were dismissed. *Write instead*: Five thousand employees were dismissed.). However, if the number is too long, you should rephrase or rewrite that sentence.

Figures are always used to designate dates, book divisions, street numbers, mathematical and technical numbers, percentages, decimals, postal codes, and exact units of time, fractions, distances, weights, and measures.

Examples:

April 3, 1995	1 May 1995	1990–1994	1999/2000
the 1900s	page 978	Act III, scene 2	
112 Seventh Avenue	546 East 49th Street	66 Berkshire Place	
Channel 13	Interstate Highway 40	County Highway 17	
Policy No. 223887	Invoice No. 194	Account No. 875	
11:35 A.M.	14:36 P.M.	32 degrees celsius	68 degrees fahrenheit
33 percent	12.4 percent	0.764 percent	.38 caliber

$.95 (95 cents) $0.07 (7 cents) $76 $108.73

£4.6 million   DM 88.1 million   FF 12 billion

13′ by 19′ (13 feet by 19 feet)   3″ × 4″ × 8″ (3 × 4 × 8 in.)

0.75 square inch equals 4.8387 square centimeters

1 cubic centimeter (cm^2) = 0.061 cubic inch (in^2)

A comma is used to separate thousands and millions. The use of a comma in four-digit numbers is optional.

Examples:

1,000 (or 1000)   3,345 (or 3345)   9,899 (or 9899)

12,543   1,345,890   45,785,002   318,654,772

In legal documents, price quotations and on checks the amount of money is usually written in both words and figures.

Examples:

eight hundred and sixty-three dollars ($863)

sixty-five U.S. dollar cents (US $0.65) per unit

eleven thousand two hundred and four and 29/100 dollars ($11,204.29)

Index